WRESTLING W
The Story of

Lloyd Geering

BRIDGET WILLIAMS BOOKS

First published in New Zealand, 2006, by Bridget Williams Books Limited, PO Box 5482, Wellington, in association with Craig Potton Publishing Limited, PO Box 555, Nelson

Reprinted 2006, 2007

Reprinted by Bridget Williams Books, 2008

National Library of New Zealand Cataloguing-in-Publication Data
Geering, Lloyd George.
Wrestling with God : the story of my life / Lloyd Geering.
Includes index.
ISBN-13: 978-1-877242-36-6
ISBN-10: 1-877242-36-5
1. Geering, Lloyd George. 2. Theologians—New Zealand—
Biography. 3. Presbyterian Church of New Zealand—Clergy—
Biography. I. Title.
230.092—dc 22

Cover design by Neil Pardington, BaseTwo
Printed by Astra Print, Wellington

To Shirley

CONTENTS

Jacob was left alone; and someone wrestled in the dust with him until the breaking of day. When he saw that he had not won the victory over Jacob, he struck him on his hip socket so that Jacob's hip was dislocated in the struggle. Then the man said, 'Release me for the dawn has come up'. But Jacob said, 'I will not release you unless you bless me'. So the man said to him, 'What is your name?' and he replied, 'Jacob!' Then he said, 'No longer shall Jacob be the name by which you are called, but Israel, for you have persevered with God and with men, and you have won the victory'. Then Jacob questioned him and said, 'Please tell me your name'. But he said, 'Why is it that you ask for my name?' So then and there he blessed Jacob. Then Jacob called the name of that place Peniel, 'For I have seen God face to face, yet my life has been preserved'.

Genesis 32: 24–30

Note: In Hebrew there is linguistic similarity between 'Israel' and 'persevere', and between 'Peniel' and the 'face of God'.

PREFACE

Why write an autobiography when its publication can be so readily interpreted as an exercise in self-promotion? It might be argued that, in my case, it marks an attempt to set the record straight after my involvement in a cause célèbre forty years ago – one that resulted in a variety of conflicting images preceding me wherever I went. Yet how could that perhaps justifiable aim be achieved when an autobiography is of necessity subjective and hence biased? On the other hand, since no two portraits of a person (whether literary or graphic) present quite the same image, biography is never as objective as one might think. Indeed, over the years many brief profiles of me have appeared in the press, a few of them so warped that they simply added to the confusion.

In former times, such a state of affairs might have inclined one to say that the real inner self is 'known only to God'. But in this secular age that would be tantamount to conceding that no one can know the inner self. And that in turn raises the question of whether there is an inner self – apart, that is, from the impressions one has of one's self, together with the personas perceived by others. The Buddhist tradition began to struggle with that issue two and a half thousand years ago.

It is my hope that those who read this book will come to recognise that the real reason for writing it is not personal but theological. I am endeavouring to describe how my thinking about religion in general and God in particular has changed and developed over the years by setting this evolutionary process in the context of the chief influences and events in my life that have helped to shape it. This book is, if you like, a theological diary, written retrospectively.

When writing *Every Moment Must be Lived*, the story of my late wife Elaine, I noted that I had tried to keep myself out of that portrait as far as possible. But because our lives had been intertwined for over fifty years, it was inevitable that her story would also contain part of my own. The two or three hundred people who have read Elaine's story may observe a few overlaps, but for the most part I have narrated those sections a little differently here.

In the present task I have been indebted to a number of people, three of whom in particular I must acknowledge here, for their contributions now lie hidden within these pages. I am grateful to my friends Tom Hall of Foster, Rhode Island (a skilful wordsmith) and Allan Davidson of St John's College, Auckland (a probing church historian): they both read the initial draft, chapter by chapter, and made many valuable suggestions, nearly all of which have been included. I am also grateful for the continuing encouragement of Bridget Williams, for this is now the fifth of my books she has published.

Lloyd Geering
Wellington, July 2006

Chapter One

WHO AM I?

People sometimes say that they are trying to find out who they are. Since this expression was never heard when I was young, I suspect its current use reflects the increasing awareness of the absence of the traditional certainties that once taught people from childhood just who they were and where they stood in society. In the Christendom of the past, people were shaped by the Christian view of reality in which God had a plan for the world and for everyone in it. Since for the most part this conviction enabled people to face life with some degree of confidence and equanimity, they had no need to ask who they were.

In today's more secular society we enjoy much more freedom, both in choosing a career and developing our individuality. This breadth of choice means that we have more responsibility for the kind of person we become, but the erosion of traditional certainties leaves us more vulnerable when we encounter life's many perplexities. Increasingly, it seems, even middle-aged people set out quite consciously on a spiritual quest for ultimate meaning or purpose in life. It is in such circumstances that they say they want to discover who they really are, for having a sense of personal identity and finding a purpose in life are closely connected.

It was almost universally assumed in our cultural past (and still believed by many today) that one's essential self is a spiritual or non-physical entity – a soul – that can exist quite independently of the physical body in which it temporarily resides. The presence of this belief in Christian culture reflects the enduring influence of Plato, who indeed regarded the physical body as a kind of prison from which the soul seeks to be free. If there were such an entity as an immortal human soul, separable from the body, it would be logical to conclude (as Plato himself did) that the soul not only survives the death of the body, but also had some sort of prior existence. In his essay 'Dream Children', Charles Lamb mused upon such a possibility. But early Christian thinkers never entertained this notion in the same way as they adopted the Platonic view that the soul survives death.

In modern times this view of the self as an immortal soul has been slowly eroding, mostly because the human sciences have helped us to understand the essential relationship of the self-conscious mind with the brain and central nervous system. Even before that, the Scottish philosopher David Hume, in his essay 'On the Immortality of the Soul', had drawn attention to the obvious correlation between soul and body: he observed that in infancy they are both immature; they grow to maturity in tandem; and in old age they show equal signs of decay. Increasingly, we have ceased to understand the self in terms of the concept of an immortal human soul, but rather acknowledge ourselves to be psychosomatic organisms. This means that the self (or soul) comes to an end when the body dies; we humans live a finite existence between conception and death, just like all the other innumerable forms of planetary life. If any part of us outlasts death (though without quite attaining immortality), it is to be found in our genes. These we inherit from our ancestors and pass on to our progeny; and most of them we have in common with the other higher animals.

But unlike those animals, including even the other anthropoids, the human species lives within a language-based culture that humans have created over many millennia. It is this that distinguishes us from all other creatures and has enabled us to attain the self-consciousness we now enjoy. Human cultures have been evolving for more than a hundred thousand years; and because each new generation too readily took for granted the language and culture into which it had been born, the resulting human self-consciousness commonly led to the conviction that our essential selves are so different from our physical bodies that they can exist independently.

But this conviction is illusory. The body, mind and spirit, which humans formerly distinguished from one another, now turn out to be facets of the same indivisible entity. I do not *have* a body, a mind and a soul. I *am* a body, a mind and a soul, all at one and the same time. Curiously enough, the early biblical view of the human condition was already remarkably close to the one we are today coming to accept. The earlier of the Genesis creation myths states that God formed Adam (humankind) from the dust of the earth, and it was only when he breathed his own breath into Adam (a sort of divine prototype of mouth-to-mouth resuscitation) that Adam became a living being. Then at death, when a person breathes their last, the body returns to dust and the breath (or air) returns to where it came from. The Bible nowhere speaks of an immortal human soul; indeed, it declares that 'only God is immortal'.

It is a strange irony that today's more ready acceptance of human mortality turns out to be thoroughly biblical; and this development shows what great changes the Christian doctrine of the human condition has undergone since biblical times. Of course, the human sciences have enabled us to understand the human condition at much greater depth than was possible in biblical times. They clearly illustrate that when I ask myself 'Who am I?', the first part of the answer will refer to me as a historical physical person, a body – as the common terms 'somebody', 'anybody', 'nobody' still show. As a body I was conceived, born and nurtured before that organism ever developed a self-conscious 'I'. Strangely enough, then, this 'I' did not exist at my birth; what then existed was a helpless infant that had to go through rapid neurological development and absorb much from the culture into which it was born before it could develop self-consciousness and eventually speak of itself as 'I'.

My physical body provides the continuity between that newly born infant and the person I now am. It also provides the visual image by which others recognise me, even though that image has undergone consider-able change over the years, particularly in my early life. Moreover, it is a photograph of the uppermost portion of this physical body that appears on my passport and driving licence to provide evidence of my identity. Passport authorities do not ask me about my thoughts and beliefs, though they may ask me how I earn my living. Yet, when we ask the question 'Who am I?', we are expecting the answer to include much more than a photograph and an occupational title. So what is this 'I' that is a physical body and yet much more?

When the self was believed to be an immortal soul, it was tempting to conclude that the essential 'I' is a permanently fixed and pre-ordained entity. If that were the case, then the exercise of 'finding out who I am' would be the task of discovering what God, the supposed creator of souls, had already ordained for me to become and to do. In Christian culture it was common for people on reaching adulthood to ask themselves, 'What has God planned for me to do?' I found myself in just that situation nearly seventy years ago, as I wrestled with the issue of whether I was being called by God to enter the Christian ministry.

Over the years I have slowly come to recognise that I neither *have* nor *am* an immortal soul. I long ago found Buddhism's basic teaching of *anatta* (there is no permanent soul) very congenial. I am a historical human being, forever tied to a particular segment of earthly time and initially shaped by a particular culture. My personal identity, while always including the outward appearance of my physical body, consists more importantly of the experiences I have had, the memories I have accumulated, the beliefs I currently hold, and the resulting stream of thoughts flowing through my mind.

At any one moment, the 'I' who is thinking, deciding and acting is largely dependent on the sum total of my past experiences, some of them active in my storehouse of memories and others now beyond recall but embedded in my unconscious. This 'I' is far from static and unchangeable, partly because my body is constantly ageing and partly because I keep having new experiences and new thoughts. The 'I' who wakes up each morning is a slightly different person from the 'I' who went to sleep the night before. I am certainly a very different 'I' from when I was a boy, yet the continuity is maintained through my physical frame and my storehouse of memories. While I remain alive I am a continually unfolding story. In one sense, I *am* my life story, as yet still open-ended and unfinished. Thus, to find out who I am, I must recall the story of my life, as clearly and honestly as I can.

Such an enterprise is not as simple and straightforward as it may at first appear. 'What I have become' has been shaped by two sets of factors, the one genetic and the other cultural. Today a great debate rages as to which element is dominant in such areas as learning ability and criminal behaviour, but the fact remains that each of us has been shaped by both

– and initially, at least, we had no choice about either of them. (This fact, incidentally, is the one element of truth in the otherwise misleading doctrine of predestination promoted by Calvin and others.) Our personal genetic code (inherited from multiple lines of ancestors) and the culture into which we were born are the two 'givens' out of which our personal identity has evolved.

With great joy and expectation we examine infants and young children to see which of their parents or grandparents they most resemble, and find likenesses that may disappear or reappear throughout their lives. Particularly as we grow older, we may find ourselves resembling one of our forebears at the same age, noting similarities not only in appearance but also in skills, interests and mannerisms – though again, opinions differ as to the relative strength of genetics and unconscious imitation. In spite of all this, of course, each one of us is a unique person, a fact that can now be scientifically established by our DNA.

The cultural factors naturally tend to be subtler than the genetic ones, for over the long pre-modern period, when our forebears lived in a largely monocultural environment, they knew little of the importance of cultural influences in the shaping of their identity. In today's global and multicultural environment, we have become keenly aware of cultural shaping. We now know that there are as many different ways of being human as there are basic cultures. Although we may acquire several languages, the one we learned 'at our mother's knee' remains our 'mother tongue'. Still, although we are initially shaped by the culture into which we were born, we may become critical of some of that culture's characteristics, even to the point of openly rejecting them as we grow to maturity. This phenomenon is increasingly common in today's globalising, diversifying and rapidly changing cultural climate.

Thus, before we develop a unique and self-conscious 'I', each of us has been initially shaped both genetically and culturally. The development of self-awareness starts when, at the age of about two, we learn to refer to ourselves as 'I' or 'me' and not by our given name. But the evolution of that self-identity still has a long way to go, and the time periods and circumstances that bring us to deeper levels of self-consciousness vary from person to person. Carl Jung once described his own growth to self-awareness (at the age of about eleven) as the experience of coming out of a mist and realising his personal identity. I vividly remember such a moment in my own life; it occurred unexpectedly and in the oddest of circumstances. As a schoolboy of about fourteen I was walking down George Street in Dunedin during a lunch hour, when I experienced a sudden flash of illumination about myself. There was nothing around me to trigger this moment of enlightenment; yet it was as if, up until that moment, I had taken myself for granted and now I was suddenly aware that 'I' was 'I'.

But such a moment of illumination does not in itself answer the question of who I am. It marks only one milestone in a continuous and ever-changing process. There is no permanent and unchangeable 'I'; rather there is an ongoing flow of consciousness that is continually having new experiences and thinking new thoughts.

Although I have a number of vivid memories of events that occurred during my lifetime, a great deal of what I have thought, said, experienced and done is quite beyond recall. It can be disconcerting to find that others remember things about me that I have long forgotten. Sometimes, they even claim to remember the very words I said to them on a particular occasion. In certain cases they may well be right, and occasionally those close to us become convinced that they know us better than we know ourselves.

Even the most authentic biography of a person will always tell the story differently from that person's autobiography – partly because it can be more objective, but also because it is drawing on a different selection of data. Carl Jung has helped us to understand that the whole self – the real 'I' – is more than the conscious ego, and more even than the memory bank that is open to ready recall.

As I now attempt to recall my story to find out who I am, I shall necessarily be retracing past events and thoughts in the light of my current values and priorities. I have come to believe, for example, that the most awe-inspiring mystery in this vast universe is life itself. We observe it around us and we experience it within us. But by the time we have developed sufficient self-awareness to reflect on it, we have already been experiencing life first-hand for quite some years. Unfortunately, this means that we tend to take life for granted and so miss the wonder of it. It seems to be possible to go through life and enjoy what it offers without ever stopping to recognise what an extraordinary phenomenon life is. And the more we learn about the vastness of the physical universe, the more miraculous the presence of life within it seems to be.

Even growth in self-awareness does not automatically lead one to ponder the miracle of life. Such reflection requires that one learn something about the phenomenon of life on this planet in all its diversity of expression. Ever since Darwin, much popular debate has focused on the question of how life began: were all species created by divine fiat or did they evolve? Not only do I find the account of biological evolution much more convincing – consistent as it is with the greatly expanded view of the universe being made known to us by biologists, anthropologists and cosmologists – but it is eminently more awe-inspiring. The alternative story – that all forms of life suddenly appeared on earth by divine command – is staunchly defended by fundamentalists on the sole grounds that it appears in the Judeo-Christian Scriptures. In fact, it offers no real explanation of origins, but simply declares that all creatures are as they are because they were originally made that way by an invisible power. Not only is this 'creationist' view unconvincing, but it denies us the great gift of spiritual wonder. By contrast, contemplating the evolution of planetary life over some three billion years leaves one speechless with awe.

The universe is not static and unchanging – it can be described in narrative form. Planetary life is not static – it also can be described in narrative form. And quite near the end of the long and complex story of planetary life to date is the equally amazing story of the evolution of humankind – one we are now painstakingly piecing together from the fossil remains of our past. The personal life of each one of us is also a story – a story within a story within a story within a story.

My story is one of millions within one cultural story, which is itself one of thousands, and the many cultural stories in turn are all chapters in the evolving story of the universe itself. The little stories are partly shaped by the bigger narratives within which they unfold. My own story has been much affected by the radical changes now taking place within the post-Christian Western culture into which I was born. These changes in turn have been caused in part by the new story of the universe that has been taking shape through the discoveries of Copernicus, Galileo, Newton, Darwin, Einstein and hosts of others. Although their origins

17

go back several centuries, these changes have especially characterised the twentieth century. Since my life has been largely coterminous with that century, it is only to be expected that it will reflect those momentous changes.

Perhaps of greatest significance within the changing character of Western culture has been the changing conception of God. At the beginning of the twentieth century nearly everyone in the Western world conceived of God as the creator of everything. God was the eternal reality upon whom everything depended. God was all-powerful and all-knowing. This God was the same for everybody, whether they knew it or not. For the majority of Western people this seemed to be a self-evident fact, and only a very few dared to call themselves atheists. God was the solid rock upon which everything stood. But by the end of the century we were beginning to see that even God had a story. Karen Armstrong made a daring and important contribution in 1993 when she attempted to tell that story in her bestseller, *A History of God*.

Given that my own life largely spanned the twentieth century, it is hardly surprising that my story became increasingly involved with the rapidly changing story of God. Perhaps I recognised this most clearly when in 2004 I was invited to go to Sydney and contribute to a series of public lectures in which each speaker sketched what God had meant in their life. The series was entitled 'God *and Me*'. Such a title, on first hearing, seems to smack of consummate megalomania, particularly if God is conceived of in more traditional terms. But the more I thought about it, the more I saw that 'this has been the story of my life'.

The task of preparing for that lecture resulted in what proved to be the initial sketch of this book. It made me understand that, from the time I decided, as an impressionable and immature adolescent, to respond to what I took to be the call of God and to train for the Christian ministry, my story and the story of God began to converge ever more closely.

Of course, my earliest notion of God was fairly similar to the traditional one – a supernatural, spiritual being who thinks, plans, creates, and exercises ultimate cosmic control. But slowly my conception changed and developed until 'God' came to be the personified, verbal symbol that both reflected the values I hold most dear and pointed to the mystery of the universe. With Archbishop Anselm of old, I am still able to say that

'God is my highest idea'. With traditional theology, I am still able to say that the attributes of this God are the values I honour and try to practise – such as love, truth, goodness, honesty, compassion. This God is the foundation of my hope for the future. It is my response to this God that makes my life meaningful.

At the same time, however, I recognise that it is because of the culture into which I was born that I continue to use the word 'God', even when my life experiences, coupled with the changing nature of the culture in which I live, have been constantly altering the way I think about God. Thus God is no longer for me an objective and supreme being, open to public enquiry and the same for everybody. Being a verbal symbol inherited from our mythological past, God is a human concept we have created and used to find and express meaning in our collective and individual experience. Indeed, it is not even a necessary symbol, for human beings have created many symbols, concepts and languages to perform this task. But this is the symbol that comes most readily to me, simply because of the culture that initially shaped me; just as English is my mother tongue, so the now rapidly changing Christendom is my indigenous culture.

In now attempting to find out who I am by telling the story of my life, I find myself talking more and more about God. Indeed, I have engaged in more creative thinking about God since I have been teaching within a secular environment than I ever did when working within the ecclesiastical institution. This is the fourth of my books to have 'God' in the title, the others being *God in the New World*, *Tomorrow's God* and *Christianity without God*.

But what I am talking about is not necessarily everybody else's God: it is 'my God'. Just as each of us is a unique, individual person, so we each have our own unique way of interpreting life; we each conceive of God (if we choose to use that term) in a unique way. And clearly, people have been doing this ever since the term 'God' came into common use, even though they were not aware of it. Even the biblical writers unconsciously acknowledged this when they used such terms as 'the God of Israel', 'the God of Abraham', 'the God of Jesus Christ', 'our God', 'my God'.

When I speak of God, then, I am always referring to 'my God'. Yet as a human being, I readily acknowledge that I share many of my values, hopes and goals with other human beings, particularly those who have been shaped by the same culture. And therefore, it is possible to speak of 'our God'. Yet even as we do so, we must not be blind to the many subtle differences that make each of us unique. In the days when God was conceived of as an objective being who was the same for everybody, these differences were often repressed and crushed; people were expected to conform to a model supposedly prescribed by that God. This is why fundamentalists – whether Christian, Muslim or Hindu – demand that all people, and indeed society itself, conform to the particular model they believe their (objective) God has ordained. And as committed believers, they are ready to use force to achieve their ends. But with the coming of the modern era, we are at last beginning to acknowledge the value of diversity within the human species and the uniqueness of each individual.

My personal experiences of life, together with my attempts to understand the changing culture around me, have shaped the way I think about God, while what I think about God has in turn helped to shape my life and supply it with meaning. 'My God' and 'I' revolve around each other like a binary star; they are like the two foci of the ellipse that forms the ever-enlarging boundary of the world of my experience. Although I lay no claim at all to mystical experience, I warm to the words of the mediaeval mystic, Meister Eckhart: 'The eye with which I see God and the eye with which God sees me is one and the same eye'. My story and my theology are closely intertwined, as will be seen in the chapters that follow.

Chapter Two

CULTURAL ROOTS

I do not know when I was first introduced to 'God'. Indeed, for the first nineteen years of my life it was rare for any thought of God to enter my mind. Some people tell me that they have been aware of the reality of God or of some divine presence from as far back as they can remember. That is not so with me. The family in which I was reared was not one that regularly went to church, and I cannot remember ever hearing the language of traditional religion on the lips of my parents. I doubt if I ever heard anything about God from them; even if they had their own thoughts on the subject from their own upbringing, like many people in those days they would have deemed it inappropriate to talk about God outside the church setting. Reference to God was best avoided for fear of being guilty of blasphemy – a sin shunned by most people, church-goers or not.

Yet my parents were good honest people – community-minded citizens who clearly had respect for Christian customs. My father, for example, even as a farmer, never engaged in any unnecessary work on a Sunday. I suspect that their reductionist and more passive form of Christian living may have derived from a more active connection with the church long before I was born; but if so, they never spoke of it to me.

My paternal grandfather, John George Geering, came from Kent. He was a plumber by trade, and my father remembered him as a tall, strong and impressive man. He married an Amelia Butt, one of a family of nine. My father was born in Kent on 4 December 1875, and was christened George Frederick Thomas.

Jim, the eldest of the Butt family, had run away from home in his early teens and worked his way to New Zealand as assistant to the ship's cook. By the age of about twenty he had established himself on the outskirts of Christchurch. Having done well for himself, he suggested that his family join him. So most of the Butt family decided to emigrate, some to New Zealand and some to South Africa; that is how my father (then aged three) and his elder sister Bertha were brought to New Zealand in 1879 to settle in Christchurch. My grandmother's sister Charlotte (Aunt Lottie to us) had married a Robert Norrish (Uncle Rob) from Devonshire, and they came to New Zealand also.

Although my father had been baptised in the Church of England, on migrating to New Zealand and settling in Kaiapoi the family found the local Anglican church too 'high' for their religious comfort, and they became Methodists. Even so, my father never attended a Methodist church during my lifetime, and whenever a Presbyterian minister paid us a pastoral visit he excused his non-attendance on the grounds that he was a Methodist.

My mother, on the other hand, was born of Scottish parents and that explains my Presbyterian connection. My maternal grandparents, Andrew and Helen Johnston, migrated from Galashiels in Scotland to Mosgiel some time in the 1870s. My mother, Alice, was their third child, born in Mosgiel on 10 February 1879, her older siblings being Robert (Uncle Bob) and Helen (Aunt Nellie). Tragically, her mother died a few months after her birth and lies buried in the East Taieri cemetery in an unmarked grave. Some time later her father, a carder in the woollen industry, shifted to Kaiapoi, where he subsequently remarried and had two more children.

It was not the most successful of marriages, and my mother carried very unhappy memories of the way she was treated by her stepmother. As I was growing up, she often told me stories of how her half-brother and half-sister received preference over her. Being the youngest of the three step-children, she no doubt felt the loss of her mother more than the other two. I suspect that her childhood may have been somewhat happier than the impression she gave me. Her complexion was unusually fair, and she loved to relate how she was chosen to represent the lily in a church presentation in which she was singing. She was a good singer and learned the piano. Yet she must have been quite young when her schooling came to an end in Standard IV. Some time in her teens she became a weaver in the Kaiapoi woollen mill.

I am fairly sure my maternal grandparents never had any of their children baptised, such an omission being much more common among the Scots than the English. I suspect that my grandfather (whom I knew only briefly) was more of a freethinker than a churchman, for the only direct religious influence he exerted on me was to give me, when I was about ten, Joseph McCabe's *The Ice Ages*. This book opened my eyes to the great age of the earth and the probability of evolution. It is possible that my grandfather went to hear McCabe, a Jesuit-turned-atheist, explaining evolution when he came to New Zealand in the early 1900s in the course of his world tour. (McCabe, incidentally, influenced the Presbyterian minister, James Chapple, grandfather of Maurice Gee, who based his celebrated novel *Plumb* on Chapple's public life.)

It was in the Kaiapoi woollen mill that my parents met, my mother being a weaver and my father a loom-tuner. I imagine my mother was a shy and unsophisticated young woman; she remained a gentle, caring person throughout her life, rarely discontented, happy to follow wherever my father's initiative led. As was the norm in those days, she saw her chief role to be that of a loyal, supportive wife and a loving mother; and this she always was. (When my brother Ira died of tuberculosis at the age of thirty-three, she felt it very deeply and took several years to come to terms with it.)

Having lost his own father at the age of twelve, my father had early thrust upon him the adult responsibility for the care of his mother and elder sister Bertha. When his mother remarried during his late teens, he was, as he told me later, somewhat embarrassed at being required to 'give her away' at her wedding. Although my father's education never went beyond primary school, he took a keen and active interest in politics and public affairs, and served on several borough councils.

About my parents' courtship I know nothing, except that it must have taken place over a period of some years, for my father was twenty-six and my mother twenty-two when they were married in my grandfather's home at the end of January 1902. My father had a new house built for them both, and before long they had a family of three boys – Ray, Ira and Fred (whom I, when I arrived in the family much later, came to call 'Way', 'Yi-yi' and

'Peb'). For the only time in her life, my mother had a servant girl to help her in the house. My father was elected to the Kaiapoi Borough Council and found himself the youngest and only clean-shaven man there.

Whether my father used to get itchy feet or merely used every chance to better himself I do not know, but during much of his working life he rarely seemed to stay in one place for more than about four years. Even before he trained as a loom-tuner he had spent some time in his late teens working on his uncle's cattle farm near Midhurst in Taranaki. In about 1910 he decided to leave Kaiapoi and take the whole family down to north Invercargill, where he worked at the Rosedale woollen mill. This move had the advantage of bringing him closer to his sister Bertha, who had married a farmer, Len McVicar, down in Mataura.

This led in turn to the next move. Perhaps because of his earlier experience of farming in Taranaki, my father decided to leave the woollen industry and take up a smallholding at Mataura. In any case, it was a good opportunity for my brothers to get to know their many McVicar cousins. They stayed there for some four or five years, long enough for my father to be elected to the Mataura Borough Council.

In about 1915 my father decided to move back to Canterbury, this time to Loburn, near Rangiora, where he had bought a sheep farm. As was common in those days, my mother did not have much say in the matter, though I later used to hear her complain about the primitive nature of the farmhouse. It had sod walls, a common enough form of building in those days, but was evidently large enough for our family and did have the advantage of holding the heat in the winter.

The family seemed quite settled there. My eldest brother attended Rangiora High School, the younger two went to the Loburn Primary School, and my father was elected to the Ashley County Council. I imagine it was quite a surprise when my mother found herself pregnant again, after a gap of eleven years. I was born in the Rangiora Maternity Home on 26 February 1918. My mother was hoping for a daughter, while another woman in the home gave birth to a daughter when she was hoping for a son. The nurse confessed to them both how tempted she had been to make a switch. I have more than once pondered the several contingencies inherent in my unplanned conception and the contemplated intervention; if it had occurred, I would have become a very different person!

The Great War had already entered its fourth year, and the British Prime Minister was Lloyd George. So, as my father's name was George, I was given the names Lloyd George. In my earlier years I was quite proud of this association. But the day came (I was about ten or eleven) when, on being introduced to a stranger, I was informed that my namesake had unfortunately fallen from grace in the public eye. Thereafter I found the association somewhat embarrassing, and have always had sympathy for those who bear the names of famous people.

Of course I have no memory of my Canterbury origins. Before I was two years old my father had sold the farm (for reasons I never found out) and moved the family to Invercargill, where we lived in Herbert Street for some time while he worked once more at the Rosedale woollen mill. At some point during 1920 he moved us again, this time to a dairy farm of some 300 acres (120 ha) at Mokotua in eastern Southland, where he milked a herd of about eighty cows.

My earliest memory stems from the day we moved onto the farm. I wandered up to the stables, which housed the four-horse team required for the agricultural work, and there I became frightened by a dog. Whether I was actually bitten or not I cannot now be sure; but it is to this experience that I trace my longstanding distrust and even fear of dogs, and this despite my later attempt to overcome it by having a pet collie in my early teens.

Sited some distance from the road was the large and comfortable farmhouse that was to be my home for the next four years. Two miles (3 km) away on one road were the railway station, store and cheese factory; on another road, the school. Although there was as yet little mechanised farming, my father did buy a Model A Ford car that carried us into Invercargill at regular intervals and to a very occasional picnic at the beach.

I remember those days as a happy childhood in a very harmonious family, to all of whom I was greatly attached. Ray and Ira worked on the farm from the beginning, and were later joined by Fred when he left school. My paternal grandmother, now widowed for the second time, also lived with us. On one occasion I was strongly rebuked by my mother for having said to her in the course of a game we were playing, 'Oh, Gran, you're dotty!' I suspect now that there may have been a grain of truth in this quite innocent remark. It was not long before she left us, eventually to reside in a home for the elderly in Invercargill, and I never saw her again.

Only many years later did I learn that I had been sheltered from the few family disagreements that did take place. One had to do with the care of my grandmother; it led to a falling-out between my father and his sister, with the result that I lost touch with a large family of cousins, of whom I have no memory at all. The other was the decision of my eldest brother to leave home at the age of nineteen to become an apprentice electrician at a time when my father desperately needed him on the farm to work the four-horse team. That was the beginning of the dispersal of the family. By the time I turned eight my other two brothers had also left home, so from then on I was brought up as an only child.

With the rest of the family largely occupied with their various duties on the farm, and no playmates within miles, I had mostly to amuse myself for my two pre-school years. I began to absorb the various bits of information out of which, unconsciously, I was constructing my view of reality. The raw material for this consisted of the many fairy stories I eagerly listened to, and the adult conversations I overheard, some of which I did not understand. For example, I kept hearing people say things like, 'He went to the front and never came back'. (It was only three years since the end of World War I.) The only 'front' I knew was the front door of our house, which, being on a farm, was never used. So for a long time I treated the front of the house with great awe, only occasionally venturing near it from the outside in an attempt to learn for myself why people so commonly disappeared when they got there.

No doubt the relative loneliness I experienced also stimulated me to use my imagination. I still remember the very primitive and childish picture of the universe I constructed for myself as a result of being impressed by the tale of Jack and the Beanstalk. I imagined that we were living inside the stomach of a great giant, and that whatever he ate and drank eventually descended upon us as rain and hail. Then I surmised that the same process could be happening to very tiny people living in our own stomachs. But, if so, this could go on indefinitely in both directions. Thus, at an early age, I began to develop the concept of infinity. (Only much later, of course, did my mathematics teacher teach me to call it 'infinity', and he explained it with a rhyme which bore some resemblance to my childish view of the universe: 'Great fleas have small fleas/ upon their backs to bite 'em/ And small fleas have smaller fleas/ and so ad infinitum'.)

In 1923, on reaching the age of five, I started my formal education at the one-teacher Mokotua School, which had a total enrolment of about twenty pupils. It stood on a little hill about 2 miles (3 km) from our farm. I walked to and from it every day; on my return journey it was my task to call in at a neighbouring farm to pick up the daily newspaper for my father to read that evening. I remember this duty well, for the kindly neighbour's adult daughter often gave me a juicy apple, the like of which I have never tasted since. As Proust noted, tastes and smells seem to leave lasting impressions on us when we are young: to this day the smell of an orange still conjures up the feeling of Christmas because of the two oranges I found in my Christmas stocking when I was about four.

My religious education, such as it was, also started about this time. Each Sunday my brother Ira took me on the back of his motorbike on his way to meet his girlfriend and deposited me at the Sunday School that was held at my school. Here for the first time I was told Bible stories, heard the name of Jesus, and was no doubt introduced to God. For me, it was simply an extension of school and I enjoyed it in the same way. The only other church connection occurred when, on odd occasions, my father took us all in the car to the morning service at the Oteramika Presbyterian Church, a few miles beyond the school. In addition, my mother taught me to say the well-known bed-time prayer, 'Gentle Jesus, meek and mild/ look upon a little child/ Pity my simplicity/ Suffer me to come to thee.'

I continued this practice until my very early teens, although not so much as an act of devotion as a superstitious ritual. I suspect that it is common for children of that age to believe that if they do not faithfully follow established routines some unwanted calamity will occur. This has little to do with fear of an angry God, but more with the belief that one must not upset the various cycles of activities that constitute the cosmic order. For similar reasons, as I was to learn much later, the ancient Babylonians feared the spring would not return if they failed to perform the annual New Year festival.

I was too young to understand why it was necessary for us to leave the farm in the spring of 1924. Only much later did I piece together the story of how, as a result of the economic downturn in 1923, my father found himself in serious debt and had to let the farm return to the previous owners, losing all the equity he had put into it. We had to get ready for a clearing sale in which all the livestock and implements were auctioned. During the preparations I suffered an accident that could have been very serious. While riding in a dray that was being used to collect unused concrete culverts for the sale, I climbed inside one of them, quite unaware of any danger; but as the dray lurched over some bumpy ground it fell out, taking me with it. I could easily have been killed or suffered a broken spine. My father, who always prided himself on the ambulance training he had received as a young man, carried me home and strapped my back. Fortunately, I came to no harm whatsoever.

Our furniture and personal belongings went into storage while my father found employment. For a month we stayed with friends in Invercargill and I was enrolled at the North Invercargill School. In November we moved to Dunedin and found lodgings in Howe Street, from which I was enrolled for a month at George Street School. From there we moved to St Kilda, and if it had not been for a polio epidemic which closed all schools for a month at the beginning of 1925, I would have been enrolled at yet another school – Musselburgh. All in all, I attended six primary schools and two high schools. These seemingly unimportant details may help to explain why I came to hate being the 'new boy' at school.

By the time the epidemic was over we had moved to St Clair, where we were offered accommodation with my father's uncle, a one-legged bachelor. He was the curator of the St Clair Pavilion, which was much used in those days by people coming to St Clair beach for picnics in the summer, but has long since been dismantled, along with the house we lived in. My great-uncle set up a merry-go-round each summer in the pavilion grounds, and though only seven or eight years old I was often employed on Saturdays to push-start it.

I remember our two years at St Clair as a more settled time in my life. I attended St Clair School for Standards I and II and made one life-long friend, Eddie Chrisp, who lived a little further up the hill from us in Bedford Street. If we were not together listening to his crystal radio, playing with his Hornby train, or looking for freshwater lobsters in the nearby stream, I was on the beach, never seeming to notice any inclement weather. Over the summer of 1925–26 I frequently attended the Dunedin and South Seas Exhibition; my father was in charge of the Southland Court, and I went off with him nearly every day. The exhibition made a great impression on me; I knew every corner of it and could readily escort adult visitors to particular exhibits they wished to see.

For some reason that I never discovered, my mother sent me to the local Methodist Sunday School rather than the Presbyterian one, even though the latter was nearer to our home. One of its activities for children was the Band of Hope, established by the powerful Temperance Movement to counter the evil influence of alcohol. So at the age of seven I enthusiastically went up to the stage at one meeting to sign the pledge never to imbibe intoxicating liquor except for medicinal purposes. To families like ours that never had any alcohol in the home, the evil it caused seemed all too self-evident. It was very common to see men drunk on the streets immediately after the pubs closed at 6 o'clock.

Occasionally my mother and I attended the Methodist evening service; on returning home after one such occasion, I arranged the kitchen chairs to form a pulpit from which I preached to an empty room. This memory now looks like a premonition of things to come, but to tell the truth no such thought entered my head again until more than a dozen years later. Yet I was influenced for a while by a book I received as a Sunday School prize. It was called *Christie's Old Organ* and I read it several times. The story was set in a British slum, where a mission hall sought to bring salvation to lost souls, and it focused on a boy befriended by an organ-grinder and his monkey. Today I rather cringe to recall how this sentimental story with its typically evangelical language brought me to tears every time I read it.

After the exhibition closed, my father once again found himself unemployed, and this time he decided to seek his fortune in Australia. I still remember how sad we felt after saying goodbye to him on the Dunedin wharf, from which he set sail across the Tasman. My great-uncle so filled my head with stories of Australian snakes and the many murders committed in cities like Sydney and Melbourne that I feared I would never see him again, and suffered some nightmares. But soon we learned that he had found work as a loom-tuner, first in Sydney and then in Geelong in Victoria, and arrangements were made for my mother and me to join him there. Once again we were on the move, this time taking an exciting sea journey on the ss *Maheno*, leaving from Dunedin and calling at Lyttelton and Wellington on the way to Melbourne.

After celebrating Christmas in Wellington with friends, my mother and I were reunited with my father in Melbourne just before New Year 1927. For the next three months we had rooms in Swanson Street, Geelong, where I slept out on a verandah. It was very warm, and in the evenings we went for walks to the beach with its coarse yellow sand. I was placed in Grade IV at Swanson Street School, just opposite where we lived. On either side of the school were the hospital and the gaol. Each day, prisoners were brought out onto the street under armed guard to break stones. On Sunday mornings we could hear their choir singing the popular 'Prisoners' Song'.

That autumn, in order to take up a better position at another woollen mill, Dad moved us once again to the coastal town of Warrnambool, about 180 miles (288 km) west of Melbourne. There, at 187 Fairy Street, we lived in a two-storeyed house made of the local sandstone, but with neither electricity nor sewerage. It was in that house that I had my only experience of living within an extended family, for during the next year we were joined by Grandad Johnston and my mother's recently widowed sister, Aunt Nellie. And before their return to New Zealand, we were joined by my brother Ray and his bride Eva, whose wedding we had been unable to attend because of the great distance.

For three years I attended Warrnambool Elementary School and did very well, going on to Warrnambool High School the following year. (In Victoria the average age for moving from primary to secondary school was about a year younger than in New Zealand.) Although I topped my class in all subjects there, I found more enjoyment in the woodwork classes than in French or English. Indeed, I so much delighted in working with my hands that I sometimes wondered whether I should have gone to the technical school instead. In those days, nearly as many pupils chose to go to technical colleges as to the more academically focused high schools.

After only a few months in Warrnambool my mother sent me off to the St John's Presbyterian Sunday School. I treated Sunday School much as I treated school, where every week we had what was called Religious Instruction. I was not aware of anything particularly sacred about Sunday School, and enjoyed going more because it had the best children's lending library in the city, where I could change my books every Sunday.

I *was* aware that there were different kinds of churches. A girl of my age from the Catholic family next door told me with pride that in her church

God was kept locked up in a box on the altar. But already I had absorbed sufficient of the widespread Protestant prejudice against Catholics, in that pre-Vatican II era, to dismiss this claim as just another of the many Catholic superstitions. Only much later did I learn that she had been referring to the 'reserved sacrament' in the Tabernacle.

I do remember that, at the age of eleven, I discussed at some length with a friend who did not go to Sunday School whether Christianity was really true. He contended that it wasn't, but I argued that it must be, or else people would not spend so much money building big churches. That was the level of my reasoning, yet in spite of my argument I never went to any services at the church whose Sunday School I attended. The two or three services I did attend were church parades of the Wolf Cub Pack, whose weekly activities and occasional camps I thoroughly enjoyed. This troop was attached to the Anglican church, and I remember being startled to find that people there knelt for prayers, and to see the vicar dressed in a long skirt.

So, in spite of Sunday School, my life remained very secular. It was during my days at Warrnambool that I graduated from the comics I used to read at St Clair to the weekly boys' magazine *The Champion*, and at last to full-length books. I even won prizes at the annual Speech and Music Competitions, where I submitted to memory tests of what I had read, and recited speeches from Shakespeare; I still have the leather-bound *Works of Shakespeare* which I chose to buy with the prize money. My other hobbies consisted of collecting cigarette-cards and stamps; the latter interest I have resumed from time to time throughout my life.

My days in Warrnambool came to an end when my parents decided to return to New Zealand. My mother had been feeling homesick, particularly since my three brothers and a new grandchild were there. So we sold our furniture, packed our special possessions and returned to New Zealand on the ss *Maheno* in January 1931, landing at Bluff. On the previous day, the ship had taken us into Milford Sound; this proved to be a memorable occasion, for although it was raining we were treated to the panorama of many waterfalls cascading down the steep slopes.

After being reunited with my three brothers, and various other friends and relatives, we settled temporarily in Dunedin where we had the use of a holiday 'crib' next door to where we had lived in 1925–26. I enrolled as a pupil at Otago Boys' High School, but being a week late had to attend without a school uniform for my first few days. Thus I was not only the new boy once again, but a very conspicuous new boy, a situation made even worse by the fact that four years in Victoria at a very formative age had left me with a strong Australian accent. For some time this continued to be the bane of my existence, for both teachers and classmates made fun of it.

There was some doubt as to what class I should be put in. On the one hand, I did not have the Proficiency Certificate from primary school that was necessary in those days for a free place at high school; but on the other hand, I had already had one year at high school in another country. After sitting some exams on my first day to assess my level of competence, I was eventually placed in IIIA, the top third form. While I had an advantage over the others in knowing some French and Algebra, I was well behind them in my English language skills – a deficiency which, through hard work, I more than overcame by winning the English prize.

Not until much later did I realise how fortunate I had been in landing up at Otago Boys' High, for it had an excellent reputation among New Zealand secondary schools both for the calibre of its staff and for regularly winning one or more of the thirty University Entrance Scholarships available each year for the whole of New Zealand. The Rector, 'Jerry' Morrell, had come from Balliol College, Oxford with a degree in 'Greats'; he was also Chancellor of the University of Otago, and his son Willy later became Professor of History there. The head of the Mathematics Department was 'Nigger' Martyn, an extremely able teacher; and the head of the French Department, 'Dreamy' Watt, and his brother Michael, another teacher, were the sons of one of the pioneering Presbyterian ministers of Otago.

The one teacher I disliked (as many others did also) was 'Barney' Campbell, head of the English Department. But I must concede that I learned more about the English language from him than from any other teacher. Unfortunately, he once set me the task of writing a critical assessment of a passage from Shakespeare, without explaining what 'literary criticism' entailed; I naively proceeded to be critical of the passage, only to have my essay returned with a low mark and the cryptic comment 'Shakespeare poor!!'

While I was adjusting to this very different educational environment and making new friends, my father went looking for work. He soon came to realise that he had chosen quite the wrong time to leave a good position in Australia; the Great Depression was already setting in, and no woollen mill anywhere needed him. So after three months, he decided to buy a small poultry farm at Abbotsford, on the southern outskirts of Dunedin; from there I travelled to school by the suburban train. We had been there only six months when a keen buyer persuaded my father to exchange the farm for a new house in the Dunedin suburb of Carlton Hill. I suspect that my father judged this to be a good move financially. Certainly, we had a fine new home with a beautiful view of the city – and enjoyed the luxury, unknown except for the two years at St Clair, of having electricity in the house. But since it entailed a big mortgage and my father still had no job, six months later we moved again, this time to Mosgiel Junction, 10 miles (16 km) south of Dunedin.

My father rented a 30 acre (12 ha) unstocked farm, known as Cosy Dell, for £1 a week. The picturesque house, with its large garden and orchard, was set down the hill from the main road; but it had neither electricity nor running water, and the farm needed to be stocked. (Today the southern motorway runs right through the middle of it.) Here we weathered the Depression for the next four years by milking six cows, running twenty sheep, fattening six pigs, and selling eggs from the one hundred hens, along with such produce as lettuce, early potatoes, raspberries and plums. At weekends and during school holidays I was allotted many different jobs connected with this very mixed farming, one of which was to cut down blue gum trees to provide firewood for the kitchen range, since we could not afford coal.

Although there were many happy occasions in this more than usually settled period of my young life, my primary recollection is of constant routine, with something always needing to be done. I have never sub-scribed to the common view that one's schooldays are the happiest days of one's life. For four years I walked a mile every weekday to the Mosgiel railway station to catch the 8.15 a.m. train to Dunedin to attend Otago Boys' High School. I was no sooner home at 5.15 p.m. than I had to round up the cows for the evening milking, and only when that was done could I settle down to two to three hours of homework. This meant sitting in my tiny bedroom at a desk I had constructed myself and, because there was no heating in the house, wrapping myself up in a dressing-gown and rug, with a hot-water bottle at my feet and sometimes gloves on my hands, working away by the light of a kerosene lamp. So burdensome was this daily grind that I eventually registered a protest by writing for the school magazine a short article in which I argued that all of our learning should be done at school. I ended with a parody of Thomas Gray's *Elegy written in a Country Churchyard*, two lines of which I still remember:

The schoolboy homeward plods his weary way,
To plough through homework after tea.

My first foray into print left the form teacher, 'Dreamy' Watt, not altogether pleased.

Despite all this I found much in school life to enjoy, such as debating, drama and, particularly, hockey. Coming from Victoria, where I was used to Australian football, I could not make head nor tail of rugby and was relieved when some friends dragged me along to hockey. The after-school practice midweek and the competition game on Saturday were the highlights of my week. I also liked cricket, but being a 'train boy' I was not free in the summer to stay after school for practice. On odd occasions I would stay in the city for the evening and go to the pictures, but it was usually on my own. Although I had school friends, I had none at all in the vicinity of my home.

No doubt the weekly grind was a valuable discipline, and it certainly helped me with the external examinations I sat each year from 1932 to 1935. My year in the Fourth Form coincided with the very last Senior Free Place Examination, which had to be passed to gain free education at a higher level. In the following years I sat University Entrance (then known as 'Matric'), and University Entrance Scholarship (twice). The need to get a scholarship spurred me on, for I knew that without it my academic career would come to an end. The job market, though improving slightly, was still very bleak; the boys who suddenly disappeared from the classroom because they had been offered employment were considered the lucky ones. All in all, I did very well at school, gaining many prizes and ending up Dux of the school in 1935 and winning the award for 'Best All-round Boy'.

It is strange to reflect on which particular incidents from those years have left a lasting memory. In my first year at Boys' High, 1931, the speaker invited to give the address at the prize-giving ceremony was the Revd

Allen Stevely, a Scottish minister who had just recently been inducted into First Church. He spoke passionately, and evidently with some effect as far as I was concerned, on the theme 'Play up, Play up, and Play the game'. In my final year, 1935, the ceremony was held in the impressive Dunedin Town Hall. The speaker on this occasion was Dean Cruikshank of the Anglican Cathedral. He spoke for only two minutes and then, to everybody's surprise, sat down. Ah, but how well I remember his chief injunction: 'Be gentlemen!' And I learned the important lesson that brevity is a virtue in public speaking.

Although all of my teachers left a lasting impression on me, the one who taught me the most about morality and common sense was perhaps the gymnastics instructor, J.P. Northey. I always looked forward to our time in the gym and felt annoyed if he spent too much time talking to us, as he loved to do. Yet many of his little stories had morals that have stayed with me over the years. For example:

> When a man who had just had his nose punched remonstrated with his aggressor, only to be told that this was a free country, he retorted, 'Your freedom ends where my nose begins!'

Many years later, when I was invited to address the school, I mentioned this story. Mr Northey beamed with pride, since he had long suffered from being regarded by the academic teachers as being of a lower class.

On the last day of the school year there was an interesting little ritual. After the closing ceremony, those boys in the upper forms who would not be returning filed out of the assembly hall, past the staff rooms and through the front door, which otherwise the boys never used. There we were greeted by a few of the more notable Old Boys of the school; the last of them said to me, 'You're out in the cold, cold world now!'

I was a very immature seventeen-year-old, often ill at ease in strange surroundings, and somewhat bashful in personal relationships, having had almost no contact with girls of my own age for some five years. I had reached this age with no strong convictions that either affirmed or denied Christian beliefs. An aunt had once presented me with a Bible, which I started to read. But I began to lose interest when I reached the genealogies in Genesis. Since my Sunday School days ended when I left Victoria, I had no further connection with the church for the next six years.

Strangely enough, our home at Cosy Dell was in the Presbyterian parish of East Taieri, in whose churchyard my grandmother lay buried. But I never once thought of going to church there; nor did anyone representing the parish ever pay us a visit.

In my last year or two at school I had joined the small Student Christian Movement (SCM) group which had lunch-hour discussions, mainly about the world religions and moral issues. My religious beliefs at that time could probably be categorised as a vague agnosticism, though I doubt if I had even heard of the term at that stage. But I do remember once puzzling my father. I said to him, 'I have great trouble imagining nothing. I think of the universe and then I try to eliminate, in turn, the moon, sun, stars and finally the earth – and then I get stuck!' My father looked at me as if I had taken leave of my senses, said nothing, and returned to reading the newspaper. I never really gave God a thought.

Chapter Three

STUDENT DAYS

With my first year out of school, 1936, came a marked increase in both my personal freedom and the number of responsible decisions to be made. My school friend John Lyth and I decided to celebrate our new-found liberty with a camping-cycling trip around Southland – the first of many such tours of New Zealand. For this I would need a new bicycle; the old bone-shaker that some years before had cost 10s was clearly inadequate. In those Depression days, when family cash was very scarce, such a purchase was a formidable hurdle indeed. Up until then, my only pocket-money had been earned by gathering mushrooms or trapping the occasional rabbit.

Perhaps business had been rather slow the morning I diffidently approached the cycle shop owner, for to my happy surprise he offered me 25s for my battered machine as a trade-in on a new bicycle. (Since the full price was £6.5s, my father gave me £5 to meet the difference. Many years later, the insurance company paid me £5 for this bicycle when it was destroyed in a shed fire; thus I can claim to have done thousands of miles of cycling round New Zealand for a net outlay of 10s! I judge that to be one of the best deals I have ever made.)

Equipped with John's tent, we set off with great excitement. Our chosen route took us through Balclutha, Owaka, the then little-known Chaslands area, Curio Bay, Invercargill, Winton, Gore and back home, travelling in rather short stages. By today's standards, particularly with geared bicycles, that seems little more than a leisurely jaunt; but for us it was a great adventure, during which we had to cope with rain, sandflies and (mostly) unsealed roads.

Two events of significance occurred while we were away. The first was the announcement in the newspapers of the University Entrance Scholarship results. I found to my relief and delight that I had achieved a high place on the list: thus my university days were now assured. The other event was the death of King George V, which we learned about after three or four days of isolation in the Chaslands. How strange it felt, some days later, to ride through the main street of the little country town of Winton and find everybody standing still as if to welcome us – and how embarrassed we felt on discovering that the whole nation was observing two minutes of silence to mark the funeral of the late king!

The end of February found me commencing my academic career by enrolling at the University of Otago. My teachers and other advisers had urged me to choose either medicine or science. But because I had no clear convictions about a future career and felt more comfortable just continuing with what I had been doing well, I opted for an Arts degree majoring in Mathematics. My high mark in Scholarship Mathematics (largely due to the good teaching at Otago Boys' High) prompted my Mathematics professor and course adviser, R.J.T. Bell, to enrol me for both Stage I and II Pure Mathematics in my first year, even though regulations then prevented me from sitting examinations in more than one stage per year. More than any natural ability, it was this good start that enabled me to excel in pure Mathematics, averaging 96 percent in the degree examinations. More than half of my BA degree was devoted to Mathematics, to which I added French, Latin, Greek and Psychology.

I soon came to enjoy the freedom and variety of student life, and began to look back on my schooldays as a kind of prison. I entered with great enthusiasm into such extra-curricula activities as debating, drama, and Capping concerts, as well as playing hockey on Wednesday and Saturday afternoons. In addition I decided to take lessons in ballroom dancing so that I could feel more confident in going to the Saturday night 'hops'. Students then were not nearly as hard-worked as they are today. With no internal assessment, and but few required essays or assignments, one could neglect one's studies in favour of other activities and then, before the November examinations, consolidate the year's work by doing a 'big swot' in October, which was free of all lectures.

On the other hand, we treated university classes too much as an extension of high school education. We were passive recipients of knowledge, too content to simply write down what was given in lectures and then try to absorb the information before summarising it in examination answers. I was never encouraged to use the library, as students are expected to do today; I did not even bother to attend the first-year tutorials, assuming they were only for those who needed extra help. I now wish I had shown more initiative in undertaking collateral reading in a number of subjects.

My Entrance Scholarship provided a boarding allowance, and I opted to live in Dunedin rather than commute by train as I had done to high school. The allowance also meant that, apart from the £6 my father gave me for the first few weeks' board, I was thereafter able to pay my own way in the world. Of far greater importance was my fortuitous choice of lodgings, for in the long run it did more to determine my subsequent career than my carefully weighed course selections. Indeed, I have noticed that seemingly insignificant events often lead to important outcomes. The 'chaos theory' proposed by modern physics may apply to human destiny as well!

What happened was this: my fellow 'train boy', Ossie Pringle, was a Roman Catholic who had attended Christian Brothers' High School; and when I told him of my intention to find board in Dunedin, he invited me to join him in the home where he lodged – not surprisingly, that of a Roman Catholic family. What is more, it was a very devout home. The landlady, Mrs McLintock, had a son who was a priest and an only daughter who had entered the closed order of the Carmelites. One of the other boarders was the chauffeur for the Bishop, and another was a young woman who had decided to enter a convent at the end of the year, and whom I coached in Algebra, seeing she was to become a teacher in the Dominican Order. I was as impressed by the devoutness of these people as I was warmly received by them, non-Catholic though I was; I even began to read the Catholic weekly, the *Tablet,* which I found lying about, and was happy to join them in eating fish on Fridays.

All this made me begin to question where I stood as a nominal but non-church-going Presbyterian; yet it did not prompt me to take any action, in large part because I always went home for the weekends. At the end of that year, however, I was invited to a Sunday evening meal in the home of Ellis Dick, a medical student who had been in my classes all through high school. After the meal, Ellis invited me to join the family in their customary attendance at the Sunday evening service in First Church. I recall thinking during the service that going to church would do me no harm, and perhaps something could be learned from the preaching.

Another coincidence was beginning to form itself into an influence, although its effect would take somewhat longer. Ellis suggested that I join him in his summer vacation job of picking fruit in Central Otago. Thus began my long, though intermittent, association with Cromwell. It was then a charming little town left over from the gold-rush days, situated at the picturesque junction of the Clutha and Kawarau rivers, and had the further appeal that my brother Fred, who worked on the railways, was stationed there.

So Ellis and I worked for three months on the orchard of J.R. Webb and Sons. We thinned apples and stone fruit, tied up and delateralised outdoor tomato plants (a job we all hated because of the discomfort of having to crouch down), and finally picked peaches and apricots. J.R. Webb had died prematurely and the business was carried on by his widow and her two sons, Harry and Jack. She lived in the old homestead with Jack, and cooked for all their employees. The meals were very good, and the dessert, as one would expect, was very often stewed apricots or peaches. We had no inkling then that in only a few years some of our number would be killed in World War II.

One of the permanent employees was George Wallis, a Londoner with a cockney accent. Being long accustomed to farm life, I gladly shared with him the task of milking the one or two cows kept for home use. Best of all, by combining the six or seven of us who lived in, the two Webb brothers, and a few day-workers, we were able to make up a cricket team. We practised each evening after work until we were ready to challenge the local clubs of Cromwell, Luggate and Nevis Valley. All in all, it proved a highly enjoyable and lucrative way of spending the long vacation.

When I returned to university for 1937 I found board in George Street, this time in the home of an Anglican widow with a daughter and schoolboy son, whose room I was to share. Now that I was living in the city full time, I decided on the first Sunday I was there to go to the evening service at First Church (to which Ellis Dick had invited me the year before). In those days the evening services were always better attended than the morning ones, but at the social gathering for supper afterwards the only face I recognised was a student from my previous year's French class. I introduced myself to her and found she was Joyce M—, the daughter of a Presbyterian minister and now enrolled at Teachers' College.

In a very short time I found myself joining the Senior Bible Class (several of whose members I knew from high school), attending church twice on Sunday, singing in the choir, and even teaching in Sunday School. I also accepted Ellis Dick's invitation to join him in the activities of the Student Christian Movement, and this soon absorbed my interest even more intensely than did the church. Indeed, while I was still in that formative period the SCM became the chief influence on my life.

As I look back now, I am puzzled by the way the direction and style of my life came to be changed so suddenly. The year 1937 was indeed a turning point; one could even characterise it as a religious conversion. Yet it all seemed to have little to do with God. It never occurred to me to say I had found God, or even that God had found me. What attracted me was the fellowship. Insofar as I thought of God at all, 'he' was simply part of a total package. Still, I was of course fully aware that I was consciously embracing the Christian tradition and making a positive decision to walk the Christian way.

But why did I do so – not only willingly but enthusiastically? No doubt influenced by the Catholic environment of the previous year, I had gradually become aware of a kind of spiritual vacuum in my life, though I would not then have used those terms. I used to go for long walks at night, looking at the stars, pondering over the universe, wondering what to make of life generally. Now plunged, more by accident than design, into the activities of the church and of the SCM, I found my life taking on structure and meaning that had previously been lacking.

First, there was the social aspect of my new life. Not having experienced much social life outside school for the last five years, I revelled in the many new contacts I was making. I was very impressed by the people I met in the SCM, and with the spirit of the week-long camp I attended that May at Pounawea. I did not miss a camp for the next six years.

Although it had been my good fortune to have loving and caring parents, I lacked brothers and sisters close to my own age. Now, active

41

membership of two Christian organisations nurtured a hitherto dormant personal need. I had been drifting along as a loner, dutifully meeting the expectations of parents, teachers and peers, but lacking any goal or clear ambition. Presently, I began to see life through new eyes. Not only did loneliness vanish in a warm and supportive group, but the practice of the Christian tradition provided a framework of reference that lent direction and meaning to everything I did.

Being part of this extended community was at first more important than the Christian tradition that held it together. Of course I knew the rudiments of Christianity from my Sunday School days, and I simply proceeded from there. As one of a fellowship of liberal-minded Protestant Christians, I found no problems with what they believed or did. Yet I was neither gullible nor wholly uncritical. When thinking about becoming a communicant member of the church, and remembering my initial introduction to the Bible, I asked a minister, 'I am not expected to believe all that stuff about Adam and Eve, am I?' 'Oh no', he said, 'No one in the church takes that story literally these days.' Though reassured by his answer, I was later to discover that many people in the church still did just that.

I should note that this change of lifestyle brought with it no conviction of any special relationship with God like that which others have described. Following the practice of my new friends, I did adopt a daily routine of personal devotional exercises, assuming it would lead me to some experience of the reality of God; but the closest I came to that was a growing but still indefinable sense of being intended to study for the ministry.

Through its study groups and the invited speakers at its popular 'Sunday teas', the SCM introduced me to a kind of Christianity I found very congenial, though it was challenging more than comforting. Two of our heroes were Albert Schweitzer, the missionary scholar in Africa, and Martin Niemöller, the founder of the Confessing Church, who was then taking a stand against Hitler's National Socialism. Even Jesus seemed more a hero than a saviour, challenging us by his teaching rather than offering us salvation from our sinfulness. Concern with his miracles and his virginal conception was far from being central to our thinking.

One of the largest student societies in the university, the SCM was more interested in Christian action than in the orthodoxy of Christian belief, and reflected the current liberal theology. One theological student caused a mild sensation by declaring himself to be a Barthian, but I knew nothing about Karl Barth at that stage. Those Christian students who took the Bible literally, who rejected evolution, and who placed great emphasis on spiritual conversion, chose to join the Evangelical Union. But in the SCM we studied the Bible with the aid of the modern commentaries – though to be sure our use of Jack Bates' little booklet, *Foundation Truths*, kept us aware of the basic theological issues of sin and salvation. A few in the SCM became caught up with the Oxford Group (later renamed Moral Rearmament). Notable among them were some whom the SCM regarded as its mentors, such as Harold Turner, Jim Linton and Hubert Ryburn. But although I was slightly attracted to this movement at first, I did not join it; I found its intensity discomforting, and even then, without clearly knowing why, I was a little suspicious of its emphasis on absolutes.

During 1937 the SCM had organised a mission to the university. It was not successful in attracting the unchurched, but it did have the effect of deepening the conviction of those who were already members. The two missioners – one of whom was Hubert Ryburn, then minister of St Andrew's in Dunedin, and later Master of Knox College and Chancellor of the University – made such an impression on me that I first formulated in explicit terms the notion that perhaps I was being called to the ministry. But having no idea what such a call should be like, I found it difficult to make any decision, and hoped the issue would become clearer over the summer vacation.

Once again I was planning to work at Webb's orchard, and this time I took with me Watson Rosevear, a friend who had already decided to enter the Anglican ministry. We had been in the same class for several years at high school, and in 1937 had met up again in the SCM. As before, bicycles were our means of transport, our route taking us down to Gore, up to Lumsden, along the new scenic road from Kingston to Queenstown, and then down the Kawarau Gorge to Cromwell. Watson was an especially valuable addition to the Webb's workforce, being a much better cricketer than I!

My return to Dunedin for the next year's classes was facilitated by Ron Viney, a permanent Webb employee, who arranged for me to board with his parents; but I still had no clear plans for the future. In this state of indecision I applied to the Presbyterian Church to be accepted as a theological candidate, secretly hoping to be rejected as unsuitable because of my lack of church background. This would have shown me that any thoughts I entertained of being called by God were the false promptings of psychological aberration. Indeed, I felt no attraction to the life of parish ministry, about which I knew precious little; rather, I was driven by an inner compulsion to offer myself in service.

With its all too frequent lack of wisdom and insight, the church committee accepted me – a decision that was to shape the rest of my life. When I told my family of my intentions, they were understandably surprised: my father tried to be encouraging by saying it might lead eventually to a political career, which I sensed would have been his preference; my brother Fred warned me that all the churches would be closed in thirty years. My mother was happy for me to do what I thought fit, and subsequently began attending her local Presbyterian church where, in her seventies, she became a communicant member.

From this time onwards, I found myself classed among a group of students known to all as 'Divs'. The move made little difference to my current course structure, for I was advised by the church committee to enter the Theological College only after I had completed my Honours degree in Mathematics. Yet I vividly recall finding great satisfaction in having a goal and purpose for my life – as well as feeling both joy and relief that the decision had been made for me. And thus it was that I began to look forward to my theological education.

Early on in the academic year I was joined at my lodgings in Forth Street by Walter Metcalf, a friend from Mathematics classes with whom I had already done some cycling and tramping. We soon discovered other common interests, such as church and SCM. Walter was a very keen violinist and also led the Scout troop at Knox Church; we boarded together for more than two years.

Walter and I also shared convictions about war and peace. During 1938 the Munich crisis became an issue of worldwide interest, and brought to a head a conviction that had been forming in my mind for some time. Not only were my earliest memories filled with accounts of the terrible conditions in the trenches during the Great War, but in about 1934 my whole school was taken to see a film set in that unspeakable carnage. I found it difficult to believe that humans could do such things to one another. Of course I was not alone in these feelings, for a wave of pacifism had swept over Europe during the early 1930s, expressed by such writers as Beverly Nicholls.

Nonetheless, the confrontation between Hitler and Neville Chamberlain posed the possibility of a second world war, and we were forced to reassess where we stood. Neither Walter, who had been in the church all of his life, nor I, a recent convert, could reconcile military force with the sincere practice of the Christian way of life, based as it was on 'loving one's enemies'. Indeed, during that year many Divinity students declared themselves to be pacifists. Having so recently embraced the Christian faith, and having taken it seriously enough to make it the focus of my professional career, I became an even more ardent pacifist than Walter. Such intensity is not uncommon in recent converts, and on at least one occasion he quite rightly rebuked me for my unreasonable statements. In the long run, he paid more dearly than I for our pacifist stand, as will be described later.

Still, it was all too easy to marginalise the topic of war and the rumours of war while engaged in a very active student life. In 1938 I was secretary of the Arts Faculty Students' Association, went for nightly runs to keep fit for hockey, and spent a great deal of my time helping to plan SCM activities. A little incident at the end of the year indicates that I was growing in self-confidence. It used to be the custom at the end of each university course for someone to thank the lecturer on behalf of the class. When my rather large Psychology class called on me to do this, I was in a quandary, for I knew very well that students had grumbled loud and long about the quality of this man's lectures. My relatively new Christian convictions led me to believe that I should always speak with sincerity and honesty; and, to the embarrassment of some of my classmates, this I proceeded to do, voicing the discontent of the class but tempering it by referring to the lecturer's often favourable relationship with the class. Two days later I was surprised to learn that the lecturer had informed his fellow staff members that my sincerity had made it the best speech of thanks he had ever received. The following year he went so far as to recommend me as a tutor to a parent seeking help for her secondary school boys, but he warned her that I could sometimes be 'a little blunt'.

By now there was yet another claim on my attention, for I had been drifting into a closer relationship with Joyce. In 1937 our respective lodgings were only a block or two apart, and we found ourselves walking together to First Church for Bible Class and morning service. Soon we began to spend more and more time in each other's company, and not only because we were both fully involved with the SCM. Yet even with all my social and extra-curricula activities, I did sufficiently well in the final examinations to become Senior Scholar for New Zealand in Pure Mathematics.

At the end of 1938 a fellow Divinity student, George Jeffreys, persuaded me not to return to Cromwell for summer fruit-picking, but to accompany him to the West Coast and work at Bruce Bay. The Public Works Department was then engaged in building the road over the Haast Pass to link up with the West Coast. (This work came to a halt during the war, and only at a later date was it completed to become the popular scenic route it is today.) We took the train to Cromwell and then hitched a ride to the Public Works camp near Haast Pass. From there we tramped some 70 miles (112 km) down the Haast River and up the coast to the other end of the road. Fortunately we took enough food to last us ten days, for we were delayed for several days by heavy rains that made it impossible to ford the rivers and streams.

Arriving at Bruce Bay, we were allotted a Public Works hut, ate our meals in the community cookhouse and fraternised with the men, some of whom proved to be very interesting characters. One came from an upper-class English family and had been a major in the Indian Army until alcohol got the better of him. Another was a tough Irish West Coaster who told us how he found himself homeless, penniless and hungry during the Depression. So he put his foot through a plate-glass window and waited for the police to arrive. His arrest and subsequent imprisonment provided him with satisfactory meals and lodgings for the next four weeks. Although my friend George had intended our Public Works venture to be a sort of mission to the unsaved, I think we were the learners, for we certainly had our eyes opened to how other people lived and thought. We did, however, establish a Sunday School for the few children at Bruce Bay, and we even broadcast one or two services over a ham radio owned by one of the settlers. Whether anyone heard them we never found out, but we were assured that in those isolated parts people were often glad to tune in to a friendly local voice.

We both wished to attend the SCM national conference, which that year was to be held at Sumner in Christchurch, so we arranged to hitch a ride with a truck leaving for the north three days before Christmas. Unfortunately, it left without us three hours ahead of schedule. Disappointed and somewhat grumpy, we had no choice but to set out on foot, carrying our packs. That day we walked 30 miles (48 km) to the village at Fox River – and on only two slices of bread each, as we had cleared our hut of provisions and could buy no more along the way. Never before or since have I felt as hungry as I did on our arrival at Fox township. After camping the night, we were fortunate to pick up a lift the next morning as far as Ross, where we caught the train.

The conference was attended by 180 students from all four universities. Like the week-long camps I had been attending since 1937, this event was such a great inspiration that I went to every subsequent gathering until 1943. Here for the first time I heard the hymn 'Immortal, invisible, God only wise' and it became a great favourite, because for me it most aptly expressed in poetic language the mystery I associated with the term 'God', and did so without limiting 'God' by using terms I would have judged, even then, to be inadequate. The spirit of the SCM community I found to be much more alive and congenial than that of church congregations, in large measure because it was free from doctrinal and denominational exclusiveness; indeed, the ecumenical spirit that flourished in the churches between 1940 and 1980 owed much to those who had participated in the SCM during their student days.

After the conference George and I returned to the West Coast, but this time we cycled from Ross down to Bruce Bay. After a month our time was cut short when I developed appendicitis. We were 100 miles (160 km) from the Westland Hospital at Hokitika and 90 miles (144 km) from the nearest doctor. The local nurse relayed my symptoms through to the doctor by phone, and though the acute stage passed after complete rest, it was decided that it would be safer for me to return home to Dunedin.

During the last week in February my parents celebrated my twenty-first birthday with a family party at their cottage in Allanton. Although we had sometimes marked family birthdays by the giving of small presents, we had not been in the habit of having parties; indeed, this was a very special occasion, for it included among others my brother Ira, my Aunt Nellie and my girlfriend Joyce. My mother gave me a portable typewriter, an instrument that was destined to have a considerable influence on my subsequent career. Typewriters were still relatively expensive in those days, and it was very rare for students to use them, let alone possess one.

Ordinarily, that year (1939) would have been devoted wholly to doing Honours in Mathematics; but having taken some Honours classes the previous year, I was able to add a further unit in Philosophy in order to be better prepared for the theological courses that lay ahead. In addition to academic study I assumed the heavy responsibilities of being president of the SCM, and played hockey in the Varsity A team. My many commitments all but eliminated leisure time, but surely were a factor in my gaining one of the two Rhodes Scholarship nominations from the University of Otago.

But events took a turn for the worse in September 1939. In the fortnight leading up to the declaration of war, I listened anxiously each day to news from Europe, and similarly dreaded the latest word from Dunedin Hospital, where my brother Ira, critically ill with tuberculosis, lay in the isolation ward where we were not allowed to visit him. When a friend brought us the news of his death (for we had no telephone), I was sent to Dunedin to break the news to my brother Fred, and it was on my way there that I heard the announcement that war had been declared. It was the bleakest day of my life up to that point.

As I was trying to adjust to the loss of my brother, my mind was increasingly engaged with the war. For the first few months, things were strangely quiet on the Western front as two armies faced each other from behind the Maginot and Siegfried fortress lines built in the aftermath of the Great War. Those of us who had declared ourselves to be pacifists during the Munich crisis of 1938 now had to rethink our position. The number of theological students who were pacifist decreased rapidly; indeed, some who had previously been pacifists, such as the highly respected George Falloon, were among the first to volunteer for military service.

Walter Metcalf, my close friend Bob Sprackett and I all remained convinced pacifists. When conscription was later introduced and we were

48

called up by ballot, the Presbyterian Church asked theological students to allow it to intervene on the grounds that ministers, like doctors, were in professions that needed to be sustained in wartime. Because I acceded to this request, I was never involved in military service.

Bob Sprackett, however, believed that pacifists should not hide behind church protection, and felt constrained to bear more of a personal witness to his pacifism by lodging his own appeal on conscientious grounds. Walter Metcalf, not being a theological student, had no option but to pursue that course. When they came up before the Department of Justice tribunal, I testified to their sincerity and strength of conviction. Bob won his case and was excused from military service. Walter lost his, and was even more distressed when the Knox Church Session summarily dismissed him from his position as scoutmaster. It is not surprising that shortly afterwards he left the Presbyterian Church and joined the Society of Friends (Quakers), with whom he remained for the rest of his life. From then on, it was not unusual for those of us who were declared pacifists to be accused of being unpatriotic or lacking in courage. That was only to be expected at a time when feelings were running high, and especially when the overseas casualty lists began to arrive.

It was in such uncertain times that the academic year of 1939 came to an end. I appeared before the Rhodes Scholarship selection committee at Government House, one of eight or nine candidates from whom two were to be chosen. Although I had no high expectations, I remained hopeful. But on being presented to the committee, two or three of whom were dressed in high-ranking military uniform, I felt that my chances had fallen sharply, given my known pacifist convictions. Besides, I may well have appeared rather immature, which indeed I was. As it turned out, of course, my lack of success was of no great moment, for the war prevented the scholarships from being taken up for at least six years, by which time much in our lives had changed.

Walter had invited me to his home in Taradale, Hawke's Bay, after the interview, so we cycled there together, starting with the long climb up the Paekakariki hill. This was the first stage of my third biking tour of New Zealand, for after spending two weeks at Walter's home I proceeded on my own to Wairoa, then up the Wairoa River to the beautiful high lake of Waikaremoana and down through the isolated Urewera country to

Ruatahuna and Te Whaiti. The Urewera country was one of the last Maori areas to be penetrated by Europeans, and the Presbyterian Church had taken responsibility for spreading the Christian faith among the Tuhoe people who lived there. Sister Annie, a Presbyterian deaconess, had long been almost the only European in Ruatahuna, and I felt it a great privilege to be invited to lunch with her.

I was glad of the opportunity to spend the weekend at neighbouring Te Whaiti; this was my first real contact with the Maori people, for down in Dunedin one rarely saw a Maori. Indeed, most of my previous personal knowledge of Maori came from my father, who had considerable contact with them at the Kaiapoi Pa when he was growing up. I visited the Maori Boys' farm, went to a school concert and prize-giving, and attended the morning church service, noting to my surprise that it did not start at the appointed time, but only when sufficient people had arrived.

From there I cycled on to Rotorua to see for the first time the geysers, pools of boiling mud and all the other phenomena of that thermal area. At Taupo I took the time to tramp to the top of Mt Tauhara, then rode on past the snow-capped mountains of Tongariro National Park and down the Parapara road to Wanganui, where I was to attend the SCM national conference. After the conference I returned to Wellington, this time avoiding the Paekakariki hill because the new coastal road had just been opened.

Having spent so much time at the Dunedin Exhibition, some fifteen years earlier, I was looking forward to the Centennial Exhibition in Wellington. Scheduled to mark the centenary of New Zealand becoming part of the British Empire, it failed to achieve its hoped-for success because of the outbreak of war. One of my chief memories of the event is my unexpected meeting with my Mathematics professor, who was able to tell me that I had gained First Class Honours for my MA.

Soon I was to leave behind a world I had come to enjoy – the world of calculus, differential equations, function theory and spherical astronomy – for a new world of theology and biblical studies. I cannot say whether I was looking forward to it or not; it was simply a necessary part of the future I had chosen. Using the common parlance of church culture, I said I had been 'called by God'; but in fact I had a very nebulous notion of God and God's call. What I had chosen to do was to identify myself with the Christian community, to learn their mode of discourse, and to draw upon the Christian tradition as a way of structuring my life in order to give it purpose and meaning.

Since God was an essential element of all Christian discourse, I hardly thought to question either his existence or the idea that worship and prayer were directed to him. But this God was distant and beyond all human understanding. It certainly made a modicum of sense to say that God was the Creator of the world; but, as I later learned, that made me more of a deist than a theist. Indeed, I was rather suspicious of evangelicals who loved to ask, 'Do you believe in a personal God?', and were themselves certain that they had a very personal relationship with God, treating him as a friendly protector.

As an accepted theological student, I was already being called upon to conduct worship. I had led my first church service at Pounawea in May 1938, before a congregation largely made up of fellow students attending an SCM camp. There I spoke very nervously on the importance of expressing gratitude, basing my homily on the example of Jesus, who gave thanks to God for the five barley loaves and two fish he had received, even though they seemed hopelessly inadequate for the task of feeding the multitude.

Sometime in 1939 I had been asked to fulfil a complete Sunday supply at the parish of Waikaka Valley; I clearly remember how exhausted I was after the day's three services. In this, my second sermon, I attempted to answer the question, 'What is God like?' The very choice of topic indicates that I was already genuinely puzzled about the nature of God and was searching for an answer. The fact that it is one of the few sermons that I later destroyed shows how dissatisfied I soon became with it.

During my visit to Walter's home in Taradale, the local Presbyterian minister had invited me to preach. I chose a topic that I took very seriously, and based my sermon on the words, 'And Jesus said to them, "Follow me and I will make you fishers of men"'. It now seems significant to me that I did not present Jesus as a divine figure but as a great teacher; I even compared him briefly with the Buddha and Muhammad. But chiefly I referred to the sacrificial kind of life to which Jesus called his followers. Since I had been attracted into the church because of the 'way of life' it promoted rather than its creed, it is only to be expected that my preaching would concentrate thereafter on Christian practice rather than Christian belief. Indeed, already by the end of 1939 I was beginning to feel concern that far too many people had made church-going simply a cultural habit rather than a stimulating exercise for thinking through and experiencing the Christian way of life.

Only much later was I introduced to the terms 'orthodoxy' and 'orthopraxy'; but I now see that, from the beginning of my active engagement with the Christian tradition, I rated orthopraxy much more highly than orthodoxy. Because a concern for Christian orthopraxy was leading me into the Christian ministry and had already led me into the unpopular camp of pacifism, I assumed that other Christians would be taking the Christian way of life just as seriously. In this, I was no doubt guilty of immaturity and youthful enthusiasm; yet looking back, I see that one of my perennial criticisms of church life is reflected in Jesus' pregnant question, 'Why do you call me Lord, Lord, and do not the things that I say?'

Chapter Four

THEOLOGICAL EDUCATION

In 1940 I began training for the ministry at the Theological Hall in Knox College, Dunedin. There has always been much confusion in the public mind as to how this institution (usually referred to simply as 'the Hall') was related to Knox College. Although the latter was founded for the express purpose of housing the Hall, it was also a residential college for students of all faculties. Divinity students, unless married, were expected to live in Knox College. This was good for their general education, and also fostered many long-term friendships; in later years, having lived in Knox College often proved a common bond between a parish minister and the local doctor.

During the Great Depression, Divinity students had found it increasingly difficult to afford the luxury of college life, and some opted for private board. I continued to do so until the end of the first term, when the Master of Knox College, Dr Merrington, persuaded me to become a college resident by offering to subsidise the fees from a special fund. At the time I especially regretted the ending of my close relationship with Walter Metcalf, but I have always been very grateful for the nearly three years I resided in Knox College.

Knox College had the air of a hotel for young gentlemen, and was probably modelled on the English university colleges. Most of the accommodation consisted of suites in which pairs of students had separate bedrooms and a shared sitting-room. But I was in the attics, where two shared a single room. The college was serviced by a bevy of maids who cleaned the bedrooms, made the beds, and waited on the tables in the dining-room. Most students sat four to a table in places personally chosen at the beginning of the year in order of priority, though some of the 'freshers' were ignominiously assigned to one long table known as 'the trough'. Each waitress served three tables and, after learning our choice of menu (beef or mutton), delivered our meals course by course.

Since the Theological Hall was a postgraduate institution, students not only had to be graduates (or have at least two-thirds of a BA) but must have passed entrance examinations in Greek, Hebrew, Philosophy, and the English Bible. It now seems a little ironic that the prescribed book for Philosophy was *Problems in Philosophy* by Bertrand Russell, a writer not only notorious for his atheism but well known for his popular book *Why I am not a Christian*. At any rate, I spent the first part of 1940 preparing for these entrance examinations in February, along with teaching myself touch-typing and taking the church services for Joyce's father during his month's vacation.

From the time I entered the Hall I largely accepted everything I was taught. After all, I was only an ignorant novice, and not only were my teachers supposed to know all about the Christianity I had decided to embrace, but they were all thoroughly immersed in what was known as Protestant Liberalism. They employed the modern methods of historical and literary criticism in Bible studies, and vigorously rejected the kind of fundamentalism that had recently sprung up in the United States. To be sure, a handful of students still remained conservative. One of them once said to me, 'Read such-and-such a book. You don't have to believe it but it'll get you through the exams!' That comment illustrated a kind of intellectual dishonesty I found very difficult to understand, though I have continued to meet it all too frequently in one form or another.

Modern approaches to understanding the Bible (particularly when pursued in the original Greek and Hebrew, which I enjoyed) came to be the most interesting part of my theological training. I learned that the Bible was not *one* book, but a library of books written by men over many centuries and in highly diverse cultural contexts. To understand them, one had to see what each book meant to the people of its particular place and time. Far from being the depository of absolute and eternal truths, they did not always speak with one consistent voice. The best way to reconcile the differences they manifested was to see them as different facets in a complex process of 'progressive revelation', a term much loved by one of our teachers.

This way of understanding the Bible made much more sense to me than the literalism of the fundamentalists. Moreover, it appeared to provide a clearer and more positive understanding of the Christian tradition than did the somewhat abstract discipline of systematic theology. Protestant Liberalism judged Christianity to be the historical religion *par excellence*, and assumed that the Christian message could be expounded and defended by appeal to the historical testimony provided by the Bible. Its foundation was not to be found so much in divinely revealed truths as in historical events. Divine revelation was to be found not in a dogmatic system but in historical events, such as the Exodus from Egypt, the history of ancient Israel, the historical life of Jesus, and his resurrection as the Christ. The foundation of Christianity was Jesus Christ and he was an historical figure, testified to by reliable evidence. The God worshipped by Christians was the Lord of history, even more than he was the Creator. This is what I was taught and accepted to be true.

John Dickie, my professor of Systematic Theology, had written the prescribed textbook, *The Organism of Christian Truth*, a book of some international repute; but I found his writing abstract and boring. Earlier students had found Dickie quite stimulating, but after thirty years at the task he was past his prime. His rather informal lectures consisted of discussing the text of his book, frequently punctuated by personal anecdotes, many drawn from his native Scotland. He kept asking his class abstruse questions, most of which they could not answer. This is illustrated by an excerpt from an ode one student wrote to celebrate the publication of his book:

> Does any of yer know what transcendentalism is?
> Do yer know where consubstantiation is amiss?
> What does Ostrogothic mean?
> Who was Dr Coe?
> Who was wife of Augustine?
> Does any of yer know?
>
> Can any of yer tell me what
> A lectionary is?

Do yer know what Urban got
For his Indulgences?
How early is the Book of Ruth?
Where is Linlithgow?
Whose book is out on Christian Truth?
Does any of yer know?

Although at the time I felt I did not receive much from John Dickie, I later concluded that I had been more influenced by him than I realised; and I became grateful for some of the observations I found in his book that I did not appreciate as a student. For example, instead of regarding the enterprise of theology as the task of expounding a set of unchangeable doctrines (as much of traditional theology had hitherto become), Dickie defined it as 'Christian religious conviction endeavouring to think itself out and to relate itself to all other knowledge and opinion'. As I was later to realise, this has far-reaching consequences, for it means that any theology inconsistent with current knowledge is thereby of limited validity.

Thus, while much that Dickie affirmed in the 1930s now appears very traditional, he showed himself to be a modern theologian: he not only was fully conversant with the German theology of the day, but acknowledged his indebtedness to Schleiermacher (often today called the first modern theologian), and spoke of him as the most creative theologian since the Protestant Reformers. Still, Dickie believed that Schleiermacher had gone too far, and saw himself more as a follower of Albrecht Ritschl (1822–89).

Ritschl, like Schleiermacher, abandoned the notion of unchangeable dogma, but believed Schleiermacher had made theology too vulnerable to personal subjectivity and thus in need of a supplementary appeal to the historical deposit inherited from the Christian past. The Bible, the Creeds, and the historic Confessions, while no longer to be regarded as the absolute and infallible medium of divine authority, nevertheless supplied Christians with much weighty material with which to test their own experience. This is why it was necessary to study the history of the Christian tradition, starting with a critical and thoroughgoing study of the Bible – a theological process that required a high degree of creativity.

Undoubtedly the most creative thinker in the Hall in my day was Helmut Rehbein, who later changed his surname to his mother's maiden name, Rex. Helmut was a young Lutheran minister from Berlin, who had in 1934 joined the Confessing Church, a body within the Lutheran Church but one that defied the Nazi ideology. The Nazi-controlled Lutheran Church refused to allow Helmut to marry his fiancée because she had a Jewish mother. In 1938 the couple managed to escape separately from Germany; after their reunion and marriage in London, the church assisted them in emigrating to New Zealand, with the intention of placing Helmut in a parish. In order to improve his English and familiarise himself with the New Zealand ethos, he spent 1939 in the Hall as an honorary student. After war broke out in September, the degree of anti-German sentiment in New Zealand made it impossible to place him in a parish, and for 1940 he was appointed as a temporary tutor, chiefly in Church History. So well did Helmut perform his task that his appointment was soon made permanent.

It was my good fortune to study under him during his first three years in the Hall. His very first lecture, on the Philosophy of History, gave me a whole new understanding of a subject I had abandoned in favour of Science after the Fourth Form. I had seen little point in trying to commit to memory long lists of dates and kings; but now Helmut sparked an apparently latent interest in the developing flow of human history and the successive changes taking place in ideas and culture.

In Berlin, Helmut had studied with Hans Lietzmann, who had not only succeeded the celebrated historian, Adolf von Harnack, but written a four-volume history of the early church. The first two volumes, translated into English in 1938, had just arrived in our library. Helmut encouraged me to read them, and far more important than helping me top the Church History class that year, they were my first indication that Christian faith and practice had evolved out of simple beginnings and had thereafter gone through many changes. Somewhat later, I came to see that instead of indoctrinating lay people with creeds and confessions as if they were un-changeable truths, it would have been much more enlightening to present Christianity to them as a living and ever-changing cultural tradition.

Helmut also introduced us, at least by glimpses, to the existentialist thought of Kierkegaard and the radical New Testament work of Rudolf Bultmann. Although at that stage I did not always grasp the implications of his teaching, some students were considerably upset by his ideas. As I have noted, the other teachers were quite liberal for their time, but Helmut Rex brought a touch of German radicalism to the theological climate of the Hall – just at the time I entered it.

Our other two teachers belonged to the mainstream of liberal biblical interpretation. Dr Hunter, a Queenslander who had trained in Glasgow, taught me Hebrew and Old Testament Exegesis to a standard that was to be of great value to me in later years. In some respects this was the subject I enjoyed the most, whereas many of my fellow students seemed more interested in the New Testament than the Old. Professor John Allan had been appointed to the New Testament chair only two years before I entered his classes. He was a New Zealander, trained at New College, Edinburgh, and was a man whom we greatly respected as a meticulous and honest scholar. For example, he had felt it necessary before his appointment to make it clear that he had some reservations about the historicity of the resurrection of Jesus, and later published commentaries on two of Paul's Epistles. Since both of these fine teachers were well abreast of the current biblical scholarship, I had no reason to feel anything but grateful.

In those days the University of New Zealand awarded no theological degrees, so on learning that the Melbourne College of Divinity offered a Bachelor's degree, I decided to become a candidate. I even resolved to sit the paper in Comparative Religion, although no such course was taught within the Hall. I therefore had to prepare myself from scratch for this paper, and since no textbooks covering the whole subject were available, I resorted to reading long articles in the twelve-volume *Encyclopaedia of Religion and Ethics* – an exercise that was to stand me in good stead in later years. Although the study of the non-Christian religions had begun in the German universities in the nineteenth century, it had remained a Cinderella in theological seminaries. It was almost as if they were afraid to introduce their students to other religions lest they justify the quip made by the Roman Catholic scholar Ronald Knox: 'The study of comparative religion makes one comparatively religious'. While some rationalists argued that to know one religion is to know them all, I inclined to the opinion that to know only one religion is to know none adequately.

At the end of 1940 I was able to gain further practical training for the ministry by taking over the vacant parish of Waikouaiti, north of Dunedin, for nearly five months and living in the large, empty manse during the summer vacation. Waikouaiti parish consisted of a small-town beach resort and a farming hinterland. I had to prepare two sermons for each Sunday and take three services, while during the week I paid pastoral visits. I am grateful for this experience as it helped to smooth the rough edges of a very raw recruit. It was there, for example, that I first learned to drink tea, which I was offered at every pastoral visit. So painful to me was the dismay on the faces of parishioners when I said I drank only water or milk that after ten days I surrendered, and have been drinking tea ever since.

My second year in the Hall continued much as the first, and I was now beginning to feel quite at home – so much so that I became quite bold when it was my turn to preach before staff and students. (It was then the practice, every Friday, for a second- or third-year student to preach a sermon in the chapel, whereupon we retired to the lecture room to have it criticised.) I argued to myself that for this to be a real sermon it should be directed to those present rather than to a typical, but absent, congregation. So I chose to speak on the words of Jesus, 'Woe unto you Pharisees, who bind heavy burdens and do not lift a finger to help'. I took the opportunity to look critically at the Christian ministry, and likened the current leadership in church life to that of the Pharisees. My fellow students tore my sermon to shreds. It had no Gospel message in it, they said, and though it might have served as the basis for a study group it was not at all suitable as a sermon. Some of the staff were more lenient. Professor Allan said, 'I was delighted! I did not think that Mr Geering had it in him'. He then added a warning: 'But he gave the impression of delivering his criticism of us Pharisees with some relish!' I took the warning, and although over the years I have often had cause to be critical of church practice, I have always tried to do so temperately. Suffice it to say that when the time came for my 'crit' sermon the following year, I chose a sermon that had already received warm commendation from a congregation.

Also in my second year in the Hall, two very unsettling incidents occurred. The first, in which I was involved only indirectly, was connected with my pacifism. We were now into the second year of World War II and patriotic feelings were becoming more intense, especially as New Zealand had suffered many casualties. One morning my close friend Bob Sprackett was conducting the daily chapel service, and in the course of the intercessions he prayed for 'our soldiers who are killing their fellow men'. Suddenly the chapel door slammed, and we opened our eyes to see that the Principal, John Dickie, had left in protest.

Bob Sprackett was such a caring and sensitive soul that giving offence to anyone was the last thing he ever intended. His overriding aim was to force us to face reality by removing all euphemisms when we prayed about the war. Not only was Dr Dickie offended by what he had heard, but he so firmly believed that pacifists had no place in the Christian ministry in a time of war that he took steps to have Bob suspended. On hearing this, I immediately assured Bob that if he were expelled from the Hall I would go too. Fortunately, a wise and moderate convener of the Theological Hall Committee was able to restore calm.

The matter eventually blew over, but not before Dr Dickie had taken the opportunity to preach on the subject in North East Valley the following Sunday. He insisted that the Westminster Confession (the subordinate standard of Presbyterian doctrine and ethos) condemned pacifism as a Christian option. It was his view that neither ministers nor theological students should be exempted from the current conscription for national service. He further believed that no congregation would elect a known pacifist as its minister. However, I myself never received a word of criticism about my views from the three congregations I served during the war period, and most congregations were not nearly as jingoistic and one-eyed as he had become.

We knew John Dickie in all other respects as a 'kindly soul', to echo a phrase he himself often used when referring to people in his many personal anecdotes. But devout Christian though he was, Dickie had two blind spots – pacifists and Germans. Two pacifists who had gone through his classes only a few years before us had already suffered congregational rejections since the war began, and Dr Dickie did not scruple to make derogatory remarks about them in his classes.

His antipathy towards the German people was despite having done postgraduate work in Germany and having translated Haering's *Dogmatik* into English. Perhaps it was during the Great War, when patriotism had become much more irrational than it ever was in World War II, that John Dickie developed his intense prejudice against Germans. So unyielding was it that, while most of us had great sympathy for Helmut Rehbein (Rex), seeing him as a refugee from Nazi persecution, Dr Dickie made it clear that only on sufferance had he been offered a temporary position on the staff. On one occasion, when Dickie was discussing the war in class, he astounded us by declaring that it had long been his firm opinion that there would be no chance of a lasting peace in Europe until the last German had disappeared. Not only were we shocked by such a declaration, but we found it impossible to reconcile his two blind spots with his obvious intellectual ability and his undoubted Christian convictions.

The second unsettling experience was much more personal. At the end of 1939 Joyce and I had become engaged, even though it would be three years or more before we could be married. Within some eighteen months, however, it had become clear to me that, while undoubtedly fond of each other, we were not wholly compatible – in considerable measure because I was beginning to move away from her more traditional approach to life. On seeking counselling from the university chaplain, Harold Turner, I was advised to break off the engagement. This was the most difficult task I have ever had to face, for I knew it went against Joyce's wishes. The stress I felt was sufficient to bring on an acute attack of appendicitis the night before I was due to visit her some 150 miles (240 km) away where she was teaching in a country school. My resolve to tell Joyce face to face thus meant a delay of three weeks while I underwent an emergency operation and then recuperated. Worse still, once the break had been made I had to face the wrath of her parents, who not only wrote strong letters of condemnation but threatened legal action.

For a long time I was so intensely troubled by the whole affair that I began to wonder whether I should withdraw from ministerial training altogether as one now unworthy to enter such a holy profession. My class work suffered, and I felt something of a black sheep among my fellow students. It was not until some eighteen months later that my confusion and guilt were finally relieved when I learned that Joyce had become engaged to someone else; and as it turned out, she was married before I was.

Before the year ended I was approached by Dr Allan to consider, as a summer holiday assignment, the post of student assistant to his friend Brian Kilroy, minister of St Andrew's in Wellington. I gladly accepted, seeing it as a great opportunity to learn from a man who had a high reputation as a preacher. I was to participate in the services each Sunday, and be wholly responsible for them during the minister's annual holiday. Further, it was my duty to report to Brian Kilroy in his study each day to receive his instructions; and this after a very pleasant walk through the Botanic Garden from the Glen, where board had been found for me with a parishioner. My duties consisted of paying pastoral visits to most members of the congregation, which was scattered widely around Wellington.

My parish visiting led to a unique experience. A parishioner in Tinakori Road very shyly confessed to me that a private spiritualist group met regularly in her home. She told me it all seemed so bewildering that she sometimes wondered which was the real world. Since I had been reading about spiritualism in relation to an Old Testament assignment, I immediately expressed interest. I was allowed to join the circle provided I promised not to upset the proceedings in any way.

Arriving on the appointed evening, I was introduced to about a dozen people, who to my surprise included a Presbyterian minister, a Methodist minister and an Anglican lay-reader. An elderly woman from Lower Hutt was the medium; she seated herself in the corner of the room and a white curtain was drawn across in front of her. The rest of us sat in a circle and, when the lights were turned off, we began to sing hymns. Presently we heard a succession of voices, purporting to come from deceased people. Although I assumed the voices originated with the medium, they appeared to be coming through a trumpet which previously had been lying on the ground but was now circling around the ceiling (it could be seen in the darkness because of a phosphorescent strip around it). Sometimes the voice died away and the trumpet fell to the ground.

Stranger things were to follow. It had been explained to me that in this séance the spirits would materialise, borrowing the 'ectoplasm' of the medium. Sure enough, a succession of figures appeared before us, their faces clearly visible in the glow of two phosphorescent plates left on the ground for them to pick up. Some people in the circle, on hearing their name called, stood up and stepped forward to greet the 'spirit'. One of the figures claimed to be a deceased Presbyterian deaconess (I had never heard of her), who proceeded to deliver quite a reasonable sermon. She then turned her attention to me and asked if I did not find it difficult to wake up in the mornings. On my conceding that I did, she told me the reason: because it was wartime, so many people were arriving in the spirit world unexpectedly that my spirit was being borrowed overnight to help the newly deceased to become adjusted to their new environment, and I enjoyed the spirit world so much that I was reluctant to return to the physical world! After thanking her for this surprising information and shaking hands with her, I sat down. The Methodist minister sitting next to me then went up to greet his deceased first wife and, after kissing her goodbye, sat down beside his second wife.

The séance came to a close when low groaning sounds arose from the medium as she supposedly emerged from her trance-like state and the lights were switched on. Thereupon two people displayed gifts that had been brought to them from the spirit world: one was a silver trinket and the other a bunch of lily of the valley. I was puzzled as to how the spirit world could contain such physical objects; I concluded that they must have been supplied by the medium. Still, since this was not the season for lily of the valley, I could not help but wonder where she could have obtained it. I went home feeling somewhat disturbed and, not surprisingly, had difficulty getting to sleep that night; evidently I was reluctant to leave this physical world.

I reported my visit in full to Brian Kilroy the next morning, and we discussed it at some length. Although I had witnessed things for which I had no rational explanation, several aspects of the event struck me as highly contrived. I had absolutely no doubt about the sincerity of the people in the circle, but the medium I was unsure of. Still, I had to concede that, if it *was* all done by trickery, the woman had shown herself to be a magician 'right out of this world'. I went back once more, intending to be more observant, but it was much the same. After that I never returned, having to my surprise become rather bored with it all. But whenever I related this experience in later years, I found my listeners always fascinated by it.

Before accepting the position at St Andrew's I had stipulated that I wished to take two to three weeks' leave over Christmas and New Year to attend the SCM Annual Conference in Auckland. A party of us, eleven in all, had arranged to cycle from Wellington to Auckland and back. Included in the group were Helmut Rehbein and his wife Renate, Mary

Wilkinson and her brother Andrew, Ron McNeur and his girlfriend Lynda Pye, along with Lynda's friend Nancy McKenzie, to whom I was becoming quite attached.

Just before we set out, the war took a sudden turn for the worse with the bombing of Pearl Harbour and the entry of both Japan and the United States into the world conflict. At first a wave of panic swept through the country, and mile-long queues of motorists formed at every service station, anxious to fill their tanks in readiness for a sudden exit from the city. But it was not long before we became adjusted to city black-outs, mine-sweepers hampering the speed of the inter-island ferries, and the construction of invasion defences on our beaches.

Undeterred by this turn of events, our cycling party left Wellington and eventually reached Waiouru, on the high central plateau, where we encountered such wintry conditions that three of the group decided to return home by train. The rest of us, with the permission of the kindly station-master, camped in the railway waiting-room. We had an enjoyable time, cooking our meal over the open fire and spreading out our sleeping-bags on the floor, undeterred by the tramp of soldiers passing through from the nearby army camp. From there we proceeded past Lake Taupo to Rotorua (where we celebrated Christmas camping in the Sunday School hall) and then on to Hamilton. There we received the news that the worsening of the war had caused the SCM conference to be cancelled. As a result, our party began to disband. Several of us rode south to visit the famous Waitomo caves and then caught the overnight express train at Te Kuiti, spending New Year's Eve on board before disembarking at Palmerston North. Three of us pedalled on through the Manawatu Gorge and down through the Wairarapa to Wellington. Thus ended my fourth cycling tour of New Zealand.

That February I was asked by Jack Somerville, then minister of Tapanui, to supply his parish during the year to enable him to join the army as a chaplain. After consulting with Brian Kilroy, I agreed – but somewhat reluctantly, knowing it would be a serious burden during my third and final year at the Hall. Not only would I have to prepare two sermons during the week for the three services each Sunday, but I would have to travel down by train and bus each Saturday evening, not returning until

Monday evening. Fortunately, parishioners would host me for the two nights and arrange for a quiet room where I might study for part of Monday. Looking back, I can see it was not a wise decision, but since so many people were taking on extra burdens as part of the war effort I felt some sense of duty to respond positively. I am now surprised that I succeeded as well as I did – even managing to play hockey on Saturday afternoons in Dunedin before catching the train.

In 1942 the war brought changes in the teaching staff of the Hall. The Revd John Collie, the previous New Testament professor, was recalled from retirement to allow John Allan to serve full time in the Home Guard. Although Allan had served in the Great War, on returning home he had become a pacifist, holding firmly to this position until about 1938. Since he was a man of strong convictions, it came as no small surprise that on joining the Home Guard he was not content with being a chaplain but insisted on joining the machine-gun unit.

Then in the middle of the year, after an illness of only a fortnight, John Dickie died. Hubert Ryburn, the Master of Knox College, a former Rhodes Scholar and later to become Chancellor of the University of Otago, was asked at short notice to assume responsibility for Systematic Theology. All in all, I learned more from him than from John Dickie, no doubt because I responded to his more questioning approach. I particularly remember his saying that he did not really get interested in theology until he had to think it through in the practical work of the parish ministry. That was to be my experience also.

During the year my relationship with Nancy McKenzie had been growing, even though we saw each other only during the short vacations as she was then teaching in her home town of Timaru. Our Easter meeting had been made especially difficult because travel restrictions had been imposed, making it necessary to get a permit to travel more than 100 miles (160 km) by train. But such was my zeal that I took my bicycle on the train to Oamaru and then cycled the last 50 miles (80 km) to Timaru. I had been so impressed by the reading of John Masefield's great poem *Good Friday* in our chapel service that I took a copy with me. Nancy and I celebrated Good Friday by reading it aloud together while sitting in the hay-barn at her parents' residence. I wonder now whether that struck her as an odd form of courting, but having been raised a keen Methodist she seemed as impressed by the poem as I was. Indeed, two years later we read it together in my first parish as the form of the Good Friday service.

As the academic year drew to a close and Exit students were being approached by vacant parishes, I received a visit from George Falloon, then minister of Kurow in North Otago, and a fellow-student of mine until 1940. He invited me to become *locum tenens* of his parish while he went off to the war as an army chaplain. I readily accepted, for Kurow was relatively close to Timaru, which by then had attractions of a different kind.

As it happened, Nancy by this time had been seconded to Waimate Primary School. So having completed my examinations, I travelled up there to propose to her on her twenty-first birthday. Since I had already written to her parents to gain their approval, it was no surprise to her, but still we had a joyful celebration. By odd coincidence Joyce was teaching English at Waimate High School. I rang her up and we exchanged good wishes; she was already planning her own wedding for the following March.

I then had to return to Dunedin to complete the requirements for my licensing as a minister. All students were required to submit three Exit Exercises to their presbytery. My Old Testament paper had been completed in 1941, but my parish duties at Tapanui had forced me to postpone the work on my New Testament and Theology exercises; not until Christmas Eve did I have them ready to submit to the examiner. The former paper focused on the Prologue of St John's Gospel, a passage I have always found inspiring. As to the latter, I had set myself the task of reading through all three volumes of John Calvin's famous *Institutes of the Christian Religion*, for I believed I ought to know more about the father of Presbyterianism. The result was a short dissertation on 'Calvin's Doctrine of the Law'. It was an incompetent and boring essay, which I never had the courage to re-read; indeed, I am surprised that Hubert Ryburn passed it.

That brought my required theological education to a close. Was I completely satisfied with it? I was hardly in any position to make a judgement, for I was largely unaware of what I had *not* been told. Certainly I was grateful for what I had learned in Church History and in the biblical subjects, but only in later years did I recognise that I should have learned more about the changes in Christian thought over the previous two hundred years. To be sure, John Dickie warned us not to be misled by Karl Barth's reaction to liberalism. He also delivered a course on the Westminster Assembly, whose documents had long been the Presbyterian doctrinal standards, subordinate to the Bible; but we learned to treat these historically rather than as the only authoritative way of interpreting the Bible.

But why did I hear much about Schleiermacher but nothing about Feuerbach? Why was I never told of the significance of David Strauss? Only much later, and particularly as a theological teacher myself, was I in a position to know what had been sadly lacking in my formal instruction; that will become clearer as this story unfolds.

Did I know more about God than I did before I started? I could answer the questions in a theological examination, but they had to do with theological doctrines and did not necessarily bring one closer to God. I was content to leave 'God' as unknowable. Given the limited capacity of the human mind, I argued to myself that God was the one reality that a person should be content to know little about. For me, 'God' was simply the name of the ultimate mystery of life. I felt myself on more solid ground with the person of Jesus Christ as portrayed in the Gospels. Even so, as one strongly grounded in the sciences, I remained chary of the so-called miracles.

Was I now prepared for the task of preaching which I was shortly to undertake? I have often told the story of a young curate who went to his bishop for advice on what to preach. He was told, 'Preach about God and preach about twenty minutes'. I have tried to stick to the 'twenty minute' rule, but only rarely have I preached specifically about God. Armed with the rich and diverse material in the Old and New Testaments, I saw the preacher's task as one of expounding the Bible in such a way as to provide insights on how best to live a Christian life.

Chapter Five

FIRST PARISH

On a Saturday evening late in January 1943, I arrived at Kurow by train to take up my first ministerial appointment. Kurow was at the terminus of a branch-line that ran inland from the coastal town of Oamaru. The train had taken three hours to cover the 40 miles (64 km), stopping at intervening stations to shunt off wagons. As I looked out for the first time on the village that was to be my home, I felt I had come to a Wild West township. 'So this is it!', I said to myself, wondering what I had let myself in for. My fellow Exit students had been invited to inspect their first parishes before agreeing to be called to them; but since I was accepting an interim appointment until George Falloon returned from military service, that had been deemed unnecessary. I was, so to speak, accepting a blind date.

I was met by my farmer host, Jim Chapman, whose family was to billet me for the weekend. The next day being Sunday, I was straight into it, with three services to conduct, two of them in country schools. And combined with these duties were my first driving lessons. This rural parish provided a manse car, but I had no driving licence. On hearing that I had been behind the wheel at least once before, my host insisted that I drive to each of the services, while he occupied the front passenger seat. I am surprised now that at the end of the day I neither felt a wreck nor had caused one. Actually, it was quite exciting.

The next day I was installed in the manse, which was situated about a mile from the church and village on a 10 acre (4 ha) glebe, a relic of the days when my predecessors travelled by horse and gig. The parish had kindly furnished the house with the bare essentials – table, chairs and a bed – and now left me to it. But how was I to continue driving without a licence? I set my problem before the local garage proprietor – a parishioner and grandson of a former minister – who issued the licences. On hearing that I had been driving for only twenty-four hours, he decided it was too soon to issue a licence; I should come back in a fortnight. When I asked how I should fulfil my parish duties in the meantime, he said, 'Just keep on driving!' I was beginning to learn that these good people had their own way of solving such problems.

The village of Kurow lay 5 miles (8 km) downstream from Lake Waitaki, beside the river of the same name, which had only recently been dammed to power the new hydro-electric power station, then the largest in the country. The parish extended some 12 miles (19 km) downstream on both sides of the river, 30 miles (48 km) northwards up the Hakataramea Valley, and 50 miles (80 km) upstream to beyond the Omarama basin. My most distant parishioners lived at the foot of the Southern Alps. Within this large area were sheep stations, wheat farms and orchards. The pleasant summers brought holiday-makers who came for the fly-fishing; and although the winters were very cold, I soon acclimatised and came to love the place.

My immediate ministerial predecessors were all interesting men whom I admired. Less than ten years before my arrival the minister had been Arnold Nordmeyer, who was now serving as a Cabinet minister in the First Labour Government, along with Dr McMillan, the Minister of Health, who had been the local GP during the Great Depression. During that time the two men often joined the local schoolmaster, Andy Davidson, to debate social issues in the community. (I occasionally boasted that the Social Security system introduced by the First Labour Government was formulated in the study of the manse which I was now privileged to occupy.) Nordmeyer was succeeded by Jack Bates, who became one of the first home-grown theologians of the New Zealand Presbyterian Church. He was followed by my friend George Falloon, who had made such an impression on the parish in only two years that taking his place was going to be a formidable challenge.

Since Otago had been a Scottish settlement from 1848 onwards, more than half of the local inhabitants were, at least nominally, Presbyterians.

My first task was to get to know them, a process that proved particularly tricky because of the dominant presence of the Munro family, which originally consisted of nine brothers and two sisters and was now three generations strong. The challenge was doubly daunting because both sisters had married twice, and in each case one of the husbands was Roman Catholic. For assistance I turned to the church treasurer who, being the manager of the only bank, knew everybody. Mr Crooks, who was as inappropriately named as he was helpful, spent an evening explaining all the relationships to me. As I recall, we calculated that 176 members of the parish belonged to the Munro clan. It was important to know who they were, for when they occasionally became embroiled in the usual family quarrels, it was unwise for an outsider to take sides.

It required only a month to complete the arrangements for my ordination, which took place on my twenty-fifth birthday, 26 February 1943, in the presence of a rather sparse Presbytery. The congregation presented me with a gown and cassock. These were hard to come by in wartime, and I was particularly grateful to inherit a cassock once owned by Basil Dowling, the poet. Although I was not personally acquainted with him, I felt honoured to 'wear his mantle', knowing that he had recently felt compelled to resign from the ministry because of his pacifism.

Nancy had managed to take brief leave from teaching to be present at my ordination and, suitably chaperoned by a female friend, she stayed with me at the manse. Naturally I was keen for her to join me permanently as soon as possible, for although Timaru was only 50 miles (80 km) away, petrol rationing meant that I could visit her only rarely. One such visit took place immediately after the evening service on Easter Sunday, when I excitedly drove to her home at 49 Bowker Street and we made the final arrangements for our wedding.

In the meantime I 'bached', a less than congenial state of affairs that was greatly eased when each day at noon the garage proprietor, Erskine Neave, picked me up at the manse gate and took me to his home, where his wife, the church organist, and his mother-in-law, Mrs T.A. Munro, had a hot meal ready. This and other examples of warm hospitality that I received from the congregation soon made me feel very much at home.

Our wedding was set to take place in Timaru on 22 May. The minister from Nancy's home church, Woodlands Street Methodist, officiated, but for reasons I cannot now recall the service was held in the Trinity Presbyterian Church. Nancy's sister Peggy was bridesmaid, and my good friend Bob Sprackett (then in his final year in the Hall) was best man. Because we had so little time after the wedding breakfast to catch the midday express train to Christchurch, we took the unusual step of going to the studio before the ceremony to have our photographs taken. Some people warned that this would bring bad luck, but we were never aware of any ill consequences.

Buoyed on our return by the congregation's warm welcome, Nancy and I settled down to roles that were new to both of us – married life and the parish ministry. We both had much to learn. It was no doubt fortunate that although the population was small and scattered, there was a surprising number of social activities. Many, of course, were church-related – weekly choir practice, Bible Class, Boys' Brigade, the Spring and Autumn Flower Shows (for church fundraising), and the monthly Session meetings. We arranged for the latter to be held at the manse to make them more personal, and we soon discovered that it was best to schedule them on Saturday evenings so that wives could attend the weekly local cinema and thus save on stringently rationed petrol. I also found that attending the cinema on the other Saturday evenings enabled me to keep in touch, however informally, with many of my parishioners.

In small rural communities, people's interest in one another is intense and news travels fast. While making a pastoral visit one day, I was greatly surprised to receive a phone call. Out of simple curiosity I asked the telephone operator (there was no automatic exchange) how she knew where to find me. 'Oh,' she replied, 'I saw you go past the exchange in your car an hour ago in the direction of Otiake and I took a guess as to whom you might be visiting!' Another time I made a railway booking one Friday afternoon, intending to take the train to Oamaru and on to Christchurch the following Monday. That Sunday I had to change my plans, and was quite surprised to receive a phone call at 7 o'clock on Monday morning from the stationmaster, who asked, 'Are you going on this train or not?' When I explained my change of plan he said, 'That's OK, I can let the train go now.' Such personal attention one cannot expect in the city.

It was also at this time that I was introduced to golf, encouraged by the local Anglican vicar, a bachelor named Dennis Dorman. Kurow had a small nine-hole course on a very uninteresting piece of flat land which was thoroughly strewn with stones; often these so deflected the path of the ball that we had a hard time finding it. Dennis and I were each assigned a green to keep in order, and we spent many a Monday afternoon attending to this duty, discussing church affairs and enjoying a round of golf, all at the same time.

The Bible-in-Schools movement was then in full vogue, and under the so-called 'Nelson system' ministers or other authorised teachers could offer religious teaching in the first half-hour of the school day. The requirements of the Secular Education Act were met by regarding the school as officially closed until 9.30 a.m. But Kurow did things its own way. The principal of the District High School suggested that I spend the whole of Thursday morning at school, taking the classes from Standard I to Form VI in turn for half an hour each. One year I even used the time allotted to the sixth form to teach its lone pupil Greek, since he was thinking of studying for the ministry. In the afternoon I followed a similar routine at Hakataramea Township Primary School, and thus spent one whole day a week as a teacher.

It was not long before I realised that, good and kind as my parishioners were, they had very little knowledge of the long and changeable history of the church they so loyally served. I was simply stunned on the occasion when one of the congregation's prominent women approached me and said: 'There's a question I've been wanting to ask you. Was the Roman Catholic Church in existence in the time of Jesus and, if so, did he condemn it?' Since preaching is seldom, if ever, the appropriate medium for raising the educational level of parishioners, I instituted adult study groups which met monthly in people's homes. For these I prepared mini-lectures on selected topics, which we then discussed. At a time when my colleagues were deploring the decline in attendances at traditional mid-week prayer meetings, these groups proved a more constructive and relevant activity, and one that most people appreciated and indeed commended.

From time to time, tutors arrived in Kurow from the government-funded WEA (Workers' Educational Association). One established a group to discuss international affairs, and another helped us to produce one-act plays which we staged in Memorial Hall. Soon we learned how to organise our own drama festivals and produce our own plays; we even invited a neutral judge from Oamaru. The climax of our efforts was a three-act play, Somerset Maugham's *Sheppey*, which we decided to stage on two successive nights. The producer was our local GP, Dr Aitken, a woman we came to know well. I was the stage manager.

The play tells the story of a man who wins a sweepstake, then has a heart attack; while recovering he takes to reading the Bible and, much to his family's consternation, decides to give the money to the poor. Rehearsals proceeded without a hitch until we heard that misgivings were being expressed around the parish, in considerable part because Nancy was cast as a London prostitute and I was playing a worldly young teacher, an atheist who scathingly rejected the Bible. Dr Aitken decided to seek the advice of our neighbouring minister, Jim Steele. After reading the play, Jim said he wished he could preach the Gospel half as well as the play did. So that was that, and the play was successfully performed. Amateur dramatics proved an excellent medium for encouraging natural talent and fostering community spirit, so much so that no distinction was discernable between parishioners and the other townspeople.

Once a month Nancy and I drove to Oamaru for the Presbytery meeting. In those days it seemed quite an adventure. For one thing, there was the pleasure of driving on paved roads, which were rare in the parish. Better still, it gave Nancy an opportunity to visit shops other than those of the local grocer, butcher and baker. Last but not least, I enjoyed the contact with the other ministers. So welcome were these breaks in the routine of parish life that when the 1943 meeting of the General Assembly was held in Dunedin, we decided to attend – and at our own expense, since it was not my turn to be a voting member.

Being the minister of Kurow meant that I had a special interest in what was to be the chief event of the Assembly – the election of a Professor of Systematic Theology to replace Dr Dickie. Jack Bates, one of my predecessors, was one of the two New Zealand candidates, and most people expected him to be appointed. To our surprise, the then largely unknown John Henderson from Edinburgh received the largest number of votes, partly because he came from Scotland, and partly because Jack Bates' liberal theology had aroused some opposition, especially when Henderson had specifically identified himself as evangelical. I began to see how unpredictable General Assemblies could be, though little did I suspect how much my own career would depend upon them in later years.

Proud of my 'high church' attitude to worship, I took very seriously the celebration of the Christian year, at a time when this was by no means as widespread in Presbyterian practice as it later became. This led to some surprises. On our first Christmas in Kurow, for example, we had invited as our guests some close friends who had just been married. The wife, who was the daughter of an elderly and somewhat conservative Presbyterian minister, flatly refused to attend the Christmas Day service on the grounds that it was against her Presbyterian principles. (For several centuries after the Protestant Reformation, the Church of Scotland abandoned Christmas and Easter services, along with all the Saints Days, because they had no biblical warrant; they observed only the weekly Sabbath.)

Nancy and I often laughed about this, especially because of its contrast with our second Christmas in Kurow. On this occasion we were joined on Christmas Day by a friend from student days who, having recently qualified as a doctor, was standing in for Dr Aitken. After Christmas dinner we spent part of the afternoon playing poker, and that evening our friend went to supper at the home of the Session clerk. Unsure of how to entertain him after the meal, his host said, 'I wonder what they are doing down at the manse?' 'Oh', he said, 'they're probably playing poker!' And they roared with laughter at such a preposterous idea.

Because attending the annual SCM Conference had been my standing practice since 1938, and Nancy had joined me for the 1942 Conference in Christchurch, we decided to attend the 1943 Conference in Lower Hutt as part of our annual holiday. Afterwards, we took the ferry to Picton, where our bicycles awaited us, and set forth on a camping tour around Marlborough and Nelson, which neither of us had visited before. At one point, running short of cash, we found work on a tobacco farm near Motueka for two days to fill the purse. According to plan, we arrived at Reefton, in Westland, in time for the induction of Bob Sprackett, whose wedding to Joan White we had attended in Ross Chapel, Knox College, only two months before.

From there we continued over the Lewis Pass, down into northern Canterbury, and back home to begin 1944. This was to prove an eventful year for us, as we had no sooner returned to the manse than Nancy found she was pregnant. Strange to say, both of us were so innocent in such matters that the parish knew before we did. One Thursday evening in February I excused Nancy's absence from choir practice, explaining that she was not feeling very well. If I had left it at that, no one would have suspected a thing; but I went on to offer the opinion that her illness could not be very serious, for despite an upset stomach each morning she usually felt quite normal later in the day. I was quite unaware of what must have been many smiles behind my back. But next morning Mrs Crooks, the treasurer's wife, called Nancy to explain the significance of her symptoms. No doubt the news and the comical nature of its discovery spread around the parish within twenty-four hours.

Within a few months Nancy had to curtail her involvement in previously shared activities such as taking a week to visit parishioners in the high country around Omarama. Our excitement grew as October approached and we equipped ourselves with bassinette, pram and baby clothes. But when the anticipated time arrived, the birth seemed delayed, and that Saturday morning Dr Aitken decided to perform an induction. On Sunday the hours dragged interminably, and still no news. That evening I was in the middle of the sermon when an emergency call came for Dr Aitken; as I saw her leave the church, I found it hard to concentrate on my subject. Alas, when the service was over I learned that it had been a quite different sort of emergency than I had supposed, and early next morning Dr Aitken arrived at the manse door to inform me sorrowfully of the stillbirth. (In those days, of course, much as we may have preferred otherwise, husbands were not permitted anywhere near the birthing scene.)

As we had not even contemplated such a possibility, we were devastated. Nancy was so full of grief that I immediately removed the baby furniture to a parishioner's home to avoid upsetting her, only later returning it to the shops in Oamaru. Meanwhile, since stillbirths required no formalities, the little cottage hospital instructed me as to the required depth of the grave and allotted me the task of burying our unnamed son. The place of burial remains my secret to this day.

This was a new kind of grieving for both of us; the movements of a child in the womb had seemed to manifest real personality even before birth. And because one begins to feel acquainted with the child about to be born, the loss is felt the more keenly. But what happens to such a child?

As I now look back to that time I can see that this unexpected death was already raising questions for which the traditional Christian teaching had no adequate answers. But at the time I was too personally involved to find a rational way through the tangled web of emotions, and vaguely imagined the child growing to maturity in some other world.

To help Nancy come to terms with the loss and, as people now say, 'get on with her life', I decided to take her with me to the upcoming General Assembly in Hastings. The Moderator was T.C. Brash, grandfather of current National Party leader Don Brash. What stands out in my mind about that Assembly is that, on the initiative of Dr Ian Fraser, it took the first step towards admitting women to be elders. I particularly recall that, when a spokesman for the conservative opposition argued that the Bible made no mention of women elders, Dr Fraser tartly replied, 'The Bible makes no mention of Moderators either'.

By the time we returned home Nancy was much recovered in spirit, though not yet physically fit. Since the protracted labour and forceps delivery had left her lame, we gratefully accepted the offer of an exchange of manses with the minister of Musselburgh parish in Dunedin, for our summer vacation. We thoroughly enjoyed the rest, delighted in gentle walks, went often to the cinema, and did a great deal of reading.

Wishing to keep up my studies during my ministry, I initially set myself a simple reading programme of important books, not necessarily related to the preparation of sermons. For example, I carefully read the two volumes of T.M. Lindsay's *History of the Reformation*. After some time I decided that the best discipline was to prepare for an Honours degree with the Melbourne College of Divinity, and for this I chose the Old Testament, as I enjoyed the Hebrew language. As it turned out, this proved a fruitful decision, for some years later it enabled me to embark on what became my primary career. Through much of 1945, I therefore spent all my spare time teaching myself Aramaic, as well as mastering the Hebrew text of Jeremiah and many of the Psalms, in the hope of sitting the six examination papers at the beginning of 1946.

Throughout my term in Kurow, men were continually being called up for military service, and after completing their training they came home on leave before being sent overseas. So it was that every few weeks a dance was held in Memorial Hall and a soldier was officially bid farewell by a member of the Returned Services Association. Since Dennis Dorman, the only other resident clergyman, did not dance, it always fell to me to represent the churches by making a little speech, wishing the soldier good health and a safe return, and presenting him with a pocket-sized New Testament. This was followed by a lavish supper. During my tenure in Kurow I must have consumed more cream-cake and pavlova than at any other period of my life – and this at a time when cream was officially unavailable because of the war effort.

By 1945 the news from the war zones was decidedly more encouraging. Then came VE Day, and the relief and excitement felt by everyone seemed to know no bounds. The tiny community of Kurow immediately arranged a celebratory procession through the village, concluding with a community Thanksgiving Service in Memorial Hall, at which I was invited to give the address. This was followed by dancing and other expressions of joy.

Three months later I was in the Waitaki Supply Stores when I learned of the dropping of the atomic bomb on Hiroshima. The grocery manager informed me that we had killed a huge number of Japanese civilians with an entirely new weapon. His reaction to the news was not at all typical, for he was almost livid with anger, saying he could not understand how humans could do this to one another. Although he led the Boys' Brigade, this man was not a churchman, and in fact would probably have described himself as an atheist; but he was well read, and took a keen interest in matters of social justice. I still recall the intensity of his reaction and the powerful impression it made on me; for although, over time, people increasingly expressed their moral opposition to nuclear weapons, few were then as perceptive as he. Fewer still were brave enough to speak their minds at a time when the dominant emotion was relief that the long and brutal war with Japan was over. And once again, of course, the community rejoiced and held a Thanksgiving Service in Memorial Hall.

The end of the war, welcome though it was, also meant that I would soon be out of a job when George Falloon returned to his post as minister of Kurow. I therefore wrote to Arthur Horwell, Director of Home Ministry, requesting a suitable placement and offering to go wherever the church decided I could be of most use. He invited me to go to the little coal-mining settlement of Granity, in an isolated part of the West Coast, an assignment that seemed reasonably attractive because it would take me close to my good friends Bob and Joan Sprackett at Reefton.

This time, however, I was to view the place first, and accordingly made plans to set off by train one Monday morning. But as chance would have it, Saturday's mail brought an invitation to consider a vacancy in the parish of Opoho in Dunedin. In something of a quandary, I rang my colleague and neighbour Jim Steele for advice. His response was positive and firm; he not only insisted that it would be foolish to bury myself at the end of a no-exit road on the West Coast, but urged me to cancel my plans to visit Granity and to accept the invitation to preach at Opoho. How different my life would have become had I not taken his advice! In due course I met the Opoho congregation, received their approval, and arrangements were made for my induction in October.

By this time Nancy was six months into her second pregnancy, Dr Aitken having advised her that this was by far the best way of overcoming her earlier disappointment. Although the circumstances were far from ideal, we had no choice but to prepare for our shift. In view of Nancy's condition, the congregation kindly insisted on taking responsibility for cleaning the manse after we left. And so it happened that, after putting Nancy on the morning train, I helped the carrier load our belongings into his van and rode with him to Opoho, to be ready for Nancy's arrival.

Thus ended my first real parish experience. It had been very full and rewarding – at least for me. To be sure, I had learned about some of my weaknesses (for example, I had great difficulty keeping a semblance of order among the lively youngsters of the Life Boys' team at Lake Waitaki), but I had achieved some success in teaching and preaching, and had gained a considerable reputation for my addresses to children. Furthermore, in spite of the seeming formality of those days, when people still addressed one another as Mr and Mrs, I had come to know a great number of people very well, and some of them became lifelong friends. I was sorry to be leaving Kurow, for its people had become part of me and I one of them.

But had I learned any more about God? To answer this I turn back to my sermons, for they are an extant record of what I was thinking then. From the very first sermon I wrote, and increasingly as time went by, I have felt a great dedication to honest expression. It was my early determination that I should never utter anything in the pulpit that I did not believe to be true. This meant that I could not propose the validity of an idea simply to please the congregation or to accord with orthodox Christian teaching.

Today, of course, I would not care to deliver any of the sermons that survive from that time, for my thinking has moved on and, I hope, matured. Yet few of them are now so foreign to me as to make me squirm when I read them. They were mostly attempts to expound biblical verses in such a way as to show their relevance and meaning for living the Christian life in today's world – and such exercises are unlikely to prove altogether embarrassing.

At the beginning of 1945 I began a series on the Apostles' Creed, having recently introduced its recitation as part of the Sunday liturgy, a practice then quite rare in Presbyterian circles. My aim was to link us with the many generations of Christians who had gone before us. But when I mentioned this to a senior minister, he expressed surprise and said I could not expect thinking Christians to be comfortable with the Creed in this day and age. He had a valid point, of course, and it was to bridge the cultural gap between the past and the present that I set out to explain the ancient doctrine phrase by phrase, in the hope of reconciling it with modern thought.

First, I emphasised how important it was to examine the beliefs we professed, since they 'mould us into the sort of people we become'. Then I pointed out how vulnerable Western civilisation had become, because we were 'living in the twilight of the day when the Christian Faith provides the beliefs which give purpose and meaning to people's lives'. Arguing that we modern people quite properly sought to substantiate our beliefs by evidence and cogent argument, I expressed the hope that the series of sermons would explain the reasoning behind the various phrases of the Creed.

As it happened, the series was cut short for several reasons – not the least of which was my departure from Kurow – and the only sermons I delivered were on the Deity. God, I said, was wholly different from any thing or any person known to us; it was the name of the mystery of life, which induced in us a sense of awe and wonder. In discussing the phrase 'The Father Almighty', I drew largely on the teaching of Jesus as found in the Gospels. Since I then still assumed that the Gospels offered a reasonably reliable record of the words of Jesus, and that he spoke with divine authority, I considered myself on very firm ground. On coming to the phrase 'Maker of heaven and earth', however, I took the opportunity to distinguish between science and faith. It was the task of science, I said, to unfold the story of *how* the world came into being, and hence the idea of biological evolution in no way undermined Christian faith. On the other hand, faith dealt with questions of purpose, meaning and value – all of which lay beyond the scope of science.

I now suspect that this whole exercise was as much a personal exploration on my part as it was an attempt to enlighten the congregation. At this stage of my spiritual journey, I had neither the scholastic background nor the personal confidence to challenge the long-established formulations of the Christian faith, but I was aware of the necessity of testing the boundaries. God remained for me the unknowable mystery of life; he could be neither contained in, nor explained by, any creed.

From the time I first embraced the Christian tradition, it had been for me more a way of life than a set of beliefs. Doing the right thing took precedence over having the right beliefs. The current move to Opoho fell into the former category. In the Presbyterian ethos, each ministerial move is treated as a response to a 'call of God'. But since I did not regard my move to Opoho as part of a divine plan, it would have been pretentious to think of it in such terms. I was simply responding, enthusiastically and excitedly, to the call of a congregation.

Chapter Six

AN IDEAL PARISH

Opoho must be one of the most compact parishes in New Zealand, and this was one of its attractions for me after attempting to minister to the widely scattered parishioners of Kurow. Located on the side of Signal Hill, overlooking Dunedin, Opoho has natural boundaries that limit it to three longish streets and a few short cross-streets. Since most people met regularly on the tram that served the suburb in those days, a strong community spirit existed; and as the only house of worship in the area, the Presbyterian church had become the community's spiritual centre.

Accordingly, I started by trying to learn who lived in every house, regardless of whether they were Presbyterian or not. In this task I was greatly indebted to the Morrison family. George Morrison was one of those rare men for whom the church was his life; and being the Sunday School superintendent, a long-time elder and past Session clerk, and a man highly respected in the community, he was a key figure. His wife Elsie, a lifelong resident, was a wonderfully down-to-earth person with a great sense of humour. She also served the church devotedly as organist and in many other ways. George and Elsie were so welcoming to Nancy and me that we soon felt ourselves part of their family, almost as much as their offspring Trevor, Gwen, Ngairie and Roy. Indeed, I remained in personal contact with each of them to the end of their lives.

The Morrisons were among the many families in the church that we came to know intimately, for the congregation included such friends from student days as Dick and Barbara Calvert, and Ron and Lynda McNeur. And because Knox College was within the parish boundaries, the congregation included a goodly number of students and some of the Hall staff, among them John Henderson, Helmut Rex and Hubert Ryburn. Although Opoho was then considered a small suburban parish, this congregation was full of vitality; about sixty lively teenagers filled its Bible Classes, and a group of the officers took their civic responsibilities so seriously that they had put up an independent candidate at the previous parliamentary elections.

The manse was then at 60 Signal Hill Road, only a few doors from the church. It was a very comfortable two-storied house, which Nancy and I tried to furnish (and even redecorate) within our rather meagre means. Yet because the war had caused many commodities to be in short supply, even buying carpet for the stairs became a major project. What a delight it was to procure at last a second-hand wringer for the tubs in what we then called the wash-house! In those days, most people were still boiling the clothes every Monday, and we felt grateful to have a gas copper; but owning a fridge (thought essential nowadays) was still far beyond us.

Settling into a new and interesting parish more than filled our time as I adapted to the task of preparing two sermons a week, attended to pastoral calls and hospital visiting, and also tried to keep up my preparation for the BD Honours examinations for which I had already enrolled. Even more importantly, we were concerned with the last three months of Nancy's second pregnancy. She seemed in good health and was certainly in very good spirits. Between Christmas and New Year we even hosted a number of students attending the annual SCM Conference, held that year at John McGlashan College.

Then came the great day. On 2 January Nancy gave birth to our second son, though not without some difficulty. It was again a forceps delivery, which left Jonathan with a damaged eyelid. Nancy and I had decided that this baby would be called either Jonathan or Jennifer, so Jonathan he was. Perhaps because I was a little put out when my friend Arthur Prior expressed surprise and amusement at our choice of name, we all soon came to know him as 'Johnny'.

During the week Nancy spent in the nursing home, and continuing through January, I used every available hour to work on my preparation for the examinations in late February. I did not do as well as I had hoped, partly because the Melbourne College of Divinity was less than informative about the scope of each of the six papers; but the extra qualifications I gained were eventually to serve me well. One of the immediate consequences was an invitation to teach the introductory course in Hebrew for students preparing to enter the Theological Hall.

It was now time to give my full attention to the affairs of the parish; and as it turned out, 1946–47 were to be my only two years of enjoying both normal family life and a parish ministry. The young people were a great delight to me, and now, more than fifty years later, I still meet them, mature and retired, all around New Zealand. We put on concerts, went on hikes and played games. Since Nancy and I had both played hockey as students, we aroused their interest in the game and soon established our own hockey club, which regularly fielded two women's teams and one men's team in the second grade. I suspect it was the only unisex hockey club in New Zealand. The young people were also responsible for the post-war revival of the Opoho Tennis Club, and I even found myself playing third-grade tennis as well as second-grade hockey.

It was during these early years in Opoho that I had my first experience of broadcasting. It was then the practice for the 'YA' radio stations (now National Radio) to present a ten-minute devotional service at 10 a.m. each weekday morning, and I was placed on the roster at 4YA. In addition, for a time, I became responsible for the Children's Hour at 5 p.m. on Sunday evenings. For this I wrote little plays, sometimes based on Bible stories; and after I had persuaded some of our Bible Class people to practise them in the afternoon, we went down to the studio and presented them live. Of course, this was very amateurish compared with what is broadcast over the radio today; and it is not surprising that, when I attempted to do similar little productions in Wellington in my next parish, the radio authorities were absolutely shocked and insisted that we pre-record them. Yet in spite of many deficiencies, some of our efforts were received by listeners with great enthusiasm; in one that I remember, we attempted to present the work of Flynn of the Inland, the Presbyterian minister who introduced the Flying Doctor Service in inland Australia.

It was also during these years that I was first invited to take part in the wider life of the church. The 1946 General Assembly had appointed me convener of the Statistics Committee, a task I performed for nine or ten years. As part of my report to the 1947 Assembly, I studied the growth and decline of every Presbyterian parish since 1900 and made some interesting findings. For example, I discovered that a marked decline in the vitality of the rural parishes of Otago and Southland had occurred because of migration to the cities. When my report also showed that the large inner-city parishes were likewise declining, some of the ministers concerned (several with congregations of over a thousand members) flatly denied this to be the case. As a result, nothing was done about it until some sixteen years later, when the General Assembly found it necessary to set up a special committee to study the decline of the inner-city parishes. All that time was wasted because the church refused to believe the facts.

But those problems were only symptoms of a much deeper malaise which very few people in the church, myself included, were willing to face up to: the gradual ebbing of the church's role and influence, which had been going on for nearly a century. To be sure, some ministers deplored the dwindling attendance at the traditional mid-week prayer meeting, but I saw that simply as a change in devotional habits. Most parishes still enjoyed healthy attendances at Sunday services, with many people going both morning and evening. In addition, it was still the custom, on the Thursday evening prior to the Sunday of each Quarterly Communion, for worshippers to prepare themselves devotionally to receive communion. This Preparatory Service, as it was called, was the equivalent of the Catholic practice of going to Confession before attending Mass, but is a practice that has long since disappeared. Moreover, it was plain to see that the communicant membership nation-wide was steadily growing, and new parishes were being established. What none of us seemed to notice was that this growth was not keeping pace with the expanding population. Our percentage was steadily slipping, and the church was slowly losing its status in society; but another thirty years would pass before this finally became undeniably clear to all.

But in 1946–47, with full pews and a large and healthy contingent of young people, I felt very confident about the future of the church. Indeed, the ecumenical movement then gathering momentum led me to hope that, before long, all Protestant Christians would be united in one large church. In the spring of 1947, the National Council of Churches organised a Faith and Order Conference in Wellington, and as one of the Presbyterian representatives I came away from it feeling greatly encouraged.

In the meantime, a plan had been prepared to unite the Presbyterian, Methodist and Congregational churches. Before a vote was taken in 1948, David Herron of Knox Church in Dunedin invited me to put the case for church union to his own large and influential congregation. Our best efforts were not enough, however, as conservative and evangelical Presbyterians were strongly opposed. The vote was particularly disappointing, for although a majority were in favour, so many people failed to vote that the Assembly felt it lacked a strong enough mandate to proceed.

Nonetheless, a continuing Church Union Committee was set up and I was appointed the convener. After making an initial analysis of what had occurred to date, we tried to engage in positive dialogue with those who had so strongly opposed church union. When this proved unsuccessful, we developed a policy of education within the church, and prepared a statement of Ten Propositions relating to the 'Unity of the Church and Church Union' – which, after full discussion in the presbyteries, was finally adopted by the Assembly. This enterprise was to take up an increasing amount of my time and interest, both in Opoho and in my subsequent parish.

I had not wholly abandoned my academic interests after completing the BD Honours. In those days enrolling for a PhD was not feasible, but I did take some German classes, having been encouraged to do so by Helmut Rex and John Henderson, the new Professor of Systematic Theology. I looked to them as my theological mentors and was very appreciative of their encouraging support, little suspecting that I would one day become their colleague.

To be sure, when the Old Testament Chair became vacant in 1947 with the retirement of my former teacher, Dr Hunter, it was suggested that I throw my hat into the ring; but knowing I had neither the knowledge nor the experience for the task, I was quite content to tutor in Hebrew. After his arrival from Scotland to fill the Chair, George Knight also offered great encouragement, especially during the first few months, when he and his family lived in Opoho.

In January 1948 Nancy and I visited her parents' home in Timaru for a happy summer holiday and frequent trips with Johnny to the beach. We had chosen this quiet holiday because Nancy was again pregnant, and on our return we would be caught up in the many events being organised to celebrate the centenary of the province of Otago and of the Presbyterian

Church in Otago and Southland. I had been entrusted to prepare the souvenir programme of church activities, and with Jim Oliver to compile a register of ministerial appointments in all parishes during the previous one hundred years. This latter document was to be included in the official church history being written by John Collie, and published as *The Story of the Otago Free Church Settlement*.

Two months later, our little family attended the spectacular fireworks display at Ocean Beach to celebrate the centenary. Although the total population of Dunedin was only about 80,000, the crowd was estimated at 120,000; afterwards, we were stuck in a traffic jam that took three hours to clear. Still, I associate that day with good news, namely the unexpected reconciliation of my father with his sister Bertha McVicar after an estrangement of twenty-five years. A day or so later, however, bad news intruded on the celebrations. During a routine prenatal check, Nancy was found to have an advanced case of pulmonary tuberculosis. She had evidently been suffering from it for two to three years without our realising it.

Her immediate admission to the Wakari sanatorium naturally entailed drastic changes for us all. My parents offered to come and join me in the manse and assist with the care of Johnny. That was, of course, a great help, but a more immediate need was better transport; although the hospital was only ten minutes away by car, it took more than an hour to get there by tram and bus. Because of the war, second-hand cars were nearly as expensive as new ones; but with the help of loans from friends, I bought a four-door Morris Eight for £430 – a sum greater than my whole year's salary. I had never been in such debt, but the car enabled me to visit Nancy three times a week.

Up until then, Nancy had always been full of vigour and vitality, and of a cheerful and optimistic disposition; but the sudden news had proved as great a personal blow to her as it was to me. I soon realised how much she had come to depend on my visits to keep her spirits up. One day she asked me, 'What does prognosis mean?' When I told her, I found she had been surreptitiously reading the doctor's chart, which stated that her prognosis was very bad.

I began to understand the wisdom of living a day at a time, without attempting to plan too far ahead. And the lesson was soon reinforced.

Some time previously I had applied for a scholarship being offered by the British Foundation for study in England, and had been delighted to hear I had been selected for the shortlist of six; but on hearing that I had not been chosen, I felt but little disappointment, for I knew it would have been impossible to accept.

Some of the familiar words of the Gospels came to have striking relevance to me personally: 'Take no thought for tomorrow, let the morrow take care of itself. Sufficient unto the day is the evil thereof'. Although I had previously been somewhat puzzled by the latter phrase, I found this philosophy to be a great practical help, particularly over the next few years. Indeed, I now recognise it as an essential aspect of what it means to live by faith.

But however sustaining these verses might be, they were of no help in planning to take on the responsibility of caring for a new baby. Faced with this quandary, I was completely bowled over when a parishioner came into my garden one Monday afternoon to propose a truly magnanimous solution. Despite having long yearned for the joys of motherhood, Betty Brown could have no children of her own, and had come to ask whether I would entrust to her the care of our baby, then soon to be born. Were I inclined to an evangelical faith, I would no doubt interpret her overture as evidence of divine providence. As it was, I took her up to see Nancy and together we gratefully accepted her kind offer.

In due course Nancy was transferred to Dunedin Hospital for the birth, and to our surprise and great relief it was the easiest delivery she had yet experienced. But because of her highly infectious disease, Nancy was allowed no physical contact with her new daughter, and was returned to the sanatorium. Thereupon Betty took charge of little Judith, and after a week's apprenticeship at the Karitane Hospital took the baby to her own home in Opoho, where she remained for eighteen months. I did my best to bond with Judy (as we soon came to call her) by looking after her every Friday evening to allow Betty and her husband Alan to go out on their own.

This commitment, along with my parish duties, visiting Nancy, and taking my parents back to their home in Allanton one day a fortnight to keep it in order, now imposed on my life a full and regular routine. During this time I conducted one of the most heartbreaking funerals of my career. A girl from our Bible Class was one of three nurses who perished on the Copland Pass while tramping over the Alps from the West Coast to Canterbury. After a private ceremony at her home, the family proceeded to an overflowing church. I myself felt the loss so deeply that I was unsure of my ability to retain my composure during the service. Although I rarely drank even a small glass of wine, I remember thinking I could have done with a whisky just before going into the pulpit, where I attempted to bring some words of solace and hope to a shocked and grieving community.

Such a stressful year had 1948 proved to be that, as the January holidays approached, I accepted the offer of Alphaeus Hayes (with whom I was still in contact from our Kurow days) to come and work on his farm in the Hakataramea Valley. To be engaged in harvesting wheat and other farming tasks provided not only an invigorating change of activity, but also a welcome addition to my meagre finances, which were badly strained by repaying the debt on my car.

When my parents regretfully told me they could not continue our domestic arrangement for a second year, I solved the problem by inviting a newly married couple of the congregation, John and Agnes Mayer, to share the manse with me. It gave them free accommodation at a time when John was still a student and Agnes had a secretarial post at Teachers' College. Since Johnny, now three, had started at the kindergarten close to the college, it suited John to take him there each morning in my car. By the end of March Nancy was invalided home, and although no longer confined to bed she was unable to do any but the lightest of home duties, most of which were shared by Agnes and myself. Still, for the next six months we four adults had a very happy time together. Indeed, after the midday meal (in those days the main meal of the day, for which nearly everyone went home) we often enjoyed a hand or two of bridge.

Although Nancy had to rest a good deal, she was always very cheerful and was able to go out a little, including to attend church. Once a fortnight I took her to the hospital clinic to receive her treatment, which consisted of pumping air into the cavity between the lungs and the rib-cage. On such an occasion, early in October, I slipped out of the Presbytery meeting to collect her from the clinic. On arriving I found she had suffered a black-out during treatment. Although she had by then recovered full consciousness and we were able to chat, it was thought advisable for her to remain in hospital overnight.

While I was at home putting Johnny to bed, I received a phone call from the hospital to say that Nancy had been placed on the seriously ill list. Only five minutes later a second call informed me that Nancy was now dangerously ill and I should come immediately. Arriving at the ward I found Nancy in an oxygen tent, gasping for breath and unable to speak. I held her hand, but she died a few minutes later.

The rest of that evening is vividly etched in my memory for I have relived it so often. Dazed as I was, my mind seemed to be racing ahead, thinking of all the things I now had to attend to immediately. After signing the papers necessary for the autopsy, I went straight to the funeral directors (already well known to me professionally) to make initial arrangements about the death notice and the funeral; then to the home of a parishioner whose wedding I was due to conduct two days later, to inform her I would arrange a replacement minister; thereafter to Betty Brown to acquaint her with the news; and finally home to get a message to Nancy's parents. Knowing what a shock it would be, I rang one of their friends in Timaru and asked her to break the news to them. At that point, some parishioners arrived with their teenage daughter for a pre-arranged meeting at which we were to discuss a possible wedding in connection with her unplanned pregnancy. While I was talking with them, Nancy's mother rang to hear a fuller account of what had happened. By the time the parishioners left, less than three hours had passed since Nancy's unexpected death and I had hardly had time yet to take it all in.

From the next morning, I was inundated with messages and visits. I was called to the hospital to have explained to me the cause of Nancy's death. It had resulted from an accident in her treatment: the needle used to pump air into the chest cavity had unfortunately penetrated a vein and sent a bubble of air to her heart. That was the cause of the black-out, and it was surprising that she had made even a temporary recovery. By a strange coincidence, Nancy had just been reading a detective story in which this was the method used by the murderer. When she chatted with me after her initial recovery, she wondered whether this had caused her black-out. Thus she guessed what had happened to her, even before the doctors knew.

After the funeral, which was conducted by my friend Bob Sprackett, the parish insisted that I have a break; so Johnny and I spent some ten days visiting Nancy's parents, my brother Ray and his family in Ashburton, the Hayes family in Hakataramea, and finally Bob and Joan Sprackett (then in Duntroon, next to my old Kurow parish).

It is now acknowledged that bereaved people commonly go into denial in the early stages of their grief. That may explain why I could not bring myself to tell Johnny that his mother had died. One day, in the presence of others, he suddenly asked me, 'Where's Mummy?', and I replied, 'Don't you remember how we took her to the hospital?' A few days later he slowly deduced the truth for himself and asked me point-blank. Then I realised how badly I had handled the situation. For some time I felt somewhat numbed and had little zest for living; but I knew I had to go on for the sake of our two children.

On returning to Opoho, I tried to carry on from where I had left off. But having experienced, within the space of ten years, the deaths of my brother Ira, our unborn son, and now my young wife, I was forced to think about death and its aftermath more seriously than I ever had before. The so-called Christian hope was no longer an academic question, as it had been when studying theology. I felt 'the sting of death' all the more keenly because, while visiting Hakataramea, one of my most loyal former parishioners had said to me, 'I suppose you found that Nancy's death simply strengthened your faith?' Surprised at what I judged to be an altogether too glib remark, I murmured an affirmative reply; but inwardly I knew I was quite unsure what I believed, or even what faith in eternal life meant.

I found myself going back to something my (agnostic) brother Ray had said to me when I was about fifteen: 'When you're dead, you're dead!' The Christian faith I now embraced had long taught otherwise, and I tried hard to accept its teaching. It did not bring a great deal of comfort, but simply left me in a confused state. The phenomenon of death, when it strikes close to home, not only shocks us with the sudden break in personal relationships but brings into sharp relief the mystery of life itself.

Perhaps it was fortunate that immediately on my return to Opoho I went to hear an address by Martin Niemöller, then touring New Zealand. Even during my student days, this German pastor had become one of our Christian heroes for the way he had challenged Hitler and initiated the formation of the Confessing Church within the Lutheran Church of Germany. On hearing of his faith experiences in a Nazi prison, I found myself being strengthened to resume my regular activities and personal responsibilities.

I was greatly assisted in this process by the continuing influence of Nancy herself. One of the many things she taught me in our few years together was never to feel sorry for myself. And of course she had left me her own example – fully aware that she had little time left to live, she remained bright and cheerful each day.

Yet it was difficult not to let my grieving and confused state affect my preaching. In the weeks before Nancy died, I had been delivering a series of sermons on Paul's First Letter to the Corinthians. On the Sunday prior to her death I had reached Chapter 12, and preached on the union of all Christians in the body of Christ, a theme very appropriate as it was World Communion Sunday. Before resuming this series on my return, I first preached about Niemöller and the faith and courage he had shown.

Then on Remembrance Sunday I delivered the last of the Corinthian series, expounding the famous Chapter 15, in which Paul appealed to the resurrection of Jesus as the grounds for having faith in the resurrection of Christian believers. Echoing Paul, I said:

> If the Christian faith does nothing more than present Jesus Christ to us as a teacher of good conduct, then we Christians are the most miserable of people because we have been deluded…It is because Jesus rose from the dead that we can make remembrance today of those who fell in battle, not with unrelieved sorrow but with some joy and gratitude.

The sermon was specifically intended, of course, to refer to those tragically lost in the war, for that tragedy was still very fresh in our minds. But most in the congregation were aware that I was thinking chiefly of Nancy, and I sensed that awareness even as I spoke.

During this period of confusion I read Frank Morison's *Who Moved the Stone?*, a little book so popular at the time that it had already gone through fourteen printings. Morison's scepticism about the resurrection of Jesus had led him to sift the historical evidence for himself. Focusing on the last seven days in the life of Jesus, and setting aside the obviously mythical elements in the Gospel material, he painstakingly reconstructed the actual events that led up to Easter morning. To his own considerable surprise, he came to the conclusion that solid historical facts supported the assertion that 'on the third day he rose again from the dead'. This book renewed my confidence in the genuineness of the Easter proclamation that is central to the traditional Christian faith. And so, like Paul – and many modern evangelicals – I began to base the validity of the Christian faith on the historicity of the resurrection of Jesus.

(It was not until some years later that I detected the fallacy in Morison's book. It lay not in the logical development of his argument, but in his premises: he had assumed the historicity of all the Gospel references he used for his argument. He had fallen into the logical trap of 'begging the question', just as fundamentalists do when they quote 1 Timothy 3:16, 'All scripture is inspired by God', to argue the divine inspiration of the Bible.)

I was also encouraged by a book of quite a different character, *And the Life Everlasting*, by John Baillie, Professor of Divinity at Edinburgh. This I studied with great care, finding it all the more persuasive for my having recently met the author when he was a guest speaker at our centenary celebrations. Although Baillie referred of course to the resurrection of Jesus, he based the Christian hope for the 'life everlasting' on the being of God, believing it would be inconsistent with the nature of God's love for humanity to allow us to come to a complete end at our death. Baillie concluded by claiming there are only two real alternatives – 'a radical and consequent pessimism' about the finality of death ('a dark night of the soul at which none of us can afford to sneer') or 'the hope of everlasting life with God'.

Taking new heart from these two books, I resumed my normal schedule of duties, one that now included visiting the sanatorium from time to time to see the friends Nancy had made there. As I saw them gradually decline in health, I began to feel some gratitude for the suddenness of her death. Painful though it had been for me at the time, it had saved her from the lingering death I now saw others experiencing.

Once again I spent my summer holiday at the Hayes' farm, this time taking Johnny with me; but on my return I needed to reorganise the running of the household. Since Judy was now eighteen months old, it was time for me to assume full responsibility for her so that the two children could be brought up together. The previous year's arrangement with John and Agnes had proved so successful that I invited a Baptist minister who had enrolled in a one-year course at the Theological Hall to bring his wife and teenage daughter and share the manse with me. This time the arrangement did not work out so well, partly because I was expecting too much. Our relationship remained cordial, but we soon became two separate families; and although I did not have to prepare the main meal, I had full care of both children. I ate with them in a separate room, took Johnny to kindergarten, and most afternoons left them with helpful parishioners while I attended to pastoral visiting. Life became so hectic that since then I have felt great sympathy for solo parents.

Just as this new arrangement was beginning in February, there arrived in Opoho some new parishioners, one of whom was destined to change the course of my life. During the previous year I had met Reva Kingsland at an SCM camp, and when she informed me she was coming to live in Opoho I immediately invited her to lead one of the Bible Classes. On her first morning she brought along two friends with whom she shared her flat. They were speech therapists who worked at the Dunedin Speech Clinic and had been together all through their training – Mary Keen and Elaine Parker.

When I paid a pastoral visit to their flat to welcome them into the parish – and with the hope of gaining two more Sunday School teachers – Elaine informed me we had met previously, at a wedding reception in 1949. I had officiated at the marriage of a parishioner, Nancy Gillam, her second cousin, and Elaine had been sent by her parents to represent the family. At the time my Nancy had been well enough to accompany me to the wedding, and had recognised Elaine among the guests as a friend from Timaru Girls' High School. Calling her over, Nancy had introduced us. (Elaine later loved to tease me that, since I did not at first recall that meeting, she had evidently made little impression on me. If so, that was soon to change.)

It soon became a great delight, after putting the children to bed, to leave them in the care of my fellow residents and escape for an hour or two to enjoy the company of the young women at 3 Comely Bank. The safety in numbers thus provided was an added benefit, since frequent visits to one eligible young woman by a recently widowed man would soon be talked about in such a close-knit community. I always had the good excuse that there was church business to discuss, for all three of the young women had agreed to take active roles in youth activities within the parish.

In due course Elaine accepted my invitation to go to a Repertory play, and thus began a relationship that was to last more than fifty years. But only occasionally did we go out together, lest rumours spread or the parish jump to conclusions before we ourselves knew where we were going. Since close acquaintance with an entire community makes it very difficult to conduct a courtship, most of our early friendship blossomed under the watchful eyes of Reva and Mary.

At first it was not at all clear that we would prove compatible. Observing the growing attachment, Reva commented to Elaine, perhaps as a warning, 'You're not a bit like Nancy!' Then there were our theological views: mine were considerably more liberal than those held by Elaine, who had recently come under the influence of a strong-minded friend in the Evangelical Union. Indeed, our early courtship consisted of a series of quite vigorous theological debates. But we learned to respect each other's views and to listen attentively to what the other had to say, and that laid the foundation for our lifelong mutual trust and respect. And by this time Elaine was already taking a genuine and affectionate interest in Judy and Johnny.

In the May vacation Elaine returned home to Timaru. She felt confident enough about our relationship to tell her parents about it. The news met with strong disapproval. The atmosphere in the household became so frigid, Elaine told me, that she approached her parish minister, Mac Wilson, to discuss the situation. Although considerably older than I was, Mac was a personal friend; he immediately wrote congratulating me on my wonderful choice and assuring me that it was not at all too soon after Nancy's death. Indeed, he assumed I had already proposed marriage, though we had certainly not yet reached that stage.

Since I had to go to Timaru on business in June, Elaine suggested that I go and make myself known to her parents. I innocently agreed to this, though I now see it was a serious mistake. I did not know quite what to expect, and was ill prepared for my chilly reception. Her mother had a prior engagement that evening, but her father minced no words in telling me that I should not be contemplating another marriage so soon after my wife's death. In the strongest possible terms, he explained why he and his wife believed it would be most unwise for Elaine to marry me, declaring that she was too young and inexperienced to take over the immediate responsibility of two young children. I suspect that, like many parents, they entertained their own expectations of the most eligible suitor for their daughter, thus making an impecunious widower burdened with two children quite unthinkable.

In June I was invited to consider a call to the parish of St James' in Newtown, Wellington. I was naturally receptive to the idea, knowing that if I were to remarry, it would be wise to make a new beginning somewhere else. While I was still weighing the situation, Elaine noticed that a speech therapy vacancy was being advertised in Wellington and decided to apply. In July I spent a weekend in Wellington getting to know the parish, and while I was there Elaine telegraphed me the news that she had been offered the Wellington job and intended to accept it. It was, to tell the truth, chiefly Elaine's message that led me to accept the invitation from St James'. The Presbyterian ethos understands moving from one parish to another as answering the 'call of God'; but as the old hymn tells us, God moves in mysterious ways!

While Elaine was spending the August vacation at home before setting off for Wellington, I had a second meeting with her parents. In retrospect, it does seem a little odd that while staying with Nancy's parents I should have gone to a meeting with Elaine and her parents to discuss our future; and surely, all of us found the meeting acutely embarrassing. The next day I alone accompanied Elaine to the station to catch the express train for Lyttelton. She felt that her parents were deserting her, and were willing to support her decisions only if she acceded to their wishes – a recognition that all too soon would lead to a crisis in our relationship.

In the meantime, and indeed all through 1950, I had been taking my task of preaching as seriously as ever, and striving to be honest and relevant in whatever I said from the pulpit. But in many respects I was preaching to myself, thinking through what it meant to live by faith during a period of great uncertainty. This is well illustrated by the sermon I wrote for Sunday 1 January 1950 on 'Strangers and Pilgrims on the earth' (Hebrews 11:16), in which I compared the Christian path of faith with that reflected in the Rubaiyat of Omar Khayyam, quoting such verses as:

> Ah, fill the cup: – what boots it to repeat
> How Time is slipping underneath our Feet:
> Unborn TOMORROW and dead YESTERDAY,
> Why fret about them if TODAY be sweet.

Ever since being introduced to Omar Khayyam's writing in my schooldays I have remained fascinated by this poem, and was delighted to have the opportunity to visit his tomb in Iran in 2000; but at that point in my life I was intent on appealing to the traditional Christian faith to counter his alarming yet insightful comments on the nature and uncertainty of human existence.

On Easter Sunday I naturally preached on the resurrection of Jesus, but this time with greater intensity than ever before. On rereading my sermon, I am surprised to find how aware I was that, during the twentieth century, the focus of Christian attention had been shifting to Jesus as the wise teacher and away from miraculous events that were in conflict with the scientific ethos of our age. No doubt my need to show how central the resurrection of Jesus was to Paul and the early church indicated how dependent my own faith had become on that belief. I followed this up in the evening service by sketching the evidence for the resurrection that Morison presented in *Who Moved the Stone?*

Looking back, it seems to me that I felt an unconscious need to defend the somewhat uncertain foundations on which my own commitment to Christianity had come to be based. Perhaps that is also the reason why I began a series of Sunday evening sermons on the various sects: Mormonism, Seventh Day Adventism, Christian Science, British Israelism, Theosophy and the Plymouth Brethren. In each case, after sketching their history, I indicated what I took to be the inadequacy of these radical variations of the classical Christian tradition. I suspect that my commitment to the defence of Christian orthodoxy was a protective shield that reflected my own vulnerability.

Such a tendency may have been strengthened by the fact that the

1948 General Assembly had established a Committee on Doctrine, and I felt privileged, as a very junior minister, to be appointed to it. Charged with the task of producing an official *Manual of Doctrine*, this group met regularly through 1949; and though the convener, Jack Bates, would be responsible for writing the final version, the committee determined the layout and general content. It was highly rewarding to be involved in such a creative exercise of theological expression. The work was finished in time to be approved by the 1949 Assembly for publication in 1950 as 'a layman's textbook and a basis for instruction of communicants'.

In my last sermon to the Opoho congregation, I chose to depict life as a pilgrimage. The task of packing up furniture and goods prior to departure had vividly impressed on me the idea that life is a ongoing journey through changing circumstances. Especially relevant to my experience was the description of Abraham in Hebrews 11:10: 'he looked forward to the city which has foundations, whose builder and maker is God'. Ever since that time, I have found the story of Abraham's journeyings a helpful symbol of the nature and path of faith.

The decision to move from Opoho to St James' in Wellington (known locally as St Jimmie's) was probably less than wise. Not only was Opoho my ideal parish – compact, lively and thriving – but there I had many friends and a great deal of personal support at a time when I really needed it. St James', however, although the third oldest Presbyterian parish in Wellington and blessed with an illustrious past, was now in rapid decline. I was to learn after I arrived that my predecessor had prophesied there would be only one more minister after him. Perhaps I should have heeded the organist when I went to preach for the call; looking out on the long rows of pews in that barn-like sanctuary, he said to me sadly, 'People don't come to church the way they used to'.

So why did I go? The invitation had come when I was in the midst of the confusion resulting from the loss of Nancy and the prospect of a new but as yet uncertain relationship. I was torn between remaining in a tolerable, secure situation and accepting the challenge of a new and uncertain way of life. Moreover, because of my original sense of call to the ministry, I had no ambition to aim for what some called the 'plum' parishes, but was content to go where I thought the church might need me most. This meant that I let circumstances, rather than wise planning on my part, determine where I should go; and in this case a considerable element of the 'circumstances' was Elaine's decision to move to Wellington.

Another change also had come over me. Opoho had been attractive because of its association with the Theological Hall. I had arrived there keen to further my theological qualifications, and secretly harboured the hope that I might some day gain a teaching post. Nancy's death caused me to lose all interest in academic theology. For the next few years I threw all my energy into the practical work of ministry, and except for biblical commentaries read very little theological literature.

My original plan was that I would leave Judy with Betty Brown and Johnny with the Holland family for a short time until I was established in Wellington. Then one day I happened to meet Margaret Balneaves (the sister of Agnes Mayer), who with her husband was also shortly moving to Wellington. I invited them to share the Newtown manse with me on the same terms I had offered Agnes and John. When they accepted, all that was left was the final packing and the farewells. It was exactly five years since Nancy and I had arrived in Opoho and, as I remember saying at my official farewell, they had indeed been eventful years for me.

Chapter Seven

A CHALLENGING PARISH

In early October 1950, exactly a year after Nancy's death, I arrived in Wellington to take up the challenge of St James' Church, Newtown. Elaine was on the wharf to meet me, but so also, to my surprise, were two or three office-bearers from the church. Their very kind and welcoming act caused me acute embarrassment at the time, as they knew nothing of my relationship with Elaine, and we were by no means officially engaged. It looked as though what we had successfully kept private in Opoho was suddenly to be revealed. But this was not the case – and in view of the uncertain nature of our relationship over the following months, their total discretion was fortunate indeed.

When the furniture arrived that same day, Elaine helped to arrange it in the manse; and if I remember correctly, she even attended my induction service that week, keeping herself well in the background. A week or two later, Margaret and Andrew Balneaves and their little daughter arrived. The large manse, with its five bedrooms and study, had plenty of space for all of us and all of our furniture; but being some seventy years old, it had several shortcomings. For heating water we had only a wood-burning stove in the kitchen, and since the water-cylinder was outside, it was hard to get any hot water at all in a cold southerly. We had a bath, of course, but the only shower was in the basement next to the laundry, where it had been installed for the use of the harrier club that the church had once sponsored.

Early in November I made my first trip to Auckland, to attend the General Assembly, and arranged a billet with my former roommate from

99

Knox College, Stan Hunt, who was then beginning his medical career. During the Assembly I had a long talk with Mac Wilson, the parish minister of Elaine's parents. Since Elaine had informed him of our problem, he had paid them a pastoral call, but had found it impossible to change their minds about my suitability as a prospective son-in-law.

The result was that I returned home feeling both tired and depressed. I had little hope for the future of our relationship, since it was unfair of me to ask Elaine to take on the heavy responsibilities involved and at the same time create a rift in her family; for her part, Elaine felt badly torn between her loyalty to her parents and her affection for me. After the cinema one evening we talked long into the night, and despite our deep reluctance and disappointment decided to stop seeing each other. It was just six weeks since my arrival in Wellington, where we had both come for the express purpose of giving our relationship a chance to develop. For a week or so I became more depressed than ever, and found relief only in playing César Franck's melancholy symphony on a recently acquired record-player.

Soon the holiday season arrived, and although Elaine and I were no longer keeping company we nonetheless exchanged small Christmas presents and I drove her to the railway station to catch the midnight express to Auckland. Refusing to go home to her parents, she chose to spend the summer holidays up north with her uncle and aunt. In the meantime I went to Dunedin, though not without problems arising from a national rail strike which necessitated my hitchhiking from Christchurch to Dunedin. My purpose was to attend the SCM Conference, for which I had been appointed chaplain, and, after spending some time with my parents, to bring the two children back with me. On the return journey, the children and I flew from Christchurch to Wellington – a memorable trip, for air travel then was not the commonplace event it is today.

I threw all my energy into promoting the life of the parish. One of its few attractions was that, since it owned five halls of different sizes, no time would have to be spent in expanding the facilities (an issue that had proved difficult at Opoho). But when even the surviving Boys' Brigade folded, it became all too clear that empty buildings were of little value without people and activities to make use of them. The great irony was that the rapid decline in the parish had been another of its attractions, since that left me free to experiment on the grounds that I could hardly make matters any worse. So, with my personal future very much up in the air, reversing the decline at St Jimmie's became my chief aim in life.

Another issue that consumed a great deal of my attention in the first half of 1951 was the waterfront dispute, which tied up our ports for three months. To be sure, the Watersiders' Union was *partly* to blame for what became a national disaster; yet I felt sympathetic toward them, for my working-class parish included many watersiders. The media kept referring to the dispute as a strike, when in fact it was a lockout imposed by the employers when, for quite understandable reasons, the men refused to work overtime.

Near the height of this altercation it fell to St James' (as it did four times a year) to be the church whose morning service was broadcast live on the radio. I decided to speak about the dispute, choosing as the title of my sermon 'Principles are not enough'. (Prime Minister Sidney Holland, in backing the employers, had publicly asserted that he was defending principles.) On hearing that my sermon was discussed with approval at the next general meeting of the Watersiders' Union, I felt encouraged to go to the union office and meet some of the members personally. As a result, two members of their Dispute Committee agreed to come to the manse to discuss their case with a fellow minister and me, and we reported the discussion to the Presbyterian Public Questions Committee.

Not long after this, the dispute showed signs of becoming extremely dangerous. Rumours went around of men preparing weapons in case of a clash with police or with soldiers being sent to work on the wharves. At that point the Prime Minister declared a state of emergency, which meant among other things that no opinions on the dispute were to be expressed in the newspapers or on radio. The Presbyterian Public Questions Committee requested a meeting with the Prime Minister. I was not present at that meeting, having been called away on other business to Auckland – where, incidentally, I attempted to make contact with the Auckland watersiders. The Prime Minister angrily condemned the Presbyterian deputation, declaring that it had no business interfering in the affairs of state at such a crucial time. The deputation withdrew, thoroughly chastened; yet when the Prime Minister relaxed the emergency regulations the very next day, its members justifiably concluded that their efforts had not been in vain. Eventually the Watersiders' Union could hold out no longer, and the dispute was over; the Prime Minister called a snap election and was returned with an enlarged majority.

These events and the affairs of the parish so occupied my mind that I neglected to give my children the personal attention they deserved. I had entered the ministry believing that the church always had first claim on my time, and it was not until many years later that I regretfully concluded that I had not balanced my responsibilities well. Johnny, now five, had been enrolled at Newtown School on my return to Wellington, and two-year-old Judy I cared for at home with the help of Margaret Balneaves. Yet I am distressed to recall how readily I left my children to the care of others for a fortnight at a time while I represented the wider church on two occasions in the presbyteries of Hawke's Bay and South Auckland. Along with another speaker, A.D. Horwell on the first occasion and Tom Steele on the second, I was to present to each parish the challenges of the New Life Movement on which the national church had recently embarked.

As the name suggests, the aim of the campaign was to recall the church to its pastoral mission; and for this it needed to raise an extra half million pounds to build churches in the new housing areas then springing up around New Zealand as a result of the post-war baby-boom. My earlier statistical work had helped alert the Assembly to the need for a special effort; indeed, the previous Census had shown that New Zealand had many more Presbyterians than parish figures indicated. As a result, the Assembly urged every parish to conduct a parish survey as a preparatory stage in the New Life Movement.

To fulfil this task for St James', which had around 25,000 people within its parish boundaries, I organised about fifteen of our members to spend many evenings visiting every home in the parish, enquiring about the occupants' church affiliation. Next, we collated the results and passed on the information, where appropriate, to the other denominations. Then, having compiled a more complete record of all the Presbyterians in the parish, we sent out a regular newsletter to nurture their interest.

Many of us were highly enthusiastic about the New Life Movement, particularly after the recent failure of the church union movement; only later did it become more evident that the very necessity for such an effort was due to the long-term decline of the church. It is now clear that the challenge I was facing at St James' was not simply a problem of inner-city parishes, but a symptom of the condition of the church as a whole.

One evening early in July I was drying the dishes for Margaret Balneaves when she casually remarked that I should get together again with Elaine. (Only much later did I learn that Elaine used to phone Margaret from time to time to enquire how I was faring.) Then, quite by accident and barely a week later, I ran into Elaine in the course of my hospital round on a Friday afternoon and invited her to the manse (which was just across the road from the hospital) for a cup of tea. While she was there Johnny came in, greeted her warmly, and immediately ran next door to call Judy: 'Come quickly! Elaine's here!' It seemed a very promising omen.

I invited Elaine back for an evening the following week. We seemed to be taking up again just where we had left off, almost as if nothing had happened in the intervening eight months. It all seemed so right that after outlining all the difficulties we would have to face – the problem with her parents, the responsibility of mothering two small children, the burden of living in a manse under the eyes of the congregation – I formally asked if she would marry me. Without a moment's hesitation she said, 'Yes!'

The next day, without telling her, I wrote to ask her parents' consent. I received no reply from them, but Elaine was greatly surprised when her father rang to tell her that if she proceeded with the marriage, it was entirely her responsibility and that she was 'to count them out'. In spite of that setback we went ahead and became officially engaged on Saturday 14 July. After showing the ring to Margaret and Andrew, we went to see our friends Joan and Howard Anderson in Khandallah to tell them the happy news.

Although our friends seemed delighted, our elation was a little premature. On Sunday morning Elaine rang to tell me she was having second thoughts; perhaps she had been too hasty. Although somewhat taken aback, I assured her I was not going to let her down by drawing back a second time. While I was conducting the morning service, Elaine sought motherly support and advice from Mrs Peacock who, having taken her on as a boarder, had come to treat her like a daughter. As Elaine told me sometime later, Mrs Peacock gave her a very firm talking-to, telling her she must stand on her own feet, make her own decisions, and not bow to parental pressure. This advice Elaine took on board, and from then until our wedding several months later she never wavered again. Shortly after our engagement the church held a social evening, and I took the opportunity to introduce Elaine to members of the congregation as my fiancée. It was a very proud moment for me and the news spread like wildfire, with the parishioners registering their delight. We then began to plan the wedding for 20 November.

During the August vacation Elaine went down to Timaru to visit her parents, hoping to heal the rift. But they were reluctant to show any interest in her engagement ring, refused to discuss her wedding, and when visitors came to the house made no mention of her future plans. Elaine returned to Wellington hurt, humiliated, and greatly disappointed. The wedding obviously could not be in Timaru, as she would naturally have wished, nor was her young sister Juliet permitted to attend, let alone be her bridesmaid. Elaine turned to her Wadestown friends, Mr and Mrs Ball, with whom she had stayed on first arriving in Wellington. Mrs Ball, on hearing of Elaine's plight, kindly offered their home for the wedding reception. Not only that, but Mr Ball agreed to give the bride away and their daughter Phyllis was to be her bridesmaid. The obvious place for the wedding had now become the Wadestown Presbyterian Church, some 200 yards (180 m) from the Balls' home, and we arranged for the service to be conducted by a minister friend, Duncan Hercus, then chaplain at Scots College.

The highlight of our engagement period was the social evening that the congregation arranged in our honour. The recently appointed organist at St James' was Arnold Roseveare, the son of one of my elders at Opoho. Among the many delightful numbers that members of the congregation prepared for the evening's concert were several sung by the church choir under Arnold's expert baton. Especially memorable was the parody they wrote in her honour: 'Goodnight Irene' became 'Goodnight Elaine'.

In the weeks leading up to the wedding we were both kept very busy. I had to travel to Dunedin to attend the General Assembly in the first week of November, and passing through Timaru I made one last unsuccessful attempt to persuade Elaine's parents to relent and attend the wedding. In the meantime, Elaine had assumed responsibility for both the arrangements and the financial costs of the wedding reception. Partly because she handled everything with such efficiency and calm dignity, I was hardly aware of her inward conflict – a sense of shame at being abandoned by her family, compounded by apprehension about going against their wishes.

Our wedding day was fine and warm, with plenty of sunshine to make up for an occasional patch of clouds. Determined that, as near as circumstances would allow, the wedding would be what she had always hoped for, Elaine had had a lovely white wedding gown made. The Session clerk of the congregation, Gordon Warren, was my best man, and relatives, friends and a number of parishioners attended the early afternoon ceremony. My parents had travelled up from Otago, and were to stay on to look after Johnny and Judy while we were on our honeymoon.

After the reception Elaine and I went to Wellington Hospital to visit Margaret Balneaves, who had just given birth to her second child. Finally, at about 6 p.m., we set off on the drive north for our honeymoon. The little pre-war Morris Eight I had bought in Dunedin in 1948 had just come back from an engine overhaul, which in those days meant not exceeding 30 miles an hour (48 kph) for the first 500 miles (800 km), so our journey up the island was a leisurely one. Eventually we reached a fishing bach at the south end of Lake Taupo, which I had arranged to rent from the father of my student friend Walter Metcalf. There we spent seven or eight days, wandering around Taupo and Rotorua, before returning to Wellington to face the more serious side of married life. For me it was a return to parish work and a new marital relationship. For Elaine it was a much greater and more daunting metamorphosis than I could fully appreciate at the time.

A test of our new relationship arose from the decision of the Presbyterian Church to hold 'Schools for Ministers' throughout the country in 1952. These were intended to inform and stimulate ministers with regard to the New Life Movement. As one of the team of four or five people invited to lecture at each of seven three-day schools, I was often away from home for several days at a time. Unfortunately, I failed to consider the extra burden this placed on Elaine at the very time she was trying to adjust to her new situation in life.

By way of compensation for these absences, the church invited the lecturers' wives to attend the final school at Tauranga, and to precede it with a holiday break. Leaving the children in the care of parishioners, we drove north through New Plymouth to Auckland, where we stayed with Elaine's uncle and aunt. This was our first time alone together since our honeymoon, and did much to overcome the stress of my repeated absences so early in our marriage.

I returned to the regular work of the ministry: sermon preparation in the study every morning, pastoral visiting in the afternoon, and committee meetings or more visiting in the evening. That was a fairly standard routine for ministers in the days before women joined the paid workforce and television appeared on the scene. In addition to the Sunday morning and evening services at St James', I introduced a regular service at the TB ward of Wellington Hospital, which at that stage had no full-time chaplains. And because a nearby funeral chapel served many people with no church connection, I found myself conducting a funeral nearly every week. Weddings were much less frequent.

Perhaps the most unusual extra duty I took on involved the cinema that once stood across from Parliament Buildings at the corner of Lambton Quay and Molesworth Street. During World War II the Wellington City Council had given it permission to show films on Sunday afternoons for the benefit of soldiers on leave in a city that offered few amusements. The practice continued into the 1950s, but this unique relaxation of Sabbath restrictions was conditional: before the film began, a clergyman must present a five-minute address. Today such a condition seems laughable, but then it was a serious matter. I accepted the challenge – and challenge it was – to capture and hold the attention of people who were not a bit interested, and who often went right on talking. As I had developed some skill in addresses to children, I usually told a story with some moral or spiritual implications; and for this purpose, the Bible had lots of good tales the audience were mostly unaware of. Occasionally they applauded when I finished, but no doubt this was because the film was about to begin. With this duty came a fee of £1 – a quite useful addition to our income at a time when my salary was no more than £10 a week.

With the enthusiastic support of the Session, I instituted an annual plan which, as well as celebrating the chief seasons of the Christian year, divided the year into six two-month periods. During each of these periods a Confirmation class would be offered, with new members confirmed in the last week at the regular Preparatory Service on the Thursday evening. On the Saturday following we would have a working-bee to clean up the grounds and do any odd repair jobs before celebrating Holy Communion the next day. Then, on the following Wednesday, we held a social evening to nurture the spirit of fellowship within the congregation. Because it gave form and regularity to parish activities, this plan proved very successful.

In November 1952, while I was attending the General Assembly at New Plymouth, Elaine rang me with the joyful news that she was pregnant. In due course Elizabeth was born at Wellington Hospital on 24 July 1953, the day before Judy was to start school on her fifth birthday. Elaine's mother, thereafter known as 'Nan', came to Wellington for two days to visit Elaine and the baby. Although she stayed at a hotel and I saw her only briefly, relations between her and Elaine were, if cool, at least cordial. The birth of a first grandchild was helping to thaw the ice.

We were naturally delighted to have an addition to the family. From the first, Elaine assumed that I knew more about looking after babies than she did; and while this was initially true, her own caring nature soon took over. It was just as well, for her ability to cope on her own was very soon to be severely tested. When Elizabeth was only about two months old, I caught a chill while conducting a funeral at Karori Cemetery during a Wellington southerly, and the chill soon turned to pneumonia. At first I was nursed at home, with the doctor coming daily to give me a penicillin injection; but then Peter Calvert, a student friend who was now a house surgeon at the hospital, came to see me and was so alarmed by my condition that he rang my doctor, who immediately had me admitted to hospital.

As it turned out, Peter probably saved my life, for neither Elaine nor I recognised how ill I was until she visited me in hospital and discovered I had been placed on the 'seriously ill' list. The ward sister took her aside and said, 'Mrs Geering, you realise, don't you, that your husband is a very sick man'. Elaine wrote to me some days later:

> Thank goodness there's penicillin. It wasn't till five o'clock one morning when I was feeding Elizabeth that I realised how ill you were. It was a most terrible feeling. It just hadn't sunk in before and I couldn't get to sleep again. Life without you is just unthinkable…

Later, we often thought of the dreadful situation Elaine would have found herself in, had I not recovered – after less than two years of marriage, at the age of twenty-six, being left a widow with sole responsibility for three young children, and having landed herself in that predicament against the express warnings of her parents.

Of course I did recover, and afterwards we even found little things to laugh about. For example, before taking ill I had already chosen the hymns for the following Sunday, and the person conducting the service did not change them. One of them was 'For all the saints who from their labours rest'; and we heard later that, when this hymn was announced, one parishioner leaned over to another and whispered, 'I didn't realise he was as ill as that!'

When, after nearly five weeks, I was discharged and advised to take some time off to recuperate, we arranged to spend two weeks with a second cousin of mine who ran a guesthouse at Woodbury, not far from Timaru. On the way we spent a couple of nights with Elaine's parents, where we were very cordially received – largely, no doubt, because they both took great delight in Elizabeth, then only three months old. She had become a very real bond between Elaine and her parents, and would continue and grow in that felicitous role.

While we were at Woodbury I taught Elaine to drive the car. People now recognise that it is usually unwise for a husband to teach his wife to drive, but we were blithely ignorant of that. Despite a few testy moments the marriage did not fall apart, and after only ten days Elaine received her licence. Her lack of experience, however, soon showed up on our return to Wellington. After a successful drive to Karori and back she misjudged the clearance while entering our rather narrow garage and slightly dented the left front bumper. She refused to drive again, and let her licence lapse for many years.

We were hardly back from the South Island when I became caught up in the aftermath of the Tangiwai disaster. The crater lake on Mt Ruapehu had suddenly burst through its ice-wall, sending a torrent of freezing water surging down the Tangiwai Stream, hitting a railway bridge just as the Northern Express train reached it. Much of the train plunged into the swollen river with the loss of over 150 lives. It was Christmas Eve, and I heard the first news on the radio just as I was about to begin the 8 a.m. Christmas Day service. I still recall how angry I was when the church organist asked me whether this tragedy might be an act of divine judgement because the nation was not celebrating Christmas in a Christian way.

Another unsettling experience was not long in coming. After the service I was met by a Salvation Army officer, who informed me in a commanding voice that he was 'on Operation Tangiwai', and that since many of the bodies being recovered were not readily identifiable, they were being brought to Wellington Hospital. He asked permission to use our church halls, just across the road from the hospital, as a haven for many of the relatives coming to search for their loved ones. This I readily gave, but was somewhat taken aback when he added that although the ladies of our parish were welcome to provide tea and refreshments, any bereavement counselling must be left to the Salvation Army.

Some of those lost came from our parish; one was a seven-year-old boy, an only child, who was being taken by his uncle on a holiday to Auckland. The funeral was such a tragic occasion that I could bring little comfort to the many grieving and bewildered people who attended. Yet although the disaster was certainly a tragedy, it was not, as some suggested, 'an act of God'. We should long ago have renounced that kind of theological explanation. Those who remained unidentified were accorded a mass burial in Karori cemetery, where I attended a moving ceremony. The Duke of Edinburgh was present, representing Queen Elizabeth II, who was making her first visit to New Zealand.

It was only a week or two later, in January 1954, that Elaine and I eagerly took the children down to Cambridge and Kent Terraces to see the Queen and Duke travelling to and from Government House. Elaine held Elizabeth up to see the Queen, trying to impress upon her that this was something to remember; but although she was later often told about it, she was too young to register the event.

The increasing time needed to minister to patients in Wellington Hospital led me to persuade the Presbyterian Social Service to appoint a full-time chaplain, who would also be an associate minister of St James'. After the appointment was made, my associate became responsible for the evening service, and I took two morning services, one at 9.30 a.m.

for the Bible Classes and adults, and a family service at 11 a.m. which incorporated the Sunday School. We had become concerned that the Sunday School activities were too much divorced from the church, leaving the children with no real experience of Sunday worship. To avoid dividing the congregation, and since we now had a kitchen and lounge at the back of the church, people from both congregations had the opportunity to socialise over tea and coffee between the two services. Although the arrangement seemed good in theory, and was still in operation when I left, I doubt if it was as successful as we had hoped.

During my pastorate at St James' I served on several Assembly committees and was convener of the Statistics Committee, the Presbyterian Church Union Committee, and the Joint Standing Committee of the three negotiating churches. In May 1954 the latter group held a retreat at Feilding to discuss further steps to be taken towards church union. The first was to prepare a study manual for use in the churches during 1956; and to this end I was commissioned to edit *Shall we Unite?*, a booklet containing the more important papers delivered at the retreat.

The second step was to spread the net even further by inviting all churches in the National Council of Churches (NCC) to establish an even larger joint committee to discuss a possible merger. I took great delight in writing the letter of invitation and receiving the replies. The Baptist Church declined; the Salvation Army and the Quakers were unclear as to how they could fit in; the Greek Orthodox Church never replied; and the Anglican Church said they would think about it (and took many years doing so). The only positive response came from the Associated Churches of Christ. What finally came of this initial exploration into wider church union is quite another story.

At the end of 1954 the five of us drove up to Auckland in our venerable Morris Eight. It was a snug fit: Johnny and Judy sat in the back seat separated by the bassinette, in which Elizabeth could sleep quite comfortably. This was before seat-belts, of course, but even so they had hardly any room to move. After staying the night with friends in Hastings, we continued on to Auckland, where I had arranged to have the use of the Ponsonby manse for the month of January in return for taking the services at the church – a common arrangement that allowed ministers to have a good holiday at relatively little expense. But our other aim was to visit Elaine's uncle and aunt and participate in the wedding of their daughter, Leona: I was to conduct the marriage service and Elaine would help arrange the wedding breakfast, which was held at the manse.

During that month I took the opportunity to read more theology, and found myself being drawn back to my academic interests. Up until then I had put all my energy into promoting the activities of the parish. I had managed to reverse the decline in membership and attendance, and with the enthusiastic and creative efforts of key office-bearers the parish had staged two very successful fairs. At a time when most parishes were happy if their bring-and-buy netted £30, our first fair raised £700 and the second was just short of £1,000. But much of the money raised went into repairs for the ageing buildings. Since the halls I initially regarded as an asset had become a liability, we sold the three largest ones to the New Zealand Players, and they became rehearsal rooms for the first professional theatre in the country.

In spite of the spirit generated by the New Life Movement, I was beginning to feel that the church was making no real headway. My original confidence that sound preaching of a liberal kind would build up the church was beginning to ebb away. Eventually I became the butt of a family joke, because on many a Sunday evening I would announce to Elaine that I was going to resign. I did not intend these words seriously, but they reflected my frustration and growing doubts about the church's future. It was this, among other things, that was sending me back to serious theological reading.

In May 1955 I was a Presbyterian representative at the second Faith and Order Conference held at Sumner, in Christchurch, under the auspices of the now quite vigorous National Council of Churches. I remember this conference not only for its intrinsic interest but because I was approached about being appointed Secretary to the NCC. Although strongly attracted to all things ecumenical, my interests and expertise lay not so much in administration as in teaching. And from that recognition, no doubt, arose the idea of a career change.

Thus, when I spotted an advertisement by the Presbyterian Church of Queensland seeking applications for a new Chair of Old Testament Studies at Emmanuel College, Brisbane, I decided to submit my name. I had no great sense of a call this time; I simply knew it was something I would love to do, and it did not entail the rejection of my original sense of being called. Although my chances seemed slim, Elaine and I had great fun imagining and discussing such a different future.

As it happened, we were down in Dunedin for the meeting of the General Assembly when I received the cablegram offering me the position. Almost unable to believe it, we went for a walk in the upper Botanical Gardens overlooking North Dunedin and tried to take it all in. Then we drove out to my parents' home in Allanton, on the Taieri Plain, and told them the news. While glad for our sake, they were also sad that we would be moving even further away, for in those days families did not become scattered all around the world as they so readily do today.

On returning to Wellington, we were fully occupied over the Christmas season with preparations for our departure. (Elaine jokingly told our friends that I now kept a Hebrew Grammar under my pillow to brush up on the subject.) One of the more serious matters was arranging our travel to Australia: this was some years before air travel became routine, and passage on one of the two ships regularly crossing the Tasman often had to be booked months in advance. Having been warned of this by a friend in the Union Steamship Company, I had fortunately pencilled in applications for berths some time earlier, even though this seemed to be tempting fate.

Since we could take with us only my books and our personal belongings, one of our final tasks was to auction our furniture and household effects. Our one-year-old car, a recent replacement for the venerable Morris, I sold to our organist. Then one day in late January we all boarded the ss *Monowai*, and after farewells exchanged with many members of the congregation, and the ritual singing of 'Now is the Hour', we sailed out of Wellington Harbour and into Cook Strait, en route for Sydney.

Chapter Eight

FROM A PREACHER TO A TEACHER

I had much to think about on the voyage across the Tasman, for although I was remaining within the boundaries of Christian ministry, I was embarking on a very different kind of life. Indeed, it proved to be even more of a watershed in my career than I realised at the time. But being blissfully oblivious to such concerns, I simply savoured the three and a half days of thinking, reading and eating – interrupted by some unexpected interludes with the family, such as our mild embarrassment when seven-year-old Judy won the jackpot on the poker machine.

In Sydney we were welcomed at the wharf by one of my future colleagues, James Peter, who walked up to me and said, 'Professor Geering, I presume'. I was still quite unused to what seemed such an exalted title. After hosting us around Sydney, James took us all to the airport to catch our plane to Queensland.

The city of Brisbane, our home for the next few years, was in those days commonly described as an 'overgrown country town'. Its nearly one million inhabitants were so scattered over an area of some 900 square miles (2,300 km²) that the suburbs included farms and large tracts of bush. This being the annual 'big wet', as they called the rainy season, all we could see from the air was water and trees; it seemed we were about to land in a tropical jungle. On arrival we were escorted to the Canberra Hotel, by far the largest hotel in Brisbane, but unlicensed because it had been erected by the Queensland Temperance Society. This early indication of the conservative character of the State of Queensland concerned us much less than the electricity strike then in effect, which meant we had to trudge up seemingly endless flights of stairs to reach our rooms on the eleventh floor.

That was our introduction to Brisbane, where our first task was to buy a house. Within three days we had chosen a traditional Queensland house over the newer bungalows. While cost had been a considerable factor, this choice proved advantageous in the long run; set high on wooden stumps to protect it from white ants, the house was naturally air-conditioned by the sea breeze that commonly sprang up in the late afternoon. On the other hand, we were so inept at house-buying (living in manses, one gains no experience of such things) that only after we moved in did we notice that the bathroom had a bath, but no hand-basin! Furthermore, the interior walls consisted of vertical tongue-and-groove boards so thin that what was said in one room could be clearly heard in the next. And as was the case in much of Brisbane at that time, sanitation consisted of an outdoor privy in the end of the garden, along with bath and sink drains that emptied into open gutters in the street.

But at last we were in a home of our own. That brought some unexpected but welcome changes for us as a family, for living in a manse next to the church often feels very much like living in a fishbowl. On the other hand, we were less comfortable than we had been in the large, old St James' manse. To be sure, we had a fridge for the first time in our lives (in the Queensland climate, either a fridge or an ice-box is a necessity); it had been included with the house as extra bait to clinch the deal. But when it came to furnishings we were soon out of funds, as all the money from selling the car had been needed for the deposit on the house. So at first we were very poor in Brisbane. For two years, we had to leave our sitting-room unfurnished and could not afford to have the telephone connected. In fact, I often had to rely on students who owned cars to transport me to and from the college!

Nonetheless, we settled down happily and excitedly to our new life. We had to adjust quickly to such novelties as heat, humidity and mosquitoes. (Elizabeth, then three, asked one day, 'Why did God make mosquitoes?' For once, I fear I had no adequate theological answer.) Still, the mild Queensland winters were such pleasant compensation that we soon took the hot summers for granted.

The schools were something of a shock. The younger children were still using slates to write on, and rote learning was standard, even in subjects like Social Studies. School life was highly regimented, and the curriculum prescribed in great detail. The Minister of Education used to boast that he knew what was being taught in every classroom at every hour of the day.

From the very first Sunday in our new home we attended the leading city church, St Andrew's, and not the local parish church of Indooroopilly. Although I thought the latter would have been more appropriate, our neighbours were regular attendees at St Andrew's, and for the first year they kindly drove us the four miles into the city. After having been in a pulpit nearly every Sunday for thirteen years, it was a great delight to be able to sit in the pew with my family. We soon became good friends with the minister, Bill Young, a good preacher who had been called up from Melbourne. Although I played no role in the Session, I was invited to preach from time to time. On one occasion Bill took ill during the service, and I stepped up and took over; and when he later introduced short mid-week services during the lunch-hour, I was frequently called upon to give the address.

My induction into the new Chair of Old Testament Studies took place in the Clayfield parish church, and there I delivered my inaugural lecture. I became the third member of a team of full-time teachers, the other two being James Peter (who taught Theology and Church History) and Henry Innes (who taught New Testament). James was an able young theologian who had come up from Sydney, while Henry, then approaching retirement age, was an out-and-out Queenslander on whose local knowledge we two 'foreigners' came to depend. The three of us worked together very harmoniously over the next four years. Being a small company of theological teachers we had to share out a number of non-lecturing duties, and one of my tasks was to serve as the librarian of our small but growing theological library. In my first year, I had to spend a good deal of time putting the jumble of books I had inherited into some kind of order, and appreciated anew my experience as assistant librarian at Knox College.

When lectures began, some three weeks after my arrival, they had to be delivered in St Paul's Church in the inner city, for the new Emmanuel College building had not yet been completed. Some years previously, the University of Queensland had taken the bold step of moving from its original site in the city centre to the promontory of St Lucia, in one of the large bends in the Brisbane River. This enabled an impressive building programme to begin. As the senior college of those enjoying an integral relationship with the university, Emmanuel was given the prime site. It would be the end of the first term before we moved to the brand new facilities at St Lucia. The relationship of the Theological Hall to the residential college was exactly the same at Emmanuel as it was at Knox College.

I was far from feeling a total newcomer, however, for I already had indirect connections with Emmanuel College. Dr Merrington, the Master who had enabled me as a student to take up residence in Knox College, was not only a Queenslander by birth but had played a leading role in the original founding of Emmanuel. Dr Hunter, who had taught me Old Testament, was another Queenslander, and though now retired, he happened to be in Brisbane for the opening of the new college.

I entered into my teaching duties with great excitement, although in the first year I found it very demanding to keep two lectures ahead of the students in my preparation. Fortunately, it was the practice to hold lectures only from Tuesday to Thursday, since many of the students were home missionaries who had to return to country parishes to conduct services on the Sunday. This enabled me to concentrate on preparing lectures over a four-day weekend. As it was over ten years since I completed my Honours degree in Old Testament, I had a good deal of catching up to do; but I soon discovered that the surest way of learning a subject is having to teach it.

By the time I was a student, all the great battles about the supposed Mosaic authorship of the Pentateuch had been fought. In academic circles, at least, they were now over, and one was free to study the Old Testament books historically, as a set of human documents that reflected the limited beliefs (and even the prejudices) of the people who wrote them, long after the time of Moses. But much of this new approach to the Bible never reached the people in the pews; in this respect, church life in Queensland had remained rather more conservative than it had in New Zealand. I soon found that most of the students entered their training with a literal and highly simplistic understanding of the Bible; yet they did not display the dogged resistance to what I was teaching that is so commonly found in fundamentalists. One older student said to me, 'This is all very new to us but, given time and patience, we shall be able to work our way through it'.

To help students understand the context in which the various Old Testament books were written, I developed an introductory course that sketched the history of the peoples of the ancient Middle East, among whom the people of Israel lived, and in relation to whom they discovered their own special destiny. As a student I had not been aware of this approach; but feeling the lack of it during my first parish ministry, I had made it a particular interest, especially after finding that many parishioners had no idea of the chronological relation of Abraham and Moses, to say nothing of the kings of Israel and Judah. I had constructed charts based on the biblical material, and found them invaluable for providing me with a mental picture of the order of events and people. Similarly, I developed simpler and more interesting methods of teaching biblical Hebrew, abandoning the rather dull Davidson's grammar, on which I had been brought up and which had been the standard since 1874, and replacing it with that of Weingreen, which first appeared in 1939.

The freedom I felt in explaining the Old Testament historically, and in accepting the mythic and legendary nature of many of its elements, did not yet apply to the New Testament to the same degree. Even liberal scholars commonly regarded the latter as a reasonably authentic record of the life and words of Jesus. One great exception was Rudolf Bultmann and his followers, but he did not become widely known in the English-speaking world until after World War II. His books were just being translated in the early 1950s, and up to that time I had read none of them.

This deficiency became obvious when the Presbyterian Church of Australia invited me to write a study book for the Easter camps. In dealing with both testaments, it had become my practice to accept as historical all narratives that I had no good reason to doubt. Accordingly, I decided to base my study book on the story of the two disciples returning to Emmaus, and titled it 'And their eyes were opened'. I noted in the introduction that this study accepted the account 'as substantially historical and therefore a reliable independent witness to the resurrection of Jesus'; I went on to describe it as a vivid portrait of the origin and growth of genuine Christian faith, reflecting the experience of all those Christians who had never seen the risen Christ with the physical eye, but whose 'eyes of faith' had been truly opened. In view of what I was to find myself saying about the Easter stories only ten years later, I am now embarrassed by how traditional this exposition was, and am not surprised that some liberal clergy in New South Wales accused me of being too conservative – a charge that many today will find both surprising and amusing.

Of course, the terms 'liberal' and 'conservative' are relative, and must always be understood in a particular context. What may be thought a liberal opinion at one point in time may be judged conservative a few decades later. A few of us who were teaching in the Brisbane theological colleges at that time instituted a study group in which we introduced one another to various books we had been reading. It was here that I first began to be influenced by the writings of Rudolf Bultmann and Paul Tillich. For much of my life I have found myself trying to keep up with a fast-changing cultural world, and a notable acceleration in my thinking began at about this point.

Having already learned how to reinterpret the myths and legends in the Book of Genesis, I was open to Bultmann's scepticism about much of the New Testament material and attracted to his assertion that much of the language and assumptions reflected in the New Testament belonged in the category of myth rather than history. One need only recall the angelic choir in the Christmas story, the angel at the tomb, and the ascension of Jesus into heaven to find obvious examples. Bultmann contended that the New Testament message had for too long been imprisoned in the now obsolete mythological world-view of the first century; for it to be relevant to the twentieth century, it needed to be radically reinterpreted to fit the modern world-view. (It is unfortunate that his critics often mis-interpreted his term 'demythologised' to mean 'debunked'.) Our group concluded that Bultmann was raising pertinent questions that could not be avoided, although we were not persuaded to adopt the existentialist model of faith he propounded. Without consciously recognising the fact, I was beginning to expand my area of academic interest well beyond the borders of the Old Testament.

One of our number had just returned from refresher leave during which he had studied under Tillich in New York. He introduced us to such new terms as 'being itself' and 'symbol of ultimate concern', which

Tillich had coined in order to speak more convincingly about the nature of God in a modern context. Tillich was then pioneering a seminal new theology, and the first two volumes of his *Systematic Theology* had just been published. But though attracted by both these scholars, I did not have the opportunity to study them in any depth until some years later. I remained very busy trying to keep up with my classes and to master the discipline of Old Testament Studies which constituted my current responsibility.

In 1957, however, I did take on a new task that widened my interests further. I was invited to teach the first course to be offered by the University of Queensland in what was then called Comparative Religion. More by accident than by design, I was already partially equipped for this task because in my student days I had taken the unusual option of a paper in Comparative Religion for the Melbourne BD. And of course Old Testament Studies and Comparative Religion have a natural affinity, for the former leads one to study the religions of the ancient Semitic world out of which monotheism emerged. I suspect that is why Wheeler Robinson and T.H. Robinson, two of the giant Old Testament scholars of the early twentieth century, came to write books on Comparative Religion.

This new task meant that I now had a great deal of additional reading and preparation to do, at a time when I was already fully stretched, to extend my knowledge of the Old Testament. It may have been unwise of me to accept the added intellectual challenge, but I never regretted it; indeed, it helped to prepare me for my final post as Professor of Religious Studies some fourteen years later. Nor was it without its interesting pedagogical challenges and whimsicalities. Comparative Religion lectures were scheduled for Wednesday afternoons; and in that warm climate, shortly after the midday meal, with the buzz of motor-mowers outside, it was difficult to stop the students from falling asleep. I often thought about the story of the professor who dreamt he was lecturing to a class and woke up to find that he was!

My task was made more difficult by the paucity of textbooks then available on the subject. At first I used John Murphy's *The Origin and History of Religions*. Although I had to supplement his book with material gleaned from many sources, it was Murphy who first led me to study the many different religions within the context of the long cultural evolution of humankind. He related them to their cultural contexts, characterising the most notable of these as the Primitive (food-gatherers and hunters), Agricultural, Civilised (living in cities) and Prophetic. Looking back, I see here the beginnings of the evolutionary approach to religious development that I was later to take myself.

One disadvantage of Murphy's book was that, like much of Comparative Religion at the time, it studied every religion except Christianity. By the time I repeated the course in 1959, John B. Noss's more comprehensive *Man's Religions* had just been published, and it made my task much easier. Switching to that fine text represented the progression from Comparative Religion to today's Religious Studies.

It now seems to me incredible that, as well as taking on this extra task, I spent one night a week teaching Hebrew in the city's School of Modern Languages, which was open to the general public. But spreading my activities in this way seemed quite natural at the time. And the amount of reading I had to do meant that my general knowledge was being both deepened and widened at a much greater pace than ever before. I now feel all but aghast to recall my schedule of some fourteen lectures from Tuesday to Thursday, leaving Friday to Monday for reading and preparation. As a result, the quality of my lectures fell far short of the standard I set for myself in later years; but most of them were carefully typed out in full, even when they amounted to little more than summaries of what I had read. Our next-door neighbour, a widow living alone, often told me she felt comforted by hearing my typewriter clacking away far into the night; for my part there was little comfort in that heat and humidity, as the perspiration poured off me.

Of course I also tried to give adequate attention to my family, being fully aware that during my parish days they had been too often neglected in favour of my ministerial duties. Accordingly, we spent much time together as a family during the weekends, especially after the beginning of my second year, when we acquired a car. But that was also the year in which Elaine resumed her own career as a speech therapist. This meant that I was now responsible for preparing breakfast and lunches for the whole family, for transporting the two older children to school, and for looking after three-year-old Elizabeth on Mondays and Fridays. To be sure it was a busy life, but a very happy one, made yet more enjoyable by the habit we soon developed of spending time together before the evening meal, talking over the events of the day as we enjoyed a relaxing cold drink.

Through all of this we remained healthy except for two attacks of hepatitis, which was then quite widespread in Queensland. On the first occasion, all five of us were confined to our beds for several weeks while kindly neighbours brought in food. A year later, Elaine and I suffered what was probably a relapse. At least I was able to do a great deal of reading, for after the initial few days one felt quite normal apart from the need to remain in bed.

During this period I completed the seemingly strange task of reading through the entire 1,118 pages of Brown, Driver and Briggs's *Hebrew Lexicon of the Old Testament*. My purpose was to compile a compact dictionary of every word that was used more than ten times in the Hebrew Bible. This exercise greatly increased my working vocabulary, and I regularly used my little dictionary over the next fourteen years or so.

I was also playing my part in the life of the church, taking occasional Sunday services and accepting invitations to give addresses. Sometimes my speaking engagements took me far out of Brisbane. I shall never forget the time we drove up to Toowoomba on the inland plateau, where I had agreed to speak at the high school prize-giving ceremony. Our route took us through an area that had just been swept by a bush fire; it was an eerie and somewhat unnerving experience to drive between rows of blazing tree trunks on both sides of the road.

Early in 1957 I began an association with a Hungarian church community in Brisbane. This came about as a result of the Hungarian uprising against Communist rule in late 1956. The harsh crushing of this rebellion forced many young Hungarians to flee the country as refugees, and some were accepted by New Zealand. Since the Reformed (or Presbyterian) Church of Hungary was the largest Protestant church in that country, the Presbyterian Church of New Zealand asked me to meet the refugees and offer assistance on its behalf as each of the six or seven planes transporting them touched down at Brisbane International Airport for refuelling. To help me cross the language barrier, I sought the assistance of Daniel Kobza, a Hungarian school teacher who acted as the honorary minister of the local Hungarian community.

When the first planeload arrived in January 1957, we found that not only had the refugees suffered from very cramped conditions in their two-to-three-day flight from Europe, but the only clothes they had were the heavy winter garments they had fled in; and here they were landing in the heat of summer. This led me to issue a request over one of the Brisbane radio stations and, to our surprise, a tonne of clothing was deposited at the church office in only three hours! We had more than enough to distribute among the passengers of the succeeding planes. Naturally, they were very grateful, but none more so than the young woman who mistakenly assumed that Elaine's handbag was among the articles for distribution. When Elaine spotted her interest, to my amazement she immediately emptied the handbag of her personal belongings and gave it to her. (Many years later, after my name had become widely known in New Zealand, that same woman contacted us and we went to visit her.)

After the last plane had passed through, all the remaining clothing was sent off to needy families in Hungary. The group responsible for this work then began to send regular food parcels to families nominated by the Reformed Church of Hungary. Through this activity, Elaine and I became lifelong friends of Daniel Kobza and his family, and became associated with the community he ministered to. When a newly arrived Hungarian couple wished to have their baby baptised in one of the Brisbane parishes, I was invited to perform the ceremony and, since the parents had little English, I learned sufficient Hungarian to enable them to hear a small part of the rite in their own tongue.

In 1958 the Presbyterian Preachers' Association invited me to deliver their annual lecture. Under the title 'Our Prophetic Heritage and its Place in the Preaching of the Word', I tried to raise the status of the Sunday sermon above that of a lesson or an address. On another occasion I prepared for the Faith and Order Commission, then meeting in Brisbane, a research paper on 'The Church in the Old Testament'. Here I tried to show that the community nature of the religion of the Israelites, whereby they saw themselves as 'the people of God', established the prototype for the later Christian Church. Moreover, I pointed out that early Christians were accustomed to finding the church mentioned in the Old Testament, since the Bible they used was in Greek, and the Hebrew word for the assembly of God (*qahal*) was frequently translated as *ekklesia*. This simple linguistic fact is all too little noted.

There were also the regular meetings of the Presbytery and General Assembly to attend. Because of the federal nature of the Australian States, the Presbyterian Church of Australia held its own General Assembly of Australia every two years. I was fortunate to be chosen as a Queensland representative for two of these, one in Melbourne and one in Sydney. At the first one, I found myself elected to the Church Union Committee, recently instituted to work towards a merger of the Methodist, Presbyterian and Congregational churches. This involved me in preparing draft statements for debate and occasionally flying south to attend committee meetings. I was particularly interested in this project after my service as Church Union Convener in New Zealand. As it turned out, I returned to New Zealand before the Australian union was consummated; on subsequently learning of the new divisions and bitterness it gave rise to, I was relieved to be no longer a part of it.

After three years in Queensland, we decided it was time to return to New Zealand for our summer holidays in January 1959. Taking the overnight train to Sydney, we flew from there to Christchurch. What a joy it was to renew family connections! Johnny and Judy spent most of the time with Nancy's family. Elizabeth, by then five and a half, was enthusiastically welcomed by Elaine's parents, and three years of absence had enabled Elaine to establish a much warmer relationship with them. Elaine and I also went down to Allanton to visit my father, who had been living alone since my mother's sudden death in 1957. We also travelled up to Wellington to see our friends there, particularly Duncan and May Hercus, as well as the congregation of St James', where I was invited to preach.

We particularly noticed the coolness of the New Zealand climate, even in January. Clearly, we had become acclimatised to the Queensland heat, and when our brief holiday was over we were quite glad to return to it. More importantly, we felt much more settled in Brisbane than we had been before, and were now ready to make it our permanent home. And because the post I held – teaching Old Testament Studies in a Presbyterian Theological College – was one of only four in the whole of Australasia, I saw little likelihood of moving.

So I was taken by surprise when the equivalent position at Knox College, Dunedin, suddenly became vacant. Here was something of a quandary: should I apply, or should we stay in Brisbane? Although for the first year or so we had felt homesick for New Zealand, we now felt very settled in Queensland. Yet returning to New Zealand would offer distinct advantages. Our children would not be growing up completely cut off from their relatives, and Knox College would be a stimulating place in which to teach, for the New Zealand Presbyterian Church was much more liberal than that of Queensland. On the other hand, my mother's death had somewhat diminished our family ties, and Elaine seemed to get on with her parents rather better at a distance.

Finances were a further complication. Although we had been poor on arriving in Queensland, substantial increases in my salary (it had trebled in three years), along with Elaine's earnings, had made our situation rather comfortable. A return to New Zealand would mean a considerable drop in our combined income. Still, while material advantages made a strong case for remaining, both professional and family concerns inclined us towards returning home. Thus I was able to submit an application without feeling too concerned about the outcome.

When I learned that I was to be recommended to the General Assembly for appointment, but that professorial salaries were under review and might well be downgraded, I nearly withdrew my application. Being in a position of strength, I let my application stand but instructed Ralph Byers, the convener of the Theological Education Committee, to withdraw my name if proposed salary increases were not forthcoming. Not only was I gratified when Ralph cabled to inform me that both of his motions had been passed by the General Assembly, but on arriving at Knox College I found the Theological Hall staff grateful to me for having been indirectly responsible for raising their salaries.

Our time in Australia had been much shorter than we had expected. Believing we would probably be there for life, we had done little to explore Queensland, let alone the rest of Australia. We had never been further afield from Brisbane than Maloolooba in the north, the Gold Coast in the south, and Toowoomba inland. But now it was too late, and to tell the truth it was because we had been so busy that we had not travelled more extensively. Indeed, both Elaine and I worked at our respective posts until a day or so before we left.

Despite those regrets, our time in Queensland had been a very rich experience for us all, and in later years we looked back on it with great pleasure. As I remember saying at our farewell, I had learned a great deal about the Old Testament in that time; and that had laid the foundations for my academic career. But more importantly, it had broadened my interests and horizons. I was beginning to evaluate both church life and the substance of Christian teaching within a cultural context that was both more comprehensive and more complex.

In February 1960, just four years after our arrival in Brisbane, we set off on our 600 mile (960 km) drive to Sydney. After attaching a roof-rack to the little Morris Minor for our heavy luggage, we had room inside for the four of us and our smaller bags. Judy and Elizabeth, now experienced travellers, always packed their own little suitcases. (Jonathan was not with us, having already returned to New Zealand with Elaine's sister Juliet for the start of the school year at Otago Boys' High.) We made it an enjoyable trip, taking two days to get to Sydney. There we embarked on the ss *Monowai*, setting sail for New Zealand and the new life that awaited us there.

Chapter Nine

RETURN TO MY ALMA MATER

It was strange to be returning to New Zealand in February 1960 on the same ship that had carried us away four years before. But now the circumstances were very different: we were returning to a place we knew well, and were excited to be coming home. And whereas we had set out for Brisbane at our own expense and on economy fares, the Presbyterian Church of New Zealand now provided us with first-class tickets. All in all, we were feeling on top of the world, relaxed, and confident about the future.

On arrival at Wellington we were met by two good friends, Duncan Hercus, who had married us, and his wife May, who had even brought a roll of red carpet for us to walk on to their car. We recognised the carpet – it had once been on the floor of our family room in the St James' manse, and they had bought it at our auction sale when we left.

But soon we struck a problem: our car, already booked on the Lyttelton ferry that night, was not registered in New Zealand. Worse yet, it was a Saturday and all of the relevant offices were closed. Fortunately, my friend Jack Somerville, minister of St Andrew's, was one of those people who always knew how to solve the stickiest problem. He rang a parishioner in the public service, who kindly opened his office to provide me with the necessary registration papers just in time for us to board the inter-island ferry that evening.

After stopping for a day or two at Timaru to see Elaine's parents and Nancy's family, we drove to Dunedin, a city that held so many happy memories for both of us that we felt like long-lost natives returning home. Temporary accommodation had been arranged for us in the Missionary

Manse at Opoho while we went house-hunting. After inspecting a number of properties around the city (this was one of Elaine's delights!), we finally settled on a house only two doors from the church where I had once been minister, and a mere hundred yards from Comely Bank, where we had commenced our courting.

For the two or three months before we were able to move into our new home we remained in the manse, which was not very far away and only a short walk from Knox College. Having arrived only a day or two before the start of the academic year, I had to set to work immediately. Although our furniture and all my books were still in transit, I had brought with me sufficient lecture notes to get started; it was very different from having to begin without any preparation, as I had done in Brisbane. My only regret on taking up the Chair of Old Testament Studies in my alma mater was that I was no longer teaching Comparative Religion, an area that had come to interest me greatly. On the other hand, I now found myself teaching Biblical Hebrew to a few Arts students as well as those pursuing theological studies.

Indeed, I found my task quite challenging, for a number of the students in their final year were particularly able, and I had been teaching fewer and generally less advanced students in Queensland. But my colleagues I already knew well: John Allan (New Testament), Helmut Rex (Church History), Hubert Ryburn (Master of the College) and Jimmie Salmond (Christian Education, and now Executive Secretary of the Theological Education Committee) had been my teachers. John Henderson (Systematic Theology) I had come to know well while I was his minister for five years in Opoho. Still, because they were all about twenty years my seniors, I felt very much the junior partner.

At the end of 1960 we arranged with David Calvert, minister of Cromwell, to have the use of his manse for our January holiday. We so enjoyed the area that while we were there we bought a section with a very old two-roomed cottage on it which had been shifted from a farm. Thereafter, whenever possible – for vacations and even long weekends – we drove up to Central Otago in the Morris Minor to work on it. Over the next few years I built additions to the front and back until finally we had a very comfortable holiday house. I had always enjoyed working with my hands, and now found it a refreshing change from academic work to learn the rudiments of the building trade – even mixing the concrete for the foundations.

It was not until the opening of the 1961 academic year that I was able to deliver my inaugural lecture – a long-established custom associated with an appointment to a professorial chair. When I performed the same duty in Queensland in 1956, some had criticised what I said on the grounds that it was too general and not sufficiently academic. Not wishing to make the same error twice, I now went to the other extreme, and on a very warm summer afternoon had the misfortune to put many of the large gathering to sleep.

My presentation, entitled 'The Role of Abraham in the Faith of Israel', dealt first with the question of Abraham's historicity by discussing in some detail the five different biblical sources on which we can draw. (Rereading it today, for the first time in over forty years, I am surprised by how closely it parallels the work of modern New Testament scholars, especially those of the Westar Institute in California, who have sought to recover the footprints and voice-prints of the historical Jesus, long hidden behind the figure of Christ.) I tried to show that each of the clearly varying sketches of Abraham had been reshaped by the historical context in which it was written. I concluded by saying that the historicity of Abraham was of secondary importance, and that much more significant was the slow development of a portrait of Abraham as a model man of faith who, feeling himself called to do so, went forth with no map, no Bible, no doctrinal confession, and no clear idea of where he was going. Ever since I began to preach, and later to teach, I have viewed the figure of Abraham as both a challenge and an inspiration to the church as it forever moves into a new and unknown world. Without my knowing it at the time, this theme was setting the stage for dramatic events to come.

Soon after my arrival in Dunedin, Peter McKenzie, then minister at Port Chalmers, invited me to join a study group which met regularly to discuss significant new theological books. Partly because my teaching colleagues were so senior to me, I was delighted to have ministerial companions outside the Theological Hall, men with whom I could discuss theological issues in some depth. As with the earlier study group in Queensland, this association motivated me to read books outside the subject area of the Old Testament, the latter having long taken up the greater part of my academic attention. For example, I now read Dietrich Bonhoeffer's *Letters and Papers from Prison*, in which he sketched a way of being Christian in the modern secular world, arguing that it was no longer possible to be religious in the traditional way. Strangely, I was not greatly influenced by Bonhoeffer at the time, feeling that he had received such wide attention because he was a modern martyr; it was only later that I came to realise what a creative thinker he was.

The theologian who really attracted me, and intensified my interest in the subject, was Paul Tillich, to whose work I had been very sketchily introduced when the first two volumes of his *Systematic Theology* had appeared during my time in Queensland. (I remember that one local Anglican divine was so excited by them that he was afraid he might not live to see the third volume, which was eventually published in 1964.) Now, studying Tillich more closely, I found at last a theologian who, like the biblical scholar Rudolf Bultmann, was aware he was living in the twentieth century. I did not find Tillich easy to read, for I was not used to his abstract and philosophical terminology. Nevertheless, I found it highly rewarding to work my way slowly through what he called an 'answering theology': an exploration of how the Christian message could be re-expressed to supply answers to the questions being asked by thinking people in the modern world. By moving away from the traditional dogmatic mode of expounding Christian theology (my colleague John Henderson was still calling his theological course 'Dogmatics'), Tillich was, to my considerable surprise, being read by many intelligent lay people, including university staff members who had no interest at all in traditional theology.

For me and many others, this wider interest in Tillich had first been aroused by his little book *The Courage to Be*, which came out in paperback in 1962. Tillich was revitalising the theological enterprise by creating new terms that soon became quite widespread: 'faith' was the 'courage to be'; to be religious was to be seized by 'an ultimate concern'; and God was 'the symbol for one's ultimate concern'. For Tillich, the most adequate definition of God was 'being-itself', because God should not be regarded as *a being* alongside or above other beings. (Yet even the Oxford Dictionary still defines God as 'the supreme being'.)

It was just at this time (1963) that Bishop John Robinson's book *Honest to God* appeared. Those who had been reading Tillich and Bonhoeffer found little that was new in this book; nor was it particularly well written. It bears the marks of having been composed rather hurriedly, and with passion, after the author had spent some weeks in convalescence and had used the time to catch up on his reading. But the book had a bombshell effect on an unsuspecting public.

More radical than Protestant Liberalism had ever been, this book alerted the masses to what was going on in academic theological circles. Coming from a bishop of the rather staid Church of England, it caused such a religious storm that it became the most widely read theological book of the twentieth century. Within months it was followed by *The Honest to God Debate*, which documented a number of responses to the challenges it had set forth. Theological thinking was at last coming out of the academic closet and becoming both public and newsworthy. (It is somewhat ironic that theology has for so long been regarded as boring and lacking in news value; after all, the word 'Gospel', derived from the Greek *evangel*, was originally 'godspel' – that is, 'good news'.)

Soon after my arrival the National Council of Churches set up a Faith and Order Commission, to be sited in Dunedin but assisted by working groups in other major centres. I was both pleased and honoured to be appointed as a Presbyterian representative. The task of the Commission was to prepare for a Faith and Order Conference. Two earlier such conferences had dealt with the problems of Order – church, ministry and sacraments – that divided the denominations. This one, intended to tackle the substance of the Faith that they supposedly shared, focused on such issues as the authority of the Bible, the relationship of Christianity to other religions, and the relevance of the Gospel to the modern scientific world.

Various groups and individuals throughout New Zealand were invited to supply contributions on specified topics. The Commission asked me to edit them into a study booklet for the conference, entitled 'What is our Gospel?' But on receiving the material, I reported to the committee that, in at least two of the topics, the writers had failed to come to grips with the real issues facing the churches in the modern world. Already I was beginning to feel that the churches were shutting their eyes to the many intellectual challenges that the modern world, global and scientific in its outlook, was presenting to the traditional expression of the Christian faith.

Worse yet, I feared that the churches were retreating into a ghetto of their own making, within which they felt confident and secure.

On being told that, as editor, I had the responsibility to ensure that the booklet served its original purpose as well as possible, I proceeded to write two articles to replace the unsatisfactory ones. Unfortunately I failed to tell the contributors what I was doing, and they were understandably startled and hurt when they received the published version. I quickly realised what a serious blunder I had committed, and have deeply regretted it ever since.

The Faith and Order Conference, held at Massey University in early 1964, was attended by nearly two hundred participants. Although it stimulated some, it did not achieve very much. It issued two short statements, 'What our Gospel is' and 'Message to the Churches'; but as Colin Brown observed when writing the history of the National Council of Churches in 1981, these two statements, though unanimously agreed to, were 'so general as to sound platitudinous'. The Anglican Synod of Auckland protested vigorously about the lack of balance in the original booklet. The churches were in no mood to be challenged or even questioned; in the light of subsequent events, it can be seen as a lost opportunity.

In 1963 the University of Otago commissioned a series of public lectures to mark the recent centenary of the publication by Charles Darwin of *The Origin of Species,* and intended to demonstrate Darwin's influence on various disciplines. Having been invited to examine his influence on theology, and being relatively ignorant of the subject, I was forced to undertake my first piece of real theological research. In the course of my investigation I made many unexpected discoveries. For example, Darwin's theory from the outset received a positive response from a number of well-known ecclesiastical figures, including the New Testament scholar F.J.A. Hort, Charles Kingsley, and Cardinal Newman. My primary aim, however, was to sketch the complex social and theological context of which Darwin's book was but one element. In ecclesiastical circles, for example, *The Origin of Species* was soon completely overshadowed by another text: in 1861 seven Anglican scholars published *Essays and Reviews*, in which they discussed various challenges to orthodox theology. This book caused a far greater uproar in the church than Darwin's, with thousands of clergy signing petitions in the hope of deposing some of its liberal contributors. Not only was my lecture well received, but it contains little that I would wish to change even today.

During these first three or four years, of course, many other events and activities occupied my attention. Our children were settled in their respective schools, and it gave me special pleasure to have my son at my old school, Otago Boys' High. After the first year, Elaine was invited to return to speech therapy and was appointed to the Kensington School Clinic, a post she held until we left Dunedin in 1971. In those days it was still rare for the wives of professional men to 'go out to work', and we suspected that some of my colleagues disapproved, although they never mentioned the subject to us. At any rate, her income was a welcome addition to the household during the period when our three children were engaged in their basic schooling.

I even found time to resume the stamp collecting I had begun as a boy in Warrnambool. In the intervening years I had paid it little attention, except occasionally to set aside some commemorative stamps and the annual health stamps – and therefore owned the 1931 Blue Boy and Red Boy, made rare because so few were sold owing to the Depression. Rather surprised myself by this renewed interest, I jokingly explained that the previous owner of our home (a much more serious philatelist than I ever was) must have left behind some unseen aura, for the room that had housed his valuable collection was now my study. Besides attempting to get my New Zealand collection up to date, I started to collect stamps with religious themes from all countries. This naturally included Christmas and Easter stamps, as well as many from the Vatican City.

At the end of 1962, the staff of the Theological Hall began to undergo great changes. John Allan and John Henderson retired that year, while Hubert Ryburn and J.D. Salmond followed suit a year later; Ralph Byers then became the Executive Secretary and Jack Somerville was appointed Master of the College. In November 1962, the General Assembly appointed Frank Nichol to the Chair of Theology, Evan Pollard to the New Testament Chair, and I was made Principal. Almost in a flash I had moved from being the junior board member to the managing director. Fortunately, the principalship did not entail many administrative duties, those being carried out by the Executive Secretary; but obviously it involved new responsibilities which I had to learn how to handle.

Almost my first task as Principal was to be the chief speaker at the 1962–63 Summer Conference of the Presbyterian Bible Class, that year being held at Gore. This was one of the last of these large conferences, which annually brought together as many as two thousand young people. The theme was 'God's Purpose for His People'. In the first of three major addresses, I sketched the long history of 'the people of God' through the Old Testament and ending with Jesus, who 'embodied in himself the whole role of Ancient Israel'. In the second I drew attention to the changing mission of the people of God, from Old Testament times through New Testament times and culminating in the church of today. The third focused on the church's active and sacrificial service to others as its primary mission to the modern world.

As I now read what I said to that gathering over forty-three years ago, I am surprised to find that, although my references to God and his people were couched in the customary language of the church, I was rather boldly trying to lead the young people away from the traditional approach to evangelism – which I dismissed as the kind of proselytism that, according to the Gospels, Jesus had sharply condemned. That it is the mission of the church to turn other people into committed Christians I emphatically denied. This did not reflect a change in my thinking, as from the beginning of my ministry I had always put the emphasis on Christian *action* rather than on Christian *belief*. But what led me to spell this out more explicitly than I had ever done before – and in such a context? Perhaps my seven years' experience in teaching had provided me with a firmer basis on which to take a stand. To be sure, I remember fearing some adverse reaction to my words; yet to my surprise they were enthusiastically received, and years later people who had been there still recalled them favourably.

It was with a feeling of confidence in the church of the future, then, that I took up my new role as Principal. Indeed, 1963 proved to be a very exciting year as the new staff of the Hall settled down to business. We teamed together so well that I was soon encouraged to take six months' study leave in the latter half of 1964; and when I wrote to Gerhard von

Rad, the internationally famous Professor of Old Testament at Heidelberg, he issued me a warm invitation. In those days travelling by sea was still the norm, being much cheaper than air travel; and since I had to stay behind to complete mid-year exams, Elaine, Judy and Elizabeth set off some weeks ahead of me on the ss *Fairsky*, leaving me to join them later by plane. Johnny had opted to stay and complete his seventh form year, becoming a boarder at John McGlashan College.

Eventually I left on a BOAC Comet, expecting to receive letters en route from Elaine, posted to reach me at pre-arranged destinations. One that I received at Singapore airport told me how unhappy she was with the ship and begged me to arrange our return on a different line. By curious coincidence, on my flight was an Israeli I had met in Dunedin, who was returning home to Tel Aviv. He urged me to spend more than the six days I had planned in Israel, and so it happened that, at 30,000 feet in the night sky over Afghanistan, I made two important decisions. First, we would cancel our return tickets in London and return together by air. Second, on arriving at Tel Aviv I would extend my visit to Israel to fourteen days and then fly directly to Frankfurt for a conference.

When we arrived in Tel Aviv, my Israeli friend not only invited me to his home but within an hour had worked out an itinerary and arranged all the tour bookings. As a result of this change of plan, Elaine was completely confused as to where I was when I cabled birthday greetings to Judy and Elizabeth from Jerusalem. Her puzzlement was further complicated by the fact that, since they were then sailing up the Gulf of Suez, and Israel and Egypt were officially at war, the cablegram arrived via Italy, the ss *Fairsky* being an Italian vessel.

My two weeks in Israel were an eye-opener, for they made the Old Testament come alive in a way that books can never do. Still somewhat jet-lagged, I travelled south to Beersheba, the Dead Sea, the ruins of the Nabataean city of Avdat in the Negev desert, the copper mines of Solomon, and the coastal port of Eilat on the Gulf of Aqaba. Then up north to Haifa, the Baha'i shrine on Mt Carmel, Nazareth, the Upper Galilee, and Caesarea Philippi. Of greatest interest to me were not the Christian sites long hallowed by pilgrimage (and most of them then in Jordan), but the mountains and other features of a topography that had not changed over thousands of years. One could much more easily visualise the many familiar Old Testament stories in their natural setting.

Finally, I spent four days in Jerusalem. At one stage, in an attempt to get a glimpse of Bethlehem from a distance, I inadvertently strayed into the no-man's-land separating Israel from Jordan, and a concerned Israeli taxi-driver stopped his car and called out that I might be shot by an Arab if I went any further. Unfortunately, the Old City was in Jordan, and I could tour only the Israeli sector. The highlight was going on an organised tour to see the great variety of synagogues that had evolved in the different ethnic cultures represented by the many immigrant congregations. An Iranian synagogue, for example, had two reading desks, one for the Qur'an as well as the normal one for the Torah. The Qur'an was never read, but that was how Iranian Jews had learned to compromise while living in an Islamic society.

My round-the-world air ticket allowed me to change my itinerary and fly directly from Tel Aviv to Frankfurt, where I was to attend the Conference of the World Alliance of Reformed Churches, following a three-day conference at Darmstadt especially arranged for the Presbyterian theologians attending the Alliance meeting. Of course I was not a systematic theologian, but they had graciously permitted me, as a biblical teacher, to attend. The only person I had met before was Ronald Gregor Smith, who held the Chair of Theology at Glasgow and had recently visited New Zealand. Although I felt somewhat out of place among these theological giants (as they seemed to me), I had the audacity to point out that in their discussions they kept harking back to Paul, but rarely referred to the teaching of Jesus in the Gospels and never once to the Old Testament. My rather cheeky observation was well received.

While others moved from Darmstadt to Frankfurt, I took the opportunity of the intervening weekend to go down to Heidelberg and make initial arrangements for the accommodation we would require later when I was studying at the university. There I contacted a young American who had also come to study under von Rad, and he and his wife kindly offered us the use of their flat while they went on holiday. It was high summer and beautifully warm, and I happened to strike the annual commemoration of a French invasion many years ago that had resulted in the burning of the famous castle. From the banks of the Neckar River I watched an impressive fireworks display and saw the now-ruined castle ablaze with flares.

The meeting of the World Alliance began with a service in a Calvinist church in Frankfurt; and I soon became aware that Calvinist (or Presbyterian) churches are relatively rare in Germany, most Germans being either Catholic or Lutheran. The discussions at the meeting were not very exciting, but I valued the opportunity to meet many people from other parts of the world and to get a feel for the international character of Presbyterianism. I observed with interest that when Professor Tom Torrance (the Barthian Professor of Theology at Edinburgh) stepped up to the podium, he was greeted with a kind of hushed reverence, for he was regarded as the current champion of Calvinism in the English-speaking world. (I mention this primarily because I was later to be challenged by one of his most ardent devotees.) I found myself elected to the executive body that dealt with the affairs of the Alliance in between the seven-yearly meetings; it was an office that would lead to some interesting experiences five years later. But by this time, my thoughts were more occupied with joining Elaine and the girls in London.

It was a very exciting reunion. As they had already spent some days in London, they rather delighted in showing me around. After visiting the usual sites, such as Westminster Abbey, the Tower of London and Hampton Court Palace, we took a rental car out into the countryside. We spent a week in the picturesque village of Steeple Aston, near Oxford, where our New Zealand friend Harold Turner had offered us the use of his holiday house, formerly the village inn. From there we explored Oxford, Stratford and some of the charming villages of the Cotswolds. We were so attracted to the latter that we returned several times on subsequent visits. Then we drove over to Cambridge for a day, to be shown around by one of my former students, Graeme Ferguson, with whom I had renewed contact at the Alliance meeting in Frankfurt.

We chose to travel to Germany via Amsterdam, and this led to an unexpected crisis on the way. On transferring at the Hook of Holland from the ferry to the train, I had inadvertently neglected to pay the customary tip to the porter; and when Elizabeth spotted our luggage being returned to the station, I left the carriage and went in hot pursuit, only to have the train depart without me. Thus, on her first visit to the Continent,

Elaine found herself with our two daughters, travelling on a train in a non-English-speaking environment without tickets, money, passports or luggage. Fortunately, a friendly Dutch railway guard sorted it all out, and the three of them were waiting patiently in Amsterdam when I arrived an hour later.

Our bed-and-breakfast host ensured that we saw the best of Amsterdam in our three days, including the Anne Frank house. Then we went by train to Wiesbaden, where at breakfast we had our first taste of the *brötchen* we came to love. There I bought a second-hand car and with some trepidation set off for Heidelberg, driving on the 'wrong' side of the road. During our three months in Heidelberg the car was a wonderful convenience, for besides spending the weekends exploring the castles in the Neckar Valley we also managed trips to Luxembourg, Switzerland, Liechtenstein, Strasbourg and Heilbronn.

After a few weeks in the flat lent to us by the American couple, we leased one in Gaiberg, a village about 6 miles (10 km) from Heidelberg on the hill behind its famous castle. This village was becoming a German summer resort, but with autumn already upon us we were glad of the heating and excellent insulation that this new flat offered. Although language was a problem (particularly in view of the strong local dialect), we appreciated the chance to get the feel of village life – the ringing of the church bells and the announcement of village news over a public address system in every street. Each day I drove to Heidelberg to take the girls to the Hölderlin Gymnasium, the girls' high school where Judy and Elizabeth settled in surprisingly well, since they knew no German. (The principal beamed with pleasure when, on enrolling them, I said we preferred them to become immersed in German culture rather than go to the school attached to the nearby American military base.)

At the university, I soon found that my language preparation had not been sufficient to enable me to gain full value from the lectures. Although I attended a graduate seminar conducted by the Old Testament scholar Claus Westermann, I had to be content to do my work primarily in the library, where I could read at my own speed. I had set myself the task of studying the Priestly source within the Pentateuch. I hoped that, by isolating it from the material with which it is now closely linked, I could find out whether it ever had an independent existence, as both the Yahwist and Elohistic sources are thought to have had, or whether it was compiled as the framework in which to insert the earlier sources. Although I now suspect the latter, my project was never completed, as events forced me to move quickly to more religiously relevant issues on my return home. Nevertheless, I valued the personal contact with von Rad and Westermann, both of whom treated me very graciously.

By the time we were due to return to London, the weather had become so cold that when walking down the main street of Heidelberg, we had to escape into the warmth of a shop every hundred metres or so. Even in Dunedin we were not used to winters like this. On the other hand, the cold brought people together, and made us realise why Christmas is such a joyful family time in Europe. On the way back to London we spent two days in Brussels, and found the city decked out like a fairyland with music to match. Christmas itself we spent in London, feeling quite relieved to be in an English-speaking country again.

As I had successfully cashed in our return boat tickets and replaced them with half-round-the-world air tickets, we decided to see as much of the world as we could on the trip home. In Rome we stayed at a little ecumenical pension run by some Dutch nuns and situated behind Piazza Navona, not far from the Vatican. The nuns gave us very helpful advice on how much to pay for taxis, when to see and hear the Pope in St Peter's Square, how to get to the Sistine Chapel, and what to view in the great St Peter's Basilica, which was then set up for the Vatican II Council. These friendly and somewhat worldly nuns (they smoked like chimneys!) promoted the new ecumenical spirit of Vatican II by inviting us Protestants to participate in their Sunday Mass.

The undoubted highlight of our return journey, however, was the ten days we spent in Jordan, which then included the West Bank. A rather scruffy-looking Middle Eastern Airlines plane picked us up at Beirut for the flight to Jerusalem, but a very low cloud ceiling on our arrival diverted us to Amman. From there a *bedu* dressed in flowing robes drove us at breakneck speed to St George's Hospice in Jerusalem, where we were accommodated in charming surroundings.

Having visited Israel only six months before, and had a sense of Palestinian hostility from the Jewish side, I found it fascinating to experience something of what it was like on the Palestinian side. Because my Old

Testament studies had instilled in me a deep interest in the history of the Jewish people and their ancestral claims to the land, and because of what the Jews had suffered in the Holocaust, my sympathies were mainly with Israel. Elaine, on the other hand, fell in love with Jordan at once and came strongly to espouse the Palestinian cause. Over the years we had many friendly arguments on the subject, and only in the last fifteen did we become united in our deep concern for the plight of the Palestinian people.

We wandered the quaint little streets of the Old City of Jerusalem, visited the Church of All Nations in the Garden of Gethsemane, climbed the Mount of Olives, and walked around to Bethany, thus inspecting all the sites of Christian interest. By taxi we visited the Church of the Nativity in Bethlehem, and the tombs of the patriarchs in Hebron. Then we went to Jacob's well at Nablus, entered into the Samaritan Synagogue, handled the Samaritan Bible, explored the ruins of ancient Samaria, and finally reached Jericho and the Dead Sea by taking the route to the Jordan Valley supposedly taken by Jacob when he fled to his uncle Laban. I had now had the opportunity to traverse all of the Holy Land; it became a turning point in my career, for the task of teaching the Old Testament would ever thereafter be alive with personal interest.

Returning home to Dunedin was like coming down to earth again, but in a very refreshed frame of mind. On resuming my duties, I was immediately involved with the induction of new staff members. While I was away, the General Assembly had made two appointments – Bob Paterson to a newly established lectureship in Biblical Studies, made necessary by an increase in student numbers (he took over some of my Old Testament courses, as well as some in New Testament), and Ian Breward to the Chair of Church History and the History of Doctrine, left vacant by the early retirement of Helmut Rex due to poor health. Helmut, who had been teaching since 1940, had proved so able that in 1953 he was appointed the first Professor of Church History. Now he was to be succeeded by one of his students, who had been in his final year when I returned from Queensland in 1960. Thus, in only five years, I had become the oldest and longest-serving member of the staff; and rather than being a colleague of some of my original teachers, I was now a colleague of one of my students.

At this stage, the Presbyterian Church of New Zealand seemed to be in very good heart and the Theological Hall was booming. To serve the still-expanding communicant membership, we had the highest number of students in training (between sixty and seventy in the Hall) and the highest number of staff members the Hall was ever to have. As I settled once again into the comfortable routine of teaching and administrative duties, I had no inkling that 1965 was to be the last year in which my academic life at Knox College would be quiet and undisturbed.

Chapter Ten

THRUST INTO THE LIMELIGHT…

A train of events that would soon change my life dramatically had its unobtrusive beginning in an invitation from the editor of the *Outlook* (the Presbyterian weekly) to write an article for Reformation Sunday, 31 October 1965. Taking my lead from John Robinson (who had recently published *The New Reformation?*), I confidently proceeded to discuss why such a reformation had become necessary. 'Is the Christian faith inextricably bound up with the world-view of ancient mankind, which has now been superseded', I asked, 'or can the substance of it be translated into the world-view of twentieth century mankind?' I pointed out that, 'for the man who has stepped into the twentieth century with his eyes open, the old distinction between a natural world and a supernatural world is a thing of the past'; and that, if the church continued to ignore this fact, 'the Christian faith will continue to diminish in its influence in the world at the present alarmingly rapid rate'.

When the article appeared on 25 September, some praised it and asked for more; one reader even referred to it as 'the word of God for our age!' Others took strong exception to my rejection of the supernatural world, believing this to be an absolutely essential element of Christianity. What particularly riled the evangelicals was my blunt rejection of fundamentalism. This is what I said:

> The Bible is *not* literally inerrant. The Bible is *not* 'the Word of God in written form'. The Bible is *not* a simple guide setting forth what every Christian in every generation must believe and do…[It] is a book from

the ancient world and must be studied in the light of modern scholarship and all that it can tell us about the world that bequeathed to us
the Bible.

This was hardly revolutionary; after all, it had been the basis for biblical
studies in seminaries for fifty years.

Early that November, my friend Jack Bates was installed as Moderator
of the General Assembly, and in his Moderatorial Address he took the
issue further; he hinted that any form of reformation sufficiently radical to
engage the modern mind could well lead to a form of Christian atheism.
No doubt he had in mind what John Robinson had said in an appendix
to *The New Reformation?*:

> There is so much in the atheist's case that is true, that for many people
> today the only Christian faith which can be valid for them is the one
> that takes over after the death of God as 'God' has traditionally been
> understood.

Robinson then set out the atheist's case under three headings: (1) God is
intellectually superfluous; (2) God is emotionally dispensable; (3) God
is morally intolerable.

Robinson did not go so far as to affirm Christian atheism, but did
acknowledge that he had much in common with Paul van Buren, William
Hamilton and Thomas Altizer, American theologians who during 1964–65
had become known as the leading exponents of 'the death of God'. At that
stage I was not more than faintly aware of their work, nor did I give them
careful study until the later 1960s. Nonetheless, my critics took what I
had said in my article to reflect this non-theistic position.

The most theologically able, and also the most aggressive, of my critics was the Revd Bob Blaikie. A student of the Barthian theologian Tom
Torrance in Edinburgh, he had made his presence felt soon after arriving
in New Zealand from Africa. After conducting a school of theology for
ministers, my colleague Frank Nichol complained to me that Bob had
given him a torrid time during discussion periods. Accordingly, I had
a long personal talk with Bob at the Assembly, suggesting that if he felt
compelled to attack the Theological Hall staff, he should address himself
to me as Principal and leave the others alone. In the light of later events,
that was hardly a wise thing for me to do.

Not only did Blaikie respond to my article with a sharply critical letter in the December *Outlook*, but early in 1966 he followed it up with two articles of his own. He asserted that the kind of reformation that I (along with Robinson, Tillich, Bultmann and Bonhoeffer) had been commending was nothing less than 'the religious road to atheism' and the ultimate abandonment of Christianity altogether. He warned that the coming debate would split the church into 'the church of God and the church of the antichrist'.

This proved to be an apt forecast of things to come, for even before his articles appeared, the editor of the *Outlook* invited me in January to write an article for the Easter edition, to appear on 2 April. I had just been reading Ronald Gregor Smith's newly published book, *Secular Christianity*, and chose as the focal point of my article his challenging statement:

> ...we may freely say that the bones of Jesus lie somewhere in Palestine. Christian faith is not destroyed by this admission. On the contrary, only now, when this has been said, are we in a position to ask about the meaning of the resurrection as an integral part of the message concerning Jesus.

It had become clear to me that the question was no longer *whether or not* Jesus rose from the dead, but *what meaning* the resurrection of Jesus could possibly have within the context of our modern world-view. It could not refer to a bodily resuscitation; nor could it even be regarded as a historical event in the same way as the crucifixion. I pointed out that the New Testament itself uses a variety of ways to speak of the risen Jesus, several of which are clearly figurative and thus inconsistent with one another if taken literally. For example, Paul speaks of Christians as being 'in Christ' and thereby members of his body. The story of the empty tomb is only one of the ways of speaking of the risen Christ and should be regarded as a pious legend rather than a historical event. I suggested (no doubt having been influenced by Bultmann) that what all the stories pointed back to was the continuing influence of Jesus after his death; hence, the only way to understand his resurrection as a historical event was to recognise that 'the apostles themselves quite unexpectedly became transformed men'.

Of course, I was aware that this would come as a surprise to those readers who thought of the resurrection exclusively in terms of a resuscitated body coming forth from a tomb; and for that reason I considered toning it down. After discussing the matter fully with Elaine (always my best critic) and being urged to leave it as it was, I included a warning that I had no wish to disturb the faith of those who were committed to the traditional interpretation. This discussion, I said, was for those

> ...who know that the mythical three-decker universe is not the real tangible world in which we live, and because of that are genuinely puzzled to know what the modern man is to make of such an important Christian affirmation as the resurrection of Jesus.

The storm that followed the publication of my article took me by surprise. The next issues of the *Outlook* were filled with letters to the editor – some in praise, but most in violent and angry disagreement. Additional copies of the *Outlook* were printed to meet the demand, and were accompanied by a letter from Jack Bates as Moderator of the General Assembly, who noted that 'the gap between the pulpit and pew in the understanding of the Bible has been too great for too long'. He told me on the phone that he had immediately consulted *The Manual of Doctrine* of 1950 (in the writing of which we had both been involved), and was relieved to find that it said: 'the Resurrection is not an affair of history which can be vouched for by historical tests...and belongs to the dimension which only faith can apprehend'.

As I learned later, the editor of the *Outlook*, Peter McCallum Smith, was taken aback when he received the article and sought advice from his board as to whether he should publish it. He was a very committed Presbyterian, having been reared in the Church of Scotland, and only quite recently had considered training for the ministry himself. Understandably, he was greatly disturbed to find his journal becoming the instrument of church dissension – even though, despite some immediate cancellations, circulation numbers had increased as a result.

McCallum Smith wrote to his friend William Barclay, Professor of New Testament in his native Glasgow, to gain his opinion of the original article. Barclay replied that the article largely represented his own views, but that he would never dare say so publicly in Scotland! This seems strange, since the book by Gregor Smith that I had been quoting never caused so much as a ripple in Scotland. At any rate, Barclay's reply did little to allay McCallum Smith's continuing concern; and according to his family, he developed an agitated state that may well have contributed to his premature death the following year.

Only a few days after the Easter issue of the *Outlook* appeared, the Session of Somervell Church in Auckland unanimously expressed their conviction that my two articles constituted a radical departure from the historic Christian faith, and their resolve to protest to the Presbytery and the General Assembly. The Presbytery set up a committee to deal with the issue, and the first I heard of the protest was when its convener, Frank Winton, wrote to me, seeking clarification of my views. In answering, I pointed out that I had been writing for 'that group of people in the church who were quite keen to learn how the church interprets the Gospel in the world of the twentieth century'.

For the first six weeks, the controversy was confined to Presbyterian circles. Then the newspapers reported that the Auckland Presbytery had met in private to discuss a certain controversial article, but its members were bound to secrecy. This further attracted the interest of the press, and several newspapers then printed the offending article in full. When the *Otago Daily Times* asked a local minister why the Dunedin Presbytery hadn't even bothered to discuss the article, he replied, 'Most ministers in this city are already familiar with these theories of the resurrection because they read their theological journals'.

The *Otago Daily Times* followed this with an editorial, quoting Dean Raphael of the Dunedin Cathedral; he had not only preached in support of the article, but reported what his own office-bearer had said to him afterwards: 'That is what we lay people have privately thought for a long time but kept quiet about for fear of offending the clergy'. Thus, what started as a Presbyterian debate quickly became a public one. Anglicans, Catholics and others joined Presbyterians in making public statements, both in favour and in protest. Even secular journalists of the press and radio joined in, discussing at considerable length what they thought about the reports of Jesus' resurrection from the dead.

In a very short time I found myself the centre of public attention, a situation for which I was ill prepared. I was not used to being interviewed and questioned by journalists from the press, radio and television, and not accustomed to seeing my name in the paper nearly every day, usually as the butt of attack and bitter criticism. It may be a very pleasant experience to become suddenly famous, but to be the subject of public notoriety is altogether different.

All this brought about a sudden change in my reading habits. I began to read so vigorously that my reading speed accelerated rapidly and has remained at that level ever since. My record of the books I was reading shows a sudden shift of interest away from the Old Testament, which had naturally taken up most of my reading time until then. First, I read everything I could find on the resurrection of Jesus, including a book by Hans Grass that has never been translated into English. I felt compelled to reassure myself that I had not overstepped the mark, and nearly everything I read confirmed in one way or another all that I had said.

On my own shelves was a commentary on Mark's Gospel which I had bought in 1942 but not yet read. Its author was Henry Major, who after theological training and parish ministry in New Zealand had gone to Oxford for further study and become the leading Anglican modernist in England. After discussing the three possible ways in which 'resurrection' could be conceived, Major concluded that, to make any sense for the modern mind,

> ...the mode of the Resurrection must be psychological and subjective. The belief in the Resurrection of Jesus was created...by the impact of His personality upon the personality of the disciples in the preceding period.

Hans Lietzman, the celebrated church historian whose books Helmut Rex had encouraged me to read, had likewise argued in 1937 that all attempts to discover the facts behind the Gospel narratives had to be carried out on the basis of our own experience of the way things happen. As he put it, 'the true nature of the event described as the resurrection of Jesus does not come within the province of historical enquiry into matters of fact; it belongs to the place where the human soul touches the eternal'. In short, all my research showed me to be fully in tune with the conclusions of much of the scholarly world, even if not with public sentiment in New Zealand.

I began to receive hundreds of letters, and replied to as many of them as time allowed. Both friends and strangers in great numbers offered support and told me that a burden had been lifted from their shoulders. That this was a common theme in letters I received throughout the next two years showed how many people had been trying to be faithful to their church despite the difficulty of reconciling traditional doctrine with modern knowledge.

Other letters were strongly critical, some going so far as to accuse me of being the agent of the devil. On 2 June I received the following telegram:

> YOU HAVE CAUSED UNTOLD PAIN AND DOUBTS BY THE STATEMENTS AS TO YOUR POSITION. MY WIFE HAS JUST GOT OVER A NERVOUS BREAKDOWN AND A RELAPSE IS POSSIBLE. I CHALLENGE YOU TO PUBLIC [SIC] DEBATE YOUR VIEW WITH ME. I AM A BARRISTER OF THE SUPREME COURT WITH OVER THIRTY-FIVE YEARS EXPERIENCE. PLEASE REPLY URGENTLY.

Were my words as damaging to people's health as this implied? I respectfully declined the invitation, on the grounds that public debating of that kind 'neither nurtures faith nor determines historical facts but merely confirms prejudices'.

At first I tried to respond to each letter personally, but the vast number appearing in the *Outlook* alone made this impossible. In an attempt to pour oil on troubled waters, I decided to write four more articles for the *Outlook*, explaining the background to the controversy. More than a little shocked by the sudden furore, I wanted to disabuse people of the unfortunate notion that I had set out to sow dissension. At the suggestion of the editor, I prefaced the articles with this general reply to those who had written:

> My brothers and sisters in Christ, if this article contains some plain speaking, I am even more concerned to try and ensure that I am speaking the truth IN LOVE. No personal offence is in any way intended. I have welcomed your letters and take no offence from anything you have said, for I do not doubt for one moment you are absolutely sincere. We must all agree that there is no place for bitterness and personal recriminations among Christians. We are here to witness to the truth as we understand it, and to help one another embrace it.

I naively supposed that once people were brought up to date on current theological thinking, they would soon come to see everything in a different light.

In the first article, 'Knowledge or faith? That is the question', I distinguished between knowledge (which is open to critical enquiry) and faith (which is an attitude of trust). Faith is not a matter of accepting uncritically a set of beliefs, I said, quoting one of my favourite authors. The nineteenth-century clergyman C.L. Dodgson, better known as Lewis Carroll, used *Alice in Wonderland* to make fun of people who accepted beliefs uncritically. There we find, for instance, that when Alice says she cannot believe impossible things, the White Queen urges her to practise it for half-an-hour a day, adding, 'Sometimes I've believed as many as six impossible things before breakfast'.

In the second article, 'The Empty Tomb', I showed that the historicity of the empty tomb story had not been confirmed by any secular historian. I then quoted a series of biblical scholars and theologians – including Alfred von Harnack, James Denny, Kirsopp Lake, Karl Barth and Emil Brunner – all of whom declared that faith in the resurrection of Jesus did not depend on the historicity of the empty tomb story.

The third article was titled 'The Westminster Confession – our Master or our Servant?' It was aimed at those who contended that, as a Presbyterian minister, I was bound by my ordination vows to remain faithful to the beliefs expressed in the Westminster Confession. After sketching the origin and purpose of the Westminster documents, I showed how Presbyterian churches throughout the world had, for more than sixty years, been uneasy about these subordinate standards, regarding them as no longer relevant to the modern world. Indeed, the meeting of Presbyterian theologians I had attended in Germany in 1964 had declared the continuing role of the Westminster Confession to be a dead issue.

In the final article, 'The Word of God and the Bible', I outlined how the nineteenth century had witnessed a revolution in the way we understand the Bible. I distinguished between the literal reading of Holy Scripture and the hearing of the Word of God, the latter being a personal and subjective experience. I also quoted Dean Farrar, who said in 1886, 'Whoever was the first dogmatist to make the terms "the Bible" and "the word of God" synonymous rendered to the cause of truth and of religion an immense disservice'.

These articles seemed to me at the time – as they still do today – to answer all the objections that my critics had raised. Further, they showed that I was not the isolated maverick I was being made out to be, for Christian scholars elsewhere offered wide support for everything I had said. But far from having the desired effect, my articles were like petrol thrown on an already blazing fire.

From the beginning I was loyally supported by the staff at the Theological Hall, who decided to offer an opportunity for public questioning and discussion. Some three hundred people packed into the hall at Knox College to hear us speak and answer their questions. It was an opportunity to show our solidarity, and at the same time to indicate that there was room for different viewpoints. The staff of the (Catholic) Holy Cross College arranged a similar event, but one with different results, for although open to the public its primary aim was to reassure Catholics. We were informed, for example, that Catholics believe there are three 'bodies' residing in heaven: Elijah (having been taken up in a whirlwind), Jesus (having risen and ascended), and the Virgin Mary (by virtue of the dogma of her bodily assumption).

Even the poet James K. Baxter became involved, having by that time become a Catholic. Then a Burns Fellow at the University of Otago, he wrote a poem for the student journal *Critic*, which began:

> I'm feeling ecumenical
> And yet it saddens me
> To learn that Dr Geering
> Sincerely cannot see
> That resurrection would require
> A resurrected body.

I wrote an anonymous reply, and to this day few people know who was responsible for what appeared in the next issue of *Critic*. I include it here as a little light relief, for to my surprise it was recently included in an anthology of New Zealand spiritual verse, *Spirit in a Strange Land*.

> To a James K. Baxter – Celestial Greeting!
> What joy there'll be at our future meeting.
> The 'Critic' was left by a student of late
> In the waiting-room at the pearly gate.

I began to read it when traffic was slow,
And espied your poem – jolly good show!
I passed it around and we all agreed,
That for pleas of this kind there's an urgent need.
Too few in these days have enough concern
As to whether in future they'll harp or burn.
Your keen request is received and noted,
And ready in future to be re-quoted.
But just one warning I'm bidden to give –
You can bear it in mind on earth as you live:
My good friend Paul, you may have read,
Once wrote to Corinth, and there he said,
That flesh and blood can never inherit
The Kingdom intended for those of merit.
That body of dust you must leave behind.
There's a spiritual body here you'll find.
How else do you think, for all this time,
I've wielded the keys and writ this rime?
For surely you know my bones still lie
In the city of Rome, the Tiber nigh.
This spiritual body I find much neater,
Yours truly, Cephas (Known as St Peter).

What became ever clearer, as the controversy dragged on in the press and in the church courts, was that widespread ignorance existed in both the churches and the general public regarding the radical changes that had been taking place in biblical scholarship and Christian thought in the previous hundred years. Much of what had been taught in the seminaries for decades had never reached the people in the pews, let alone the public at large. This was partly because many ministers, afraid of causing dissension in their congregations, were reluctant to share with them the new understanding of the Bible, which even the ministers themselves may have found disturbing at first. As a result, it was still widely assumed that everything in the Bible was to be taken literally.

During these months, the material appearing in newspapers was mounting rapidly. It is quite by accident that I have much of it now preserved. In 1965, well before any hint appeared of the coming controversy, the staff at the Theological Hall had been discussing whether to subscribe to a professional news-clipping service. When we finally decided it was too expensive, I resolved to undertake the project myself, though on a smaller scale. I had no sooner started than the public uproar began.

A British New Testament scholar, Dr A.R.C. Leaney, was then visiting New Zealand to lecture at St John's College in Auckland. This seemed a good opportunity for people to hear an alternative view on the resurrection from an authoritative source, so he and I were invited to engage in a televised discussion. To be sure, he was somewhat more conservative than I, and did his best to defend the more traditional view of the resurrection; but after the programme, he admitted to me privately that the traditional view did not altogether stand up. Leaney was also invited to write an article for the *Outlook*. Being the kindly person he was, Leaney was careful not to contradict anything I had said; he did not even mention the 'empty tomb', but traced the belief in the resurrection to the so-called 'appearances' to the disciples. Thus he did not bring much comfort to my critics. Then, just prior to the General Assembly, the church published my five articles in booklet form, along with Leaney's article and another by my colleague Evan Pollard.

Two other British scholars visited New Zealand at this time, and the press immediately asked them for their views. Hugh Montefiore, then Canon of Coventry but later Bishop of Birmingham, said that he agreed with me; but F.F. Bruce, Professor of Biblical Criticism at Manchester, with a background in the Brethren, declared that 'bodily resurrection is the only sense that could have been intended by the first preachers and understood by the first hearers'. He went on to say that I had set out to make people think and had certainly succeeded, but that the Bible would withstand any test of that kind.

In the meantime, as the controversy continued with deadly seriousness and at times much heat, Sir James Fletcher and Sir William Goodfellow sponsored a public meeting of Presbyterian laymen. Seventeen hundred people gathered in the Auckland Town Hall and called for a New Zealand Association of Presbyterian Laymen (NZAPL) to be established for the express purpose of restoring sound doctrine to the Presbyterian Church. A representative gathering of 120 laymen eventually approved a constitution (which provided for women to be admitted only as associate members) and elected R.J. Wardlaw of Auckland as the national chairman. The

NZAPL then began a widespread advertising campaign (Wardlaw ran an advertising firm) and held meetings throughout the country. Seven hundred people filled the Dunedin Concert Chamber, but a subsequent meeting in Invercargill ended in disorder, for the association was itself coming under severe criticism for potentially causing a split within the church.

Public advertisements for the NZAPL prompted the 'Gallery' current affairs programme to invite Bob Wardlaw and me to be interviewed by Austin Mitchell and Graham Billing. The whole exercise gave me a valuable insight into how television can manipulate people. The show was pre-recorded, and when the director decided that Bob and I had been too 'nice' to each other, he made a second recording after instructing us to be much more aggressive. Accordingly, I challenged Bob on a number of points, but later felt very bad about it, as my normal approach in theological debate was to be as conciliatory as possible within the limits of integrity. Of the thirty-four letters I received as a result of the programme, eleven were critical and twenty-three were supportive.

Following this debate, the Auckland Church of Christ (not to be confused with the Associated Churches of Christ) placed a full-page advertisement in the *New Zealand Herald*, entitled 'Was Prof. Geering right on TV?' One of its many headlines asserted, 'Heaven *is* a place, Professor Geering!' (To demonstrate how far we have moved in just over thirty years, in 1999 no less an authority than Pope John Paul II made headlines in *The Times* of London by saying, 'Heaven is *not* a place. It is a state of mind.')

While denying it was an attack on me personally, the *Herald* advertisement stated that it had been inserted in support of 'Bible-believing Christians in the Presbyterian Church'; it also cited biblical passages to show that many of the things I had said on television were in direct conflict with statements found in the Bible. This was true, of course; and it characterises a line of argument that appears to give the fundamentalists the high moral ground. Unfortunately, they conveniently ignore the fact that the Bible, being an anthology of books written by different people in different times and cultural contexts, is far from being consistent.

The national conference of the NZAPL, held in early October, decided to circulate a petition in the press, inviting public support. The petition sought the coming General Assembly to reaffirm (a) the supernatural nature of the Person of God, (b) the deity of Jesus Christ His Son, and (c) the fact of the resurrection of Christ in true, real, visible and tangible form. It also asked the General Assembly to rule that doctrines opposed to these should not be taught in the church's theological college.

In the meantime, a proposal was brought before the Auckland Presbytery calling for the resignation of all Theological Hall staff members whose thinking was incompatible with biblical faith. Although this was defeated, my long-time critic Bob Blaikie (who denied any connection with the newly formed NZAPL) succeeded in having forwarded to the Assembly an overture calling for reaffirmation of the basic Christian doctrines. This was only one of several such initiatives sent to the Assembly.

The Doctrine Committee of the Presbyterian Church had decided at its annual August meeting not to take up time in discussing my articles, as they were not published as official statements. By October, however, it was forced by the increasing tension within the church to have something ready for the coming General Assembly in an attempt to restore confidence. As Principal, I was *ex officio* a member of the Doctrine Committee, but was prevented from saying a word during its deliberations. This resulted not from any ecclesiastical restraint, but from a bad attack of laryngitis which left me completely speechless. Some judged this to be an act of God!

What the Doctrine Committee did was to assemble evidence from the biblical material to support the affirmation that Jesus rose from the dead. To my dismay, it ignored much of the scholarly work that I had so recently canvassed. What I would have said, had I been able, was that they had entirely missed the point of my original article. It had not been my concern to deny what the committee was so anxious to reaffirm – namely, that *according to the New Testament* 'Jesus rose from the dead'. Clearly, this is what the New Testament states. The problem was this: the New Testament writers believed that they lived in a three-decker universe, consisting of heaven, earth, and the underworld of the dead. Within that framework of belief, to say that Jesus rose (from the underworld of the dead) and 'ascended into heaven' made sense; for us, who see ourselves living in a space-time universe, it does not.

Even the Doctrine Committee had difficulty finding the words that would satisfy all its members, a clear indication that this was a topic on which they had a variety of views. Changes were being made to their statement right up until the morning of the Assembly, after which it was to be presented as an addendum to their annual report.

The 1966 General Assembly met in St John's Church, Wellington, in an atmosphere of tense expectancy. The newly installed Moderator was Stan Read of St Andrew's Church, Wellington, whom I had known personally ever since he officiated at the funeral of my brother Ira in 1939. That I was well known to so many of the leading ministers of the church unfortunately led many of my critics, particularly those of the laity, to assume that the support I received sprang from friendship rather than theological conviction, and that consequently they were not receiving a fair hearing.

Stan Read, however, tried to be strictly neutral, and in his opening address set the stage for the coming debate. On the one hand, he said that some contemporary theologians who attempted to relate the Christian message to the modern age were 'like the housewife who used nitric acid to take a stain off her tablecloth. It took away both the stain and the cloth'. (It was not clear whether he was referring to me or not.) On the other hand, he called upon parish ministers to have done with 'moralistic waffling' and 'pious blather', and to grapple with the problem of relating the Christian message to modern life. He called for 'an aggressive evangelism which, though Bible based, was directed to secular man'. He pointed out that the secular world was rooted in the Gospel and in biblical ideals stemming from the Israelite prophets.

This augured well for a good debate, and the church was packed to overflowing to hear it. But first, five overtures from presbyteries and sessions had to be received. Then Bob Wardlaw, in presenting a petition signed by nearly five thousand people, aroused considerable anger when he referred to the 'odd-ball college of theology'. Later the Revd Hemi Potatau, Moderator of the Presbyterian Maori Synod, received warm applause for his description of visits to the holy Christian sites in Palestine while serving in the Maori Battalion, and concluded by saying that if the Assembly did not accept the bodily resurrection of Christ, he wanted to become a savage again. Others spoke of people leaving the church as a result of its uncertainty on basic issues.

The debate lasted seven hours, during which laymen repeatedly asked for simple, easily understood declarations of faith instead of the complex theological language being used by the scholars. Eventually, after many amendments had been moved, a few accepted, and many rejected, the statement prepared by the Doctrine Committee was approved by an overwhelming majority. It said, among other things, that 'God raised Jesus Christ from the dead in triumph over sin and death to reign with the Father as sovereign over all'. This drew upon such traditional language that neither liberal nor conservative could disagree with it, simply because it fudged the issues that had been raised. It neither distinguished between theological statements and historical statements, nor addressed the question of what was meant by 'resurrection from the dead'. And that is what the controversy was really about.

Nevertheless, there was great rejoicing that the imminent split in the church had been averted, and Bob Wardlaw greeted the result as a partial victory. The Assembly then agreed on a Message to the Church, summarising the statement on the resurrection and instructing this to be read from every Presbyterian pulpit.

The Clerk of the South Auckland Presbytery announced that it was withdrawing its overture, which among other things had called for the establishment of a second, conservative theological college. This was the opportunity for the Theological Education Committee to present a statement on the 'Aims and Methods of Theological Education', in an attempt to make clear to lay people how it trained students for the ministry. At that point, I spoke for the first time in the Assembly. I said, among other things, 'Apart from the conjugation of Hebrew verbs (which allowed no variation from the established norm) we shun indoctrination of any kind and encourage students to reach their own mature convictions'. Somewhat to my surprise, my short burst was met with warm applause. In reporting the Assembly debate, the *Evening Post* noted with some humour that when People's Night of the Assembly was held in the Wellington Town Hall, the combined choirs appropriately sang, 'God has gone up' and 'The strife is o'er'.

The Governor-General of New Zealand, Sir Bernard Fergusson, had been invited to address the Assembly. Being a staunch Presbyterian from the Church of Scotland, he was very interested in the theological debate that had become the focus of the Assembly's discussions. Although he carefully avoided taking sides, he did refer to it in his remarks. Then he sent me a private message inviting me to Government House that evening to explain the issue to him over a glass of sherry.

The Assembly's decision would have been the end of the matter (as many people hoped), had it been a genuine and honest resolution. In fact, it had simply papered over the cracks with traditional yet ambiguous statements, in an attempt to restore church harmony. Few in the church were willing to face up to the reality of the theological problems that had given rise to the controversy and remained unresolved. Events were soon to show the hollowness of the unanimity that had been reached.

Still, it is doubtful whether the Assembly could have done anything else, for the floor of the Assembly is not the place to decide complex theological issues. I remember John Dickie once observing that most Christians were happy to accept the historic creeds, largely because of the authority of ancient tradition and rhetoric, yet they would never be able to agree on a credal formula articulated in modern language. We have to remember that not even the ecumenical councils of the early centuries were unanimous when they settled on the historic creeds; these *appeared* to be universal only because the vigorous minority that disagreed with them were eased out of the 'one holy catholic church'. In other words, the original creeds had been arrived at *only by causing a split among Christians*, an extremity that the Presbyterian Church of New Zealand had avoided – at least for the time being.

As 1966 drew to a close, I hoped that life would return to normal. The pressures of this public debate had made increasing demands on my time, over and above my regular duties in the Hall and at home, which naturally continued as usual. Certainly there had been less time for leisure pursuits, though I seem to recall remaining one of the friendly four golfers who went around the Ocean Beach Links on Monday afternoons. All of our children were still at home and, apart from a few quite normal adolescent problems, family life proceeded very smoothly and seemed little, if at all, affected by the limelight now being directed our way.

Chapter Eleven

…AND CHARGED WITH HERESY

The unanimity of the 1966 Assembly decision on the 'resurrection controversy' seemed to provide a climate in which theological discussion could proceed in a more relaxed style. Indeed, 1967 began in a semblance of theological calm which allowed occasional titbits of humorous exchange. An open letter to me appeared in the *Manawatu Times*, composed entirely of passages from the Pauline epistles by someone who signed himself 'Paul'. Naturally he included the words 'If Christ was not raised then neither our preaching nor your faith has any meaning at all'. The very next day came the following reply:

> Sir, I am most annoyed that it has been necessary for me to interrupt my harp lessons to correspond with you in this barbarous English tongue, but a letter in yesterday's edition, delivered up here by special arrangement, leaves me no choice. How dare one of your citizens call himself by my name – 'Paul'. As if I had not had enough of this apocryphal use of my name in the first five centuries of this era!
>
> How dare he throw chunks of my writings at your readers, out of context, to make me seem to say what I have no intention of saying. The Risen Christ I met on the Damascus Road was certainly not flesh and blood nor is my description of the after-life suggestive that we retain a physical form of life 'up here'.
>
> I have not met this fellow Geering (although he has made long-term reservations here) but he seems to be aware of the Risen Christ's presence in the world in much the same way as I knew him there.
>
> Please see that there is no nonsense about adding this letter to the Canon. – Yours, etc., 'Saint' (If you please) Paul.

But this more relaxed atmosphere was soon to be shattered once again. John Murray, then ecumenical chaplain at Victoria University of Wellington, had invited me to preach at the annual inaugural university service in March. I chose to speak about the Book of Ecclesiastes, for I saw in this book reflections of many contemporary problems. After all, it had been written by a Jewish thinker who was struggling to resolve the conflict between his religious heritage and the cultural context of Hellenistic Alexandria.

Noting that we lived in a similarly unsettling environment, I pointed out that we had already accepted many aspects of today's secular culture, even when they conflicted with traditional Christian doctrines. For example, the human sciences had concluded that 'Man is a psychosomatic creature whose psyche cannot live independently from his body. Man has no immortal soul.' Yet such a revelation, I showed, simply took us back to Ecclesiastes and even to the early Christians, for they also accepted their mortality, as we now had to do. The remarkable thing about the human condition, I continued, and that which separated us from the other animals, was not that we are immortal but that, as Ecclesiastes states, 'God has put eternity into our minds'. In other words, 'We know we must die. Yet we have glimpses of the whole human situation – of the vast universe – of time – and beyond that again of the mystery of God.'

Unlike many sermons of mine and of others, this one has stood the test of time surprisingly well. I delivered it recently without having to change a word, and in it discovered the seeds of many ideas I was later to develop in my books. I said, for example, 'There are sound theological and historical reasons why secular man has emerged out of the Judeo-Christian heritage and not from elsewhere. The Christian can welcome the birth of secular culture.'

However, when an enterprising (and religiously conservative) journalist in the congregation heard me deliver the sermon in 1966, he seized upon the words, 'Man has no immortal soul', seeing it as another radical departure from orthodoxy on my part. After it had been headlined in the next morning's news, he then telephoned various church leaders to ask them what they thought. Most appeared shocked.

Three days later, the president of the Association of Presbyterian Laymen, Bob Wardlaw, called for my immediate resignation or, failing that, my dismissal. He even wrote to evangelical students in the Theological Hall, urging them to boycott my lectures. A contrary editorial in the *Otago Daily Times* warned Presbyterians 'to consider very carefully before they think of rushing to Mr Wardlaw's support in a personal witch-hunt'. And I received further support from a most unexpected source. When addressing a conference of students at Victoria University, the Minister of Labour, the Hon. T.P. Shand, discussed my case at some length and concluded that I should be accorded academic freedom and not dismissed from my post.

As a result of Wardlaw's protest, my sermon was subsequently published in most newspapers; this was followed by widespread public discussion on the sensitive issue of what happens to us when we die. A full-page feature in the very next *Sunday News* quoted authorities from around the world and manifested conflicting views. The Anglican Bishop of Auckland asserted that to deny life after death was to deny the teaching of Jesus Christ. The Roman Catholic hierarchy, in a statement to reassure their faithful, asserted that 'The eternal God who makes man to his own image or likeness means him to live for ever...To reject this belief is to reduce man to the level of a mere animal'.

It so happened that in the previous December the Mataura Presbytery had invited me, along with Ian Breward, to discuss all the issues of the 1966 controversy at a full-day seminar open to all the lay people in Gore. To be sure, the decision to invite us had not been reached without some opposition; some in Gore would have preferred that I not be one of the two Hall staff members invited. Nevertheless, it was a more constructive way of proceeding.

Since the day chosen for the seminar turned out to be the Saturday following the outbreak of this second controversy, the atmosphere was once again very tense. Although only Presbyterians were admitted, the event drew an audience of two hundred. With two lectures apiece, Ian Breward and I had an excellent opportunity to explain theological education in general, and in particular to outline the extent and significance of the previous hundred years of revolution in our understanding of the Bible.

The press were not admitted, but were permitted to publish selected transcripts of our answers to questions we were asked, many of which naturally arose from the new controversy then emerging. For example, on being asked about the meaning of eternal life, I distinguished between it and 'life after death', declaring the latter phrase to be a contradiction in terms, since death is what brings life to an end. Death has to be taken seriously, I said, and that is why Christian theologians have never used the phrase 'life after death'. The Christian term 'eternal life' refers to the quality of life that can be experienced here and now, a quality that enables us to face both life and death with a serenity and sense of victory that take the sting out of the universal phenomenon of death.

I even dared to illustrate our ambivalence with regard to the popular view of 'life after death' by telling the story of a minister who was visiting his former parish. On meeting an old parishioner, Mrs Smith, he immediately enquired after Mr Smith, only to be told, 'Mr Smith is in heaven'. Without thinking he replied, 'I'm so sorry to hear that', only to realise that was not an appropriate response. Correcting himself, he blurted, 'I'm glad to know that', but immediately recognised that he had moved into even deeper waters. In desperation, he made one last attempt to salvage the situation by saying, 'I *am* surprised'.

On the day after the seminar, I preached in the leading Presbyterian church in Gore, and my sermon was published almost in full in the following Saturday's newspaper. I spoke about faith, distinguishing it from knowledge and orthodox doctrine. Faith, I said, is an attitude of trust in the face of both doubt and uncertainty. 'Unless you experience some doubt, you don't know what faith is. The person who believes he possesses an infallible Bible does not need to live by faith.'

The whole weekend proved very successful, particularly since Gore, along with Southland generally, was known to be a conservative area. Although not everyone agreed with our honest answers to their questions, this valuable educational and pastoral exercise demonstrated that it was far better to discuss these delicate and controversial issues face to face than to hurl invectives from a distance.

It is a great pity that this seminar did not become the prototype for many more. Instead, a largely impersonal debate continued in the public arena and mainly through the media. The New Zealand Rationalist Association offered £1,000 to anyone who could provide scientific proof that human beings possessed immortal souls. The ultra-conservative

Churches of Christ offered £5,000 to the first person to produce one clear instance of the term 'immortal soul' in the Bible. Neither amount was claimed.

Day after day the newspapers carried letters to the editor, reports of presbytery meetings, and articles on immortality by all and sundry. It is doubtful whether, at any other time, so many people in New Zealand were all thinking about the question of 'life after death'. It was such a talking point that the British Secretary of the Bible Society, on arriving in New Zealand, was immediately asked by the media whether he believed in the immortality of the soul. 'Indeed I do,' he said, 'I see no point whatever in this life if when we die we are dead and finished with.' When news of the debate reached Australia, the *Sydney Morning Herald* devoted an editorial to it and followed that up with a full-page article in its *Weekend Magazine* on whether we humans have immortal souls.

Arthur Gunn, Moderator of the South Auckland Presbytery and the leading light of the conservative Westminster Fellowship, attempted to show that I had clearly stepped outside the boundaries of allowable Presbyterian thinking. His strategy was to call the public's attention to the relevant words in the Westminster Confession, which ministers and teachers of the church were bound to uphold. But as early as 1940 John Dickie had pointed out to us students that the complicated eschatology enshrined in the Westminster Confession was based on two mutually exclusive and hence contradictory views. One – a doctrine that became dominant in the Middle Ages – was that the eternal destiny of the soul was determined immediately after death. The other was that the dead sleep in their graves until the end of the world, at which point they are resurrected to appear before the Judgement seat of God. This, he said, was the original view of both Jews and Christians, and it showed the influence of Persian religion. That is why the earliest Christian epitaph was *Requiescat in pace* (let him or her rest in peace). This second view was revived by Martin Luther but rejected by John Calvin, who scathingly condemned the notion of 'soul-sleep'.

During the gathering controversy I received a phone call from a ninety-year-old Presbyterian minister, who said, 'I cannot understand what all the fuss is about. I have been going back to my old copies of the *Outlook* that I have kept from my young days and I find that all these issues were being discussed then.' He was referring to the fact that the influential minister Rutherford Waddell had said in 1897, 'The idea of immortality as something to come…which still lingers on in many minds, is really a survival of paganism'. Thus he illustrated a perennial problem of new theological thinking: it is all too soon forgotten as a new generation arises, one that 'knows not Joseph'.

The widespread public interest in the topic caused feelings within the church to become very strained. The Moderator of the General Assembly, S.C. (Stan) Read, asked Presbyterians not to be thrown into a state of panic. As Easter drew near, I was informed that a deputation led by the Moderator was coming to see me on Thursday of Holy Week. Although unclear as to what the deputation hoped to achieve, I assumed that they wished to discuss the issues I had raised and perhaps ask me to recant. Convinced that I had no reason to retract anything I had said, I had my books ready and open to show them that it had already been said by scholars of international repute. When they said that was not their mission, I asked if they wished me to resign, indicating that I was willing to do so, however reluctantly, if it was necessary to restore harmony in the church. Again they said that was not what they sought. Rather, they asked me to do all in my power to prevent the controversy from hurting the church. This I happily agreed to, pointing out, however, that if the church did not face up honestly to issues I had raised, it would have no future.

I learned later from Evan Sherrard (who, although a recent student, had been invited to join the delegation at the last moment) that the visit had been motivated by a pastoral concern both for me and for the church, and that I was in no sense 'on trial'. All in all, the meeting was very unsatisfactory and resolved nothing, partly because I had felt so much on the defensive as to persuade the deputation that I was not open to dialogue. On their way out, the group passed my colleague Frank Nichol, who commented with a wicked smile, 'My! This must be some funeral you're planning!' And that was the feeling I was left with, for the significance of the day – Maundy Thursday – did not escape me. I went home to drive the family up to our cottage at Cromwell for the Easter break. And a very bleak Easter it was, for this was the one time throughout the entire controversy when I felt isolated from the whole of the church.

From that time onwards, I found myself increasingly singled out as the cause of widespread dissension. It was being called 'the Geering affair'. What should have been a worthwhile theological discussion, providing a number of positive outcomes, became instead a debate centred on me, as if I bore sole responsibility for the disturbance by suddenly making some outrageous claims that no one else had ever thought of.

That Easter Day, a well-known ninety-year-old New Zealander wrote to tell me that his belief in an after-life had been his sheet anchor since the death of his wife twenty-eight years before. He implied that it was his expectation of meeting her again that had enabled him to live to such a great age. There seemed to be something illogical here, for if one is so convinced of such a reunion, one would hardly take such delight in living a long life. Indeed, a few people have been known to take their own lives in order to be quickly reunited with those they love. Of course, I replied to this man as sympathetically as I could (as I did with the rest of the deluge of letters I received), even though I concurred with Paul Tillich that ministers ought to steer people away from the hope of being reunited with their loved ones in the hereafter.

In early April my colleague Frank Nichol, Professor of Systematic Theology, and my parish minister, Rod Madill, came to my support by bringing motions to the Dunedin Presbytery. After lengthy debate, the Presbytery went so far as to congratulate me on the sermon on Ecclesiastes, urged people to study it in full, and deplored the way in which words had been taken out of context to accuse me of theological error.

Although I always enjoyed warm support from my colleagues, most of the students, and those who knew me in Dunedin, the further I departed from 'home' the more uncertain I became of what to expect. At times the antagonism was not only highly personal, but also quite vicious. Some of my critics prophesied that God's curse would descend upon me in the form of fire and brimstone or some equally excruciating commodity. When death threats started to arrive, my advisers insisted that I inform the police. This I reluctantly did, and although I was offered police protection, I deemed it unnecessary. Rather than fearful, I felt staggered and ashamed that those who prided themselves on being Christian could harbour such vicious thoughts and motives.

And I was not the only target. In many ways my family suffered more than I did, for they had done nothing and were unable to defend themselves. Elaine fielded many abusive phone calls, unwelcome objects were sent through the post, and our children found that their peers could sometimes be unexpectedly cruel.

The intensely personal nature of the controversy made it clear to me that not only in the church but in society at large a very sensitive nerve had been touched. I happened to be the person who triggered the response, but it could have been any one of a large number of people. I found myself being referred to in the most extreme terms, as everything from the devil incarnate to the new Galileo. In most of this I was quite unable to recognise myself: it seemed as if a new mental image of me had formed in the collective consciousness of New Zealanders – an image that some hated and others honoured. The Christian tradition was clearly at a fork in the road. A fault-line had long been developing between traditional and popular Christian thought on the one hand, and academic enquiry on the other; now the fracture zone had become a yawning gulf.

In the midst of this intense public turmoil I was invited by the staff of Canterbury University to participate in an evening of theological discussion. On arrival in Christchurch I found I was expected to give an address, and was obliged to spend an hour or two putting my hastily prepared notes into better shape. That evening I spoke to an overflowing university hall on 'Man's Ultimate Destiny'. In the Victoria University sermon that had sparked the new commotion, I had been primarily concerned to show the relevance of the Christian tradition to a rapidly changing world. Here now was an opportunity to discuss at some length the topic of human destiny, which people had wrongly assumed to have been the point of the sermon.

First, I drew attention to the fact that all cultures and religions had evolved in order to answer the basic questions we ask about human existence, and that each of them had developed and matured over the centuries. To show the changes in the Judeo-Christian tradition, I then selected three historical cross-sections. In the first, portrayed in the Old Testament, humans accepted their personal mortality and believed their appointed role was to contribute to the ongoing destiny of their people, Israel. In the second, the period of Christian origins, human destiny was described in terms of salvation from the present evil age and the transition to a new age, the coming of a new heaven and a new earth. When that promised world failed to arrive, the third dispensation, which corresponded with the mediaeval period, came to picture the ultimate human destiny as a supernatural spiritual heaven, to be entered after death.

All three cross-sections were part of our cultural past, I said, but none of them was adequate in today's world, although the first had best stood the test of time. I concluded with some suggestions as to the most satisfying answer to the meaning of existence in today's world. The most important of these, I proposed, was that we must accept our mortality and acknowledge that all that we valued in life was bound up with our bodies and the bodies of others.

> All thought of immortal souls, life after death, heavenly existence are but pale shadows in comparison. The life we have here, with all its frustrations and finiteness, is capable of maturing to the best that we actually imagine, and that is the meaning of the Christian doctrine of the incarnation.

My lecture was received with great applause, and I felt flattered when the chairman judged it to be indicative of genuine creative thinking.

I have included this brief sketch for two reasons. First, like the sermon at Victoria University, it has stood the test of time rather well and contains the germ of much that I was to develop later. The second is that it had more immediate consequences. Having promised the Moderator not to be the cause of further dissension in the church, I had agreed to accept the invitation only on the condition that the audience would be restricted to members of the university, and that no one was to record what was said. Although the chairman made this clear at the outset, someone not only recorded the lecture but passed the audio-tape on to my accusers, with consequences that will be discussed later.

Recognising that the controversy revealed great confusion in the public mind about central theological issues, I accepted an invitation to write a book about them. In fact, I was approached by three publishers, but responded only to Hodder & Stoughton, who had been the first to contact me late in 1966. As I had never imagined myself as an author, I felt such a novice that at first I submitted a few chapters for their approval. It seemed to me necessary to leave aside the topics of resurrection and immortality for the time being, so as to explain in non-academic language what lay behind the current controversy. Thus during the first eight months of 1967, while the theological storm was swirling around me, I was producing a chapter every fortnight – although towards the end a note of urgency crept in when I realised the book would have to be finished before the meeting of the General Assembly. That is how I came to write *God in the New World*.

Just after beginning the book, I read with excitement *The Phenomenon of Man*, the magnum opus of the Jesuit scientist Teilhard de Chardin. I read it over one weekend, hardly putting it down. Here was a vision of the evolving universe, one that put all that we have come to know about cosmology, physics, chemistry and biology into one developing story. I was awestruck. This visionary sketch of a vast, immemorial process that eventually produced the human species was a more convincing description of God than Tillich's enigmatic phrase 'being itself'. God is not so much the maker of the world, the first cause or even the planner of the evolutionary process; rather, the mysterious process of an evolving universe is itself God. It is little wonder that the then popular 'process theology', originating with the philosopher A.N. Whitehead, came to be seen as consistent with Teilhard's vision.

Unbeknown to me, during these months a good deal of correspondence about my future was going on up and down the country, particularly between the Association of Presbyterian Laymen and the Moderator. The former, having failed to achieve my immediate dismissal, had called for a special meeting of the General Assembly to be held forthwith. This request was eventually declined, and it was left to the normal meeting of the Assembly in November to deal with the issue.

In view of what had happened the year before, it is understandable that the NZAPL should have reacted as strongly as it did. But curiously enough, they did not realise that on this issue they could not call on the Bible for support, as they could with regard to the resurrection, for the New Testament unambiguously declares that only God is immortal. All this was made clear in a book I had read in 1959, *The Immortality of the Soul or the Resurrection of the Dead?* by Oscar Cullmann, a New Testament scholar of international repute. The belief in immortal souls that survive the death of the body, he persuasively showed, was a post-biblical development from the second and third centuries onwards, and reflected the increasing influence of the ideas of Socrates and Plato.

In early May, the Moderator declared that the matter was now *sub judice* and was not to be discussed publicly by me or by anybody else in the church. Being unaware of how busily some were planning to bring about my downfall, I felt reasonably calm and relaxed (apart from the unsettling events of Easter weekend), and fully enjoyed some of the humorous incidents. For example, in the Auckland Presbytery Bob Blaikie raised the issue of my title; he thought the term 'Principal', an honorific I was often publicly accorded, suggested that I wielded more authority than I actually possessed. He proposed that, since the Principal did no more than chair the meetings of the theological staff (then known as the Senatus), the title should be changed to 'Chairman'. One of my friends in the Presbytery wickedly responded, 'That is a good suggestion and I would like to second it. Then we shall have Chairman Geering and Chairman Mao.' And that was the end of that!

Another incident involved an elder of Knox Church in Dunedin who suffered a sudden fainting attack in the Octagon and was carried unconscious into the nearest shop for attention. It was a milliner's shop and, on regaining consciousness, he found himself surrounded by an array of colourful hats. He concluded that he was in heaven and astounded those seeking to help him by blurting out, 'Good God! Geering's wrong!'

When my former teacher and colleague Helmut Rex died in March, he left behind a finished manuscript on the topic of Jesus' resurrection. This was published a few months later as *Did Jesus Rise from the Dead?* His widow pointed out in her preface that it was in no way intended as an 'answer to Professor Geering', since most of it had been written before the controversy arose. Rex had produced a very scholarly piece of work which arrived at a position midway between mine and that of my accusers. On the one hand he said, 'The resurrection of Jesus is certainly not an historical event in the sense in which his crucifixion is'. On the other, he defended the historicity of the empty tomb, which on his own admission some scholars, going back as far as Wellhausen in the nineteenth century, had regarded as legendary. In my view Rex, like the author of *Who Moved the Stone?*, fell into the trap of assuming the historicity of the burial story. This is simply the beginning of the empty tomb story, and it

167

is illogical to use one part of a report to prove the historicity of the other. I incline to the view that Mark's Gospel originally ended with the words 'Truly this man was the Son of God!', and that Mark 15:40–16:8 is a unit and wholly legendary, perhaps added to the Gospel just as Mark 16:9–20 was added still later.

In late 1966, the Presbyterian Publications Committee had sought to promote informed discussion by inviting J.L.Wilson, a moderately conservative minister, to write or edit a book presenting the more traditional view on the resurrection of Jesus. This now appeared as a symposium of six essays, entitled *The Third Day He Rose Again*, and containing a foreword by the Moderator. The authors included Bob Blaikie, G.N. Stanton (a former student of mine, then pursuing doctoral studies at Cambridge), B.F. Harris (a former Rhodes Scholar and then Associate Professor of Classics at Auckland University) and two conservative theological lecturers in Australia (D.W.B. Robinson of Moore Theological College, Sydney and K. Runia of the Reformed Theological College, Geelong). One of the latter wrote:

> The emptiness of the tomb was the *sine qua non* of Jesus having been raised…To claim to believe in the resurrection while holding that the bones of Jesus lie somewhere in Palestine…is to deny the resurrection.

This was a diametrical rejection of the statement by the theologian Gregor Smith, that had triggered the original debate.

During the three months leading up to the Assembly, its officials received a deluge of correspondence – to which, of course, I was not privy, but of which I received hints. Further, it so happened that in 1967 the Clerk of Assembly, Stan Read, was also the Moderator (the only year in the history of the church when this was so). Therefore, in giving advice to those preparing to lay charges of doctrinal error against me, he was often doing his best to remain neutral while wearing two very different hats. Further, he felt ambivalent on the issue itself, for like many other liberals at the time he sympathised with me but felt I had gone too far.

At one point, as I later discovered, Read privately recruited E.R.E. (Eric) Ross, Assistant Clerk and acting lecturer in Church History with me at Knox, to sound me out on how I would react if the hearing of charges against me were to be carried out in private, to avoid the adverse publicity it would otherwise bring to the church. This suggestion I unequivocally rejected, saying, 'I have nothing to hide and, having been subjected to widespread criticism in public, I insist on defending myself in public'.

Clearly, Read faced two difficulties. The first was that, under normal church procedure, any complaints about a minister's statements should be heard within a presbytery, thus leaving the Assembly to serve as a Court of Appeal. But the Dunedin Presbytery to which I belonged had already indicated its confidence in me and had no wish to lay charges. The complaints were coming from people in the Auckland Presbytery, which was becoming the centre for Christian conservatism, while liberal thought was being more readily accepted in the south. (Incidentally, this polarisation ran directly counter to the common perception of Auckland as the centre of the *avant-garde* and the south as living in the past.) Because the Theological Hall of which I was Principal served the whole church rather than one presbytery, I had no hesitation in allowing my case to be dealt with by the Assembly, even though this entailed surrendering any right of appeal.

Read's second difficulty lay in the fact that charges were being pressed by two parties presenting distinctly different arguments. Bob Wardlaw was a fundamentalist and a theologically illiterate layman, who sincerely and passionately believed that what I had said could be quite clearly disproved by quoting the Bible. As chairman of the NZAPL, he felt he could speak for the vast majority of lay people and was beginning to feel suspicious of the clergy, believing them to have become a closed shop.

Bob Blaikie, however, had considerable theological expertise. While not wanting to be associated with Wardlaw's blatant fundamentalism, he also distanced himself from the Westminster Fellowship, which was beginning to lend discreet assistance to the conservative cause. (Arthur Gunn, editor of the *Evangelical Presbyterian*, later confessed on television that he practically wrote Wardlaw's speech.) Blaikie was trying to avoid giving the impression that he was charging me with doctrinal error; but at the same time he wanted to challenge the Assembly to declare exactly where it stood on the issues that had been raised.

For this reason, the charges against me had to be laid separately. Wardlaw charged me with 'grave impropriety of conduct' in teaching doctrines contrary to the Bible and the Westminster Confession by denying (1) the Christian doctrine of a transcendent Creator God, (2) 'the Holy Scripture as the revelation of God', (3) the deity and supernatural power of Christ, (4) that Christ had been raised from the dead, and (5) 'a life to come'.

Blaikie, by far the more astute and circumspect of the two, charged me with 'gravely disturbing the peace and unity of the church by making statements which appear to be contrary to the church's teaching'. After enumerating various examples, he requested that the Assembly determine whether I had denied the substance of faith and, if so, that I be censured or otherwise dealt with as the Assembly saw fit.

When it came time for the charges to be heard before the General Assembly, to be held in Christchurch, Elaine insisted on taking leave from work to accompany me and provide moral support. Her lifelong friend, Shirley White, lived at Mt Pleasant in Christchurch, and she and her husband Ian kindly invited us to stay at their home. It proved to be a restful haven from the stress of the Assembly. Elaine and Shirley were allotted VIP seats in the balcony for the entire proceeding.

The Moderator of the 1967 Assembly, E.G. (Paddy) Jansen, had served as a missionary in China and the New Hebrides (now Vanuatu), and somewhat ironically, as it turned out, gave a moderatorial address on the 'Renewal of the Church'. On Friday 3 November 1967, I was called to the bar of the Assembly to hear the charges set forth by my accusers. The air was charged with expectancy and a good deal of drama. More than a thousand people packed St Paul's Church and overflowed into the hall, as the lamps of the television crews created a surreal glow and increased the stifling heat. The *Auckland Star* noted that Wardlaw was presenting his charges 450 years to the day since Martin Luther nailed his ninety-five theses to the church door in Wittenberg. The *Christchurch Star* observed that a perfect halo hung briefly over the church, adding that it was not of supernatural origin but was caused by four Air Force Harvards practising for an air pageant.

It had been settled beforehand that my two accusers would be given forty-five minutes each to present their charges during the Friday session, and that on the following Monday I would be allotted ninety minutes to reply. But right at the outset, Wardlaw faced a procedural problem. He sought leave to distribute to the Assembly a copy of the lecture I had delivered at Canterbury University in April. This upset and embarrassed some members of the university who were present, for they had guaranteed the privacy of that occasion. The matter was quickly resolved when I raised no objection; as I said in my address later, I had intended to bring my copy of the lecture to help me in my defence, but had inadvertently left it at home. Indeed, I was glad that the Assembly would have the opportunity to read it, however odd it might seem that words that I considered vital to my defence, Bob Wardlaw regarded as evidence of my guilt.

Wardlaw and Blaikie addressed the Assembly in turn to elaborate on their respective charges, and members of the Assembly were given the opportunity to question them. The difference between my two accusers quickly became clear. While most members of the Assembly obviously felt little sympathy with Wardlaw because of his clumsy presentation, they were puzzled by Blaikie's failure to make clear what he intended to achieve. He said he did not wish to bring charges of heresy against me, and substantially agreed with me that the Westminster Confession could not function in the modern world as it was originally intended.

On the following Monday morning, as I took my seat in the front pew, an enormous bouquet of flowers arrived for me. I never found out who sent it, but guessed that it most likely came from students of Victoria University. Then, as I listened to the opening devotions, I could hardly believe my ears. The New Testament passage being solemnly intoned was the Transfiguration story, which contains the words, 'a cloud overshadowed them and a voice came out of the cloud, "This is my beloved son; listen to him"'. Elaine told me later that she almost laughed aloud when she heard it. It was one of a number of incidents in this very serious process that must have made 'God in his high heaven laugh'; but at the time it was no laughing matter either for me or for my accusers.

My address to the Assembly lasted an hour and a half, with a recess midway for morning tea. First, I disclaimed any responsibility for 'disturbing the peace of the church'. On the contrary, I maintained that since *shalom*, the Hebrew word for peace, literally means 'wholeness', I was endeavouring to restore wholeness or integrity to the faith that the church professed. I readily conceded that those of my statements which others complained of could not readily be squared with the church's standards when taken literally. But there was a reason for that: those standards were written in times when people's view of the world was very different from what it is today: 'The creeds…of past times no longer answer the questions that men of our day are asking and we can no longer fob them off with pat answers from former generations which are no longer relevant.'

I also fully conceded that the task of reinterpreting Christianity for today's world was difficult and dangerous, and could lead to errors. But whereas my accusers had claimed that theological teachers should stay strictly within the boundaries of orthodoxy, I argued that they should be in the vanguard of change, not leaving that challenging responsibility to the parish ministers while they formed a rearguard, tucked safely away in a theological college and out of touch with daily life.

What was becoming clear, I continued, was that the controversy represented a clash between two quite different ways of understanding the Christian faith. That outlined by Wardlaw and Blaikie and their many sympathisers described Christianity as a core of fixed beliefs. In strong contrast, I saw Christianity as a living and ever-changing path of faith being trodden by successive generations of Christians who, while drawing inspiration from their predecessors, took up the challenge to express that faith in terms relevant to the culture and age in which they lived. Therefore, I concluded:

> It is faith that man needs, not past doctrines. These latter only become, like the law, heavy burdens to be borne. Faith has no security, no fixed doctrines, no infallible church, no infallible Bible, no assured revelation. I hope my accusers, along with the whole church, will see their way clear to let go their hold on whatever words, doctrines, and dogmas of the past have given them security, and launch out into this world with the same insecure faith as marked the patriarchs and prophets, the apostles and reformers.

As I finished there was a spontaneous burst of applause, swiftly quelled by the convener, W.A. Best, who had explained at the outset that there was to be no applause for any speaker. After members of the Assembly had been given the opportunity to ask me questions, Wardlaw, Blaikie and I were then allotted ten minutes each for a final reply.

After lunch, the Assembly engaged in vigorous debate for two hours.

Much to my surprise (and that of my accusers, I imagine), members hardly referred to the various doctrinal issues that had been raised. Indeed, they seemed almost to take for granted that it would be inappropriate to judge me guilty of doctrinal error; they were more concerned with finding the best way of dealing with the issue from a pastoral perspective, with an eye to the good of the church. Almost without delay, Jack Bates introduced a resolution that began, 'The General Assembly dismisses the charges against the Principal of the Theological Hall and declares that it is persuaded of his Christian integrity and conviction'. Then J.S.(Stan) Murray, a former Moderator and the Overseas Missionary Secretary of the church, who had taken a leading role in trying to resolve the tension in the Auckland Presbytery, introduced a long, seven-clause amendment which, while exonerating me, was largely in the form of a pastoral message.

The two hours were spent largely in debating the relative merits of the motion and its amendment. At last, fatigued by the emotional tension of the proceedings, the Assembly allowed the matter to be resolved more by accident than by design. Its immediate action was to pass a motion by a massive majority and on the voices alone: 'The Assembly judges that no doctrinal error has been established, dismisses the charges and declares the case closed'. Sitting quietly at the back of the church, I was greatly relieved, but much surprised to hear the Moderator next thank my accusers for their concern in bringing the charges, without making any mention of me. The following evening, after further debate, the Assembly accepted a rather hastily constructed Pastoral Letter that was to be read before all congregations. It expressed confidence in me as a minister and theological teacher, and also declared its appreciation of the faith and devotion of Mr Wardlaw and Mr Blaikie.

But although the Assembly had dismissed the charges, there was no easy way to heal the divisions that had now become public. Bob Wardlaw resigned from the church and started one of his own. A number of individuals transferred to other denominations. Nearly all the metropolitan newspapers devoted editorials to the subject, and the trial even rated a mention in *The Times* of London. The Catholic newspaper *Zealandia* was impressed by my defence and likened me to Luther, but ended (perhaps predictably) by asking, 'Where does this leave the Presbyterian church now that it has sold Christianity down the river?'

The *Sunday Times* declared that 'the Church in New Zealand has known nothing more exciting this century' and had now come of age. The *New Zealand Weekly News* commented:

> ...the Geering affair is not over. The issues he raised can't be forgotten, many platitudes of belief are destroyed and people have been forced to see religion as a commitment to be questioned rather than a comfortable habit.

It quoted a housewife present at the trial, who said, 'I've just heard my longest talk on religion and the only one I've been able to understand'. In the same issue, the Revd Ross Miller wrote, 'Nothing will ever be quite the same again'.

In many ways he was right. Nor was it ever again the same for me. Just thirty years after I embraced the Christian faith, 1967 marked the second religious turning point in my life. Along with many others, I had grown to regard the church as a holy society, different from other social institutions in that it manifested a special quality of communal life. I must confess to being considerably shocked to find that behind its customarily benign face it could harbour poisonous animosities and sheer hatred – and in the very people who claimed to be its most zealous guardians. It made me feel shame for the church; I was saddened by the recognition that, while it encompassed many fine and even noble people, the institution of the church was every bit as human as any other element of society.

Chapter Twelve

THE BATTLE OF THE BOOKS

The positive character of the Assembly's decision left me quite hopeful that the church would move forward into reformation mode. I noted with some satisfaction the judgement of the *Sunday Times* correspondent who had witnessed the Assembly:

> The real question which faced the Assembly was whether they would choose to live their faith in the context of the nineteenth, sixteenth or even the first century; or whether they would be prepared to come to grips with the real world of the twentieth century.

He correctly saw, as so many others did not, that the real crux of the 'heresy trial' was not how to deal with an 'oddball theologian' (as Bob Wardlaw spoke of me), but whether or not Christianity could transform itself into a viable faith for the modern era. 'The Reformers now have the ball at their toes', said the *Sunday Times*, 'but will the church be equal to the task?'

Some encouraging signs suggested that the church might indeed take a bold leap forward. For a few months I was kept busy accepting invitations to speak at both churches and secular organisations, and found myself being enthusiastically received. A good deal of healthy public discussion on the religious topics raised by the controversy continued through the next three years, as shown by the publication of many articles and frequent letters to the editor, many of which were strongly supportive of change.

In January 1968 John Chisholm, an elderly Presbyterian minister who was interviewed by the *Otago Daily Times* on his ninetieth birthday, reported that for years he had held virtually the same ideas as mine, and had even preached them in Knox Church, Invercargill, during the 1920s! Subsequently I heard numerous accounts of ministers whose sermons in the 1920s and 1930s had openly denied the historicity of the Virgin Birth. But if this was so in earlier times, why had such a furore erupted over one article and one sermon of mine as much as four decades later?

When I joined the church in the 1930s, liberal theology was dominant at Knox College, prevalent in many congregations, and widespread in the large and influential Bible Class movement. Since my student days, however, the percentage of evangelicals and other conservatives in the ministry had actually been increasing (and it still is); by the 1960s they had gained sufficient strength to challenge liberalism. It was my bad fortune to have become Principal of the Theological Hall just at the time when the evangelicals were preparing to challenge the liberal ascendancy for the first time since the end of the nineteenth century.

As a result of the very public controversy that had surrounded me, I became an all too visible symbol of the liberalism that the evangelicals regarded as the work of the devil; I was now a marked man, and the conservatives were ready to pounce if I said anything they disagreed with. To be sure, the Assembly's decision had dealt them a temporary setback, but now they slowly recovered and regrouped. Worse yet, some of the liberal majority who had supported me began to back away, in the face of the recent dissension in the church. Indeed, at the administrative level, the church was so anxious to show pastoral concern for those who had been distressed or confused by the controversy that it completely neglected those on the fringes or even outside the church whose spiritual interests had been reawakened by the debate. And this despite its professed concern for evangelism. As a result, newcomers often felt so unwelcome in a church intent on defending its now outmoded doctrines that they drifted away, taking others with them. Although the trend did not become conspicuous for some years, this marked the beginning of a steady decline in the communicant membership of the Presbyterian Church, a decline I found myself being publicly blamed for.

In the meantime, the controversy was entering a new phase that one might call 'the battle of the books'. First to appear was *The Heresy Trial*, in which the Presbyterian Church published the charges laid against me by my accusers, their supporting addresses, my reply, the Assembly's decision and finally its Message to the Church. While this was intended simply to make public a full and objective account of the proceedings at the so-called 'trial', it gave the impression that the church's official position on theological issues had become rather fuzzy around the boundaries. To be sure, the 'Message to the Church' neither endorsed all that I had written or said, nor accepted my theological viewpoint as the only valid one; but it did declare its conviction that, in my endeavour to restate the Christian faith in modern terms, I had not stepped outside the bounds of reasonable liberty of thought or expression of doctrine. And this was much more than some could accept.

It especially alarmed many Anglicans, in view of their denomination's current negotiations for church union. Some two hundred of them, including a bishop and many clergy, signed an open letter to their Archbishop stating that the decision of the Presbyterian General Assembly would make it impossible for them to unite with such a church. As one who had long been a passionate supporter of church union and who was serving on the negotiating committee, I naturally felt very disheartened at being even indirectly a stumbling block to achieving union.

At the very time this stir was going on, my book *God in the New World* was launched in Auckland at a literary luncheon. This enabled me to inform a large gathering as to just why and how the book came to be written. I explained that many people in the pews did not seem to realise that what they sang about in their hymns on Sunday was out of kilter with what they took for granted in the secular world they inhabited from Monday to Saturday. What I had attempted to do in this book, therefore, was to bridge the widening gap between academic theology and popular Christian thought; this I did by describing the nature of the modern world, showing how it had emerged out of the Christendom of the past, and sketching what path the Christian faith might take in the twentieth century. This was also an opportunity for me to acknowledge publicly my debt to Elaine. The very helpful criticisms she had offered as I read the draft to her, chapter by chapter, rendered the book more comprehensible to a lay readership. Indeed, it was she who thought of the title.

My chapter on 'God' ended with these words:

By God-talk we are pointing to the deepest reality we can encounter, to that which concerns us ultimately. But we do not know what that is. The God that is known is an idol. The God who can be defined is no God. It is of the essence of human existence that we live not by knowledge but by faith. It is by faith that we are led to fulfilment and our ultimate destiny, and God is the ground of our faith.

The book's publication was followed by a flood of conflicting reviews in journals and newspapers. No doubt because of the notoriety I had gained before it was published, it received much more attention than it probably deserved. I was very willing to acknowledge and learn from a number of critical comments, chiefly in the area of ambiguities and generalisations. But I observed that those reviews that condemned the book differed so much in their opinions as to demonstrate what little religious consensus exists in the post-Christian world.

A striking example of this diversity was a page of the *Otago Daily Times* on which former Moderator Jack Bates claimed that my book 'explains the real nature of the Bible', while the editor of the Catholic *Tablet* wrote that 'this book sweeps away Christian belief'. Father Ian Sanders, Professor of Theology at the Catholic Holy Cross College, wrote a long and trenchant criticism in the *Tablet*, ending with the suggestion that the book would have been more appropriately titled 'Geering in Wonderland'.

Not all Catholics were quite so abrasive. Bernard Basset, a Jesuit priest and author, was visiting New Zealand at that time, and he rang me to congratulate me on my book. News of our meeting led to a television programme in which we entered into a very fruitful dialogue about the substance of our two books, his most recent one having the intriguing title *We Agnostics*. Although we by no means agreed on all theological issues, I found Basset to be an open-minded and delightful man with a great sense of humour. When I told him of my admiration for his fellow Jesuit, Teilhard de Chardin, he explained the thorough nature of Jesuit training over thirteen years – a period so long that it led to the Jesuit joke that ordination was a reward for a life well spent.

Rather different was the television programme a few weeks later in which my views were vigorously challenged by an Anglican vicar, R.J. Nicholson, one of the signatories to the open letter mentioned above. But although he questioned and attempted to refute a number of statements he found in *God in the New World*, I rather enjoyed the face-to-face encounter, for until then most of the debate had been conducted in print, a medium that keeps the participants too insulated from one another. And when Nicholson published his counter to my book a little later, entitling it *Empty Tomb or Empty Faith?*, the producer of the *On Camera* programme invited us to a return bout. Once again it was a vigorous encounter, though carried through in a good spirit. As soon as the programme finished, a woman rang the television station to say that her son, home from school with an illness, was absolutely enthralled by it. If even the young could find a theological discussion so interesting, it is no wonder that the *New Zealand Herald* commented next day, 'This is the stuff that television is made of'. Alas, viewers get to see far too little of this kind of live television, then or now – and partly because the churches have been afraid to have their doctrines questioned in public.

The controversy that had preceded the publication of *God in the New World* ensured that it became a bestseller, and the publishers, Hodder & Stoughton, sent me a leather-bound copy in appreciation. When it was nominated for the James Wattie Book Awards, the publishers flew Elaine and me up to Auckland in October 1968 to wine and dine us before the ceremony, where I was surprised and delighted to receive an award.

In the meantime, Hodder & Stoughton had done a strange thing. Perhaps because they had originally been an evangelical publishing house, they decided, even before my book went on sale, to commission a response from a well-known conservative, E.M. Blaiklock, Professor of Classics at Auckland University. This duly appeared as *Layman's Answer: An Examination of the New Theology* and was also launched at a literary luncheon in Auckland. There the author claimed that 'the new theology menaces the very root and fabric of Christianity as no other force, assault from without or betrayal from within, has ever done'.

While the book was welcomed by all those who wished to see *God in the New World* refuted, it unfortunately reflected such a fundamentalist approach that it failed even to acknowledge the existence of the historical and theological problems that my book had attempted to answer. Strangely enough, and much to Blaiklock's disgust, I was invited by Les Gosling, the new editor of the *Outlook*, to write a review of the book for his journal, he having written the corresponding review of my book. Les and I had trained in the same year, served several years in adjacent parishes, and had remained friends even though he was a committed evangelical and a passionate opponent of church union. But he had received a good philosophical training at Victoria University and developed a critical mind. Many years later, near the end of his life, he confessed to me that he was at last beginning to appreciate the views I had championed for so long.

Although I tried to be as positive as I could in assessing Blaiklock's book (for I had long admired his skill with words), and could readily acknowledge that it would be welcomed by those who shared his assumptions, I had to say that it provided no answers for those who had penetrating questions to ask about Christianity. 'It is marred', I said, 'by that dogmatism which has done so much to bring Christian preaching into disrepute, a dogmatism that knows all the answers and will listen to no interjections.'

Indeed, this book did little to advance constructive dialogue in New Zealand, but it did have a humorous sequel. An American Baptist publisher, evidently impressed by Blaiklock's exposition, wanted to issue an American edition, but recognised that doing so would be pointless unless readers had the opportunity to read the book it claimed to rebut. Thus *God in the New World* came to be printed in the United States by a conservative publisher! I imagine few read it, but its publication was one of the many ironies produced by the controversy.

Then in 1969 another refutation of *God in the New World* appeared, this one written by a Marist priest, P.J. Gifford, and entitled *Professor Geering in Perspective*. Gifford said that my book 'abounds in gratuitous assumptions and glib half-truths', which he proceeded to identify one by one. This strategy, which had characterised many of the critical reviews, is a particularly easy way to denounce any book; its weakness often becomes evident only when the critic is challenged to write a systematic alternative.

An interesting sequel may well prove my point. Having accepted an invitation to South Africa in 1985 to lecture at Pietermaritzburgh University, I was further invited to stop off at Harare on my return journey to give a lecture there. The man who invited me was none other than Father

Gifford, who was then teaching at the University of Harare. On my arrival, he told me he had completely changed his theological position and now agreed with what I had been saying back in 1966–67!

I suspect it was primarily because I had now become a public figure that I was asked to contribute to a series of monographs designed for discussion by students in their final year at secondary school. Mine was entitled *God in the Twentieth Century*. Although only a dozen pages long, it offers a clear and concise record of how I was thinking about God at that time. Too few people, including even scholars, are aware of how greatly religious concepts and beliefs have changed and evolved over the centuries, and this was a point I wanted to get across. As the following précis illustrates, I was here sketching 'a history of God', something Karen Armstrong was to do in great detail some twenty years later in her excellent book of that title.

I began by telling how the belief in gods began, then described how Israel arrived at monotheism, and finally showed the impact of science in undermining the concept of divine revelation, thus leaving god-belief as an open question in the twentieth century. What, then, are we to make of the term 'God' in the modern scientific age? This I attempted to answer in the following words:

> When a man, in full recognition of the secular world of thought, says he believes in God, he is saying that he recognizes in human existence meaning and purpose which are themselves not ephemeral but are of an eternal character. He is further saying that the various values which both interest him and lay a claim upon him are not simply and solely conventions of human origin but are the expression of something ultimate and eternal. All the things in human experience which have for him this ultimate character are linked together in a unity and the word 'God' is a symbol of that unity which is infinite, intangible and eternal.

I now regard this statement as a little clumsy and inadequate, but it shows how far I had moved from the traditional theism of a personal God. This is no doubt why, when the monograph was published, questions were raised in Parliament as to whether it should be permitted in schools. And yet, when I delivered it the following year as a lecture to young theological students in Queensland – one of Australia's more conservative states – it was deemed quite acceptable.

It was certainly not acceptable to my accusers, however, and especially not to Bob Blaikie. All this time he had been working on his own critique of the so-called 'new theology', which was published in 1970 as *'Secular Christianity' and God who Acts*. He made it clear that, although the impetus for his book had been the controversy in which we had both been involved, it was not aimed at me personally, but directed against the 'death of God' theologians among whom he thought I should be counted. It is ironic that I by no means saw myself in the 'death of God' camp when the controversy began, but eventually found myself close to that position (as the above quote shows) largely because of the need to analyse at greater depth the doctrines Blaikie had championed.

The contrast between our respective positions, which became more accentuated as time went on, is very clearly set out in Blaikie's book under the headings 'Secular Christian World-view' (in which there is no supernatural, no miracles, no revelation) and 'Biblical World-view' (in which God creates, controls nature, acts in history, and performs miracles). The understanding of God that he insisted on defending is usually referred to as theism. Although he did not use this term, he implied in all he wrote that God was to be conceived as a supernatural being who thinks, plans and executes his will. Consequently, Blaikie had no difficulty in concluding that any secular version of Christianity (such as mine) was so total a departure from the biblical version that it was 'not a re-interpretation of Christianity but a substitute for it', and consisted of 'a whole system of radical doctrinal error'. In his view, it was an error far more serious than those of the ancient heretics, Marcion, Arius and Pelagius. It became the duty of the church, he proposed, to recognise the new theology for the falsehood it was, and to insist that its ministers be faithful to the biblical witness to the theistic God stipulated in their vows: 'the alternative being a betrayal of Christ and the Christian Faith'. Thus Blaikie's book became an apologia, an explanation of why he had charged me with doctrinal error, and why the Presbyterian Church should now vigorously pursue the matter further.

In the meantime, the 1968 Assembly had given Blaikie the assurances he sought by unanimously restating its fundamental doctrines in a way that avoided the uncertainty left by the message of the previous Assembly. Among other things, it declared that 'God raised Jesus Christ from the dead in triumph over sin and death to reign with the Father as Sovereign over all', and that 'beyond death God will raise the Christian to eternal life in direct and unshadowed fellowship with Himself and His people'.

All of this would have been perfectly at home in the sixteenth century, but it was utterly blind to the fact that in the twentieth century we had come to accept a very different view of the universe and of the human condition. While the Assembly's statement brought comfort and relief to many by reaffirming all the familiar terminology, it showed no evidence that the church was 'prepared to come to grips with the real world of the twentieth century', to use the words of the journalist quoted earlier. So when journalists asked for my response to the Assembly's decision, I declined to comment, not wishing to arouse further dissension. But what I *thought* was that ecclesiastical officialdom could not bring itself to engage in honest and creative thinking for fear of disturbing the peace of the church by upsetting the traditionalists. In particular, the faith community was unwilling to face up to the question I had posed at the very beginning: what can it *mean*, in the context of the world-view most of us share in the twentieth century, to say that 'God raised Jesus Christ from the dead in triumph over sin and death' and that 'beyond death God will raise the Christian to eternal life'?

Thus I set about writing another book, this one focusing exclusively on the issues of resurrection and eternal life. I had not done so in my first book because I felt it necessary to explain the new kind of world in which we find ourselves living, and to sketch how Christianity had helped to bring this world into being. Then in 1970, while I was still at work on this second book, two new volumes appeared: *The Resurrection of Jesus of Nazareth* by Willi Marxsen and *Resurrection and the New Testament* by C.F. Evans. Both largely supported what I had proposed in the short article on resurrection that I had written for the general reader in 1966. I was now able to draw upon these, as well as many other books, for a more in-depth study of the resurrection of Jesus.

The resulting book consisted of two unequal components. Part I, 'The Collapse of an Old Tradition', started by raising the question of what 'resurrection' *means*. I showed how the traditional view of a bodily resurrection had shifted from the miraculous to the meaningless as people came to adopt the modern world-view. If Jesus had been raised physically, as traditionalists wished to affirm, either he would still be walking the earth (since in our space-time universe he could not have ascended into outer space), or his body must have undergone a transformation. The recognition of this by biblical scholars in the last few decades had, as I showed by quoting from their books, already forced many to conjecture such a transformation; and yet there was neither biblical warrant nor the slightest mention in past tradition to support such a transformation. Thus an increasing number of biblical scholars were arriving at the conclusion that the resurrection of Jesus could not be authenticated as a historical event involving the crucified body of Jesus.

This meant that the term 'resurrection' had to be understood in some other way, perhaps through a symbolic or poetical use of language. And this, of course, opened the way to an examination of the history and development of such non-literal usages, the project I undertook in Part II.

The concept of resurrection is an idiomatic or symbolic expression of hope that has had a long history. It originally sprang from observing the resurrection of spring growth after the death of winter. It was later applied to the resurrection of the people of Israel, as in Ezekiel's famous vision of the Valley of Dry Bones. Then, under the influence of Persian thought, it became associated with the myth of the Last Judgement at the end of time. Although the belief in a general resurrection to come was embraced by only a segment of the Jewish people, mainly the Pharisees, it was already being applied to the Jewish martyrs in the Maccabaean Revolt 150 years before the Christian era. Thus resurrection language was already in use before it came to be applied to Jesus after his crucifixion by the Romans. It had been used to express the hope that martyrdom was not in vain, and that was exactly what the disciples of Jesus sought to affirm about his death. This affirmation was later amplified by accounts of visions and the legend of a tomb found empty.

The book was published in 1971 as *Resurrection: A Symbol of Hope*. It did not receive as much attention as *God in the New World*, partly because by that time I no longer held a church appointment, and partly because the topic had ceased to be of great public interest.

That the reviews fell into three main groups was, I thought, in itself an interesting commentary on the religious character of our post-Christian society. First the journalists, who often skim books looking for startling, newsworthy items, produced articles with such headlines as 'Another savage attack on the traditional teachings of the church', and 'Professor Geering Back into Battle'.

The evangelicals and Roman Catholics, who found themselves quite unpersuaded by the arguments I had advanced, were anxious to defend the traditional view. A review in a British Catholic journal described the publication as 'a very silly book'. Canon Michael Green said in the *British Weekly* that although I wrote with 'erudition, sincerity and charm', it 'required far more credulity to believe Mr Geering's far-flung theories than to believe the witness of the New Testament writers'. Now Green had himself written a little book on the resurrection of Jesus, called *Man Alive!* The very title epitomises the way in which traditionalists had come to view the resurrection in modern times: it was a miracle whereby, for the first time in history, a dead man had come to life again, and this miracle had caused Christianity to burst into life. Taking quite the contrary stand, I had tried to show that resurrection had been in the air for quite some time before being seized upon to interpret the death of Jesus not as a tragedy but as a symbol of hope.

A third group of reviews took the book seriously; of these, some were critical and some very positive. One worthy of mention appeared in the *Times Literary Supplement*. While granting that the book was 'written with great ability and distinction and with many valuable things to say', the reviewer found a 'contradiction at the heart of it. How can a non-event be regarded as a symbol of hope?...We are driven back on the need for an Easter event'. Alas, he had entirely missed the point. There *was* an event – it was the tragic death of Jesus on the cross. The symbolic language of resurrection was what the early Christians used in order to interpret that dire event in a positive light.

Certainly I was disappointed that open-minded and informed readers did not find the argument more persuasive at the time. Since the book concentrated on the issue that had sparked off the whole controversy, I judged it to be much better than my first book; it had more depth, and broke new ground by widening the historical context in which the idea of resurrection was to be understood. This was the last real clash in 'the battle of the books'; and by the time it was published and being reviewed I had already left the Theological Hall. We must now turn back to see how this came about.

Chapter Thirteen

CHANCE EVENTS PROVE ADVANTAGEOUS

With the heresy trial behind me, and feeling both relieved and vindi-
cated by the outcome, I returned to the routine of life at the Theological
Hall, fully expecting to remain in that teaching post until my eventual
retirement. In view of its fulfilment of my original sense of call to the
ministry, this was an entirely pleasant prospect. During the next three
years, however, a succession of chance events conspired to lead me in a
new direction. I say 'chance events' because most of life is (to borrow the
title of Jacques Monod's book on the evolution of planetary life) a matter
of 'chance and necessity'.

The net result of these events proved to be distinctly advantageous for
me. Of course, some of my evangelical critics might have preferred (however ironically) to call them providential, regarding them as evidence of
the 'hidden hand of God' working his purposes out. But it is we humans
who create the appearance of divine or cosmic purpose when we (often
unconsciously) select certain events to the exclusion of others and weave
them into a meaningful story. It is only in retrospect, then, that I can now
appreciate how a string of random events turned out to be an excellent
preparation for the next major turning point in my life.

During these years my family responsibilities diminished as our two
older children flew the nest to go flatting soon after they began their
tertiary education. To my shame, I must confess that during the previous
two years I had not given them the personal attention they deserved.
They had to put up as best they could with snide remarks about their

notorious father. Yet never once did they utter a word of rebuke to me; on the contrary, they were exceedingly loyal.

It was in the general area of personal relations that I began to find, to my surprise and occasional consternation, that the adverse publicity I had received had brought about some changes. Some of my former ministerial friends, liberal though I assumed them to be, began to distance themselves from me. One even refused to shake hands any more, with the result that for quite some years I deemed it prudent not to be the first to put out my hand in greeting. Indeed, I began to feel something of an outcast, even though the support of many loyal friends and colleagues testified to the contrary.

Further, I had to be on the alert for other negative responses. Take for example our quandary when it was the turn of the Theological Hall to provide the programme for People's Night at the 1968 General Assembly. The staff debated whether I, as Principal, should be the one to give the main address: on the one hand, this might be judged unduly provocative in view of the tension surrounding me at the previous Assembly; on the other, for another member of staff to give the address might create the impression that they had lost confidence in their Principal. So I duly gave the address, only to hear in the course of it some loud groans from members of the audience when I referred to the lack of historicity in St John's Gospel – although I was drawing upon books that had been granted currency in academic circles for at least thirty years.

Then in 1969, when it became known that I was to go to Beirut to attend the executive meeting of the World Alliance of Presbyterian Churches (WAPC), some Presbyterians raised public objection to church funds being used for my travel. (I had been elected to the WAPC executive in 1964, but cost and distance had prevented me from attending its yearly meetings.) The Administrative Secretary had to explain that the church was covering only one third of the cost; one third came from the Alliance, and the other third I provided myself.

This trip was to enrich me with experiences that would prove most helpful in my subsequent career. As the period following the Beirut meeting coincided with the academic vacation at the Theological Hall, I planned to see as much of the Middle East as I could on the journey home. My primary purpose for doing this stemmed from my Old Testament duties; here was a golden opportunity to study the extant remains of the ancient history of the area in the wonderful museums at Beirut, Damascus, Baghdad and Teheran. It also offered valuable experience of life in the modern Islamic world.

First came Lebanon, the Phoenicia of the biblical world. Since this was before the tragic civil war that devastated the country, I was privileged to survey the beauty and charm of Beirut when it was still the busy commercial and tourist centre of the Eastern Mediterranean. Of even greater interest to me, however, were the coastal cities of Tyre and Sidon, referred to in both Testaments, as well as the ruins of ancient Byblos, from which the Phoenicians sailed off to trade their valuable wares and spread the priceless gift of their alphabet all around the Mediterranean. Then I went to Baalbeck, the valley between the snow-capped Lebanon and Anti-Lebanon ranges, to see its impressive second-century Roman temples. On another day, a bus took me some 5,000 feet (over 1,500 m) up Mount Lebanon to view all that now remains of the once-famous 'cedars of Lebanon'.

Having had difficulty in Beirut in obtaining a visa for Syria, I accepted the invitation of a honeymooning Iraqi couple I met in the hotel to share a taxi with them to Damascus, on the chance that I would be given a visa at the Syrian border. This proved to be no difficulty at all, and I experienced the unusual comfort of travelling by taxi from the capital of one country to the capital of another.

While in Damascus I walked up the long narrow street called 'Straight' (made famous by the biblical story about St Paul), visited the chapel built over the House of Ananias (still the centre of a community of Syrian Christians), and went on to the remains of the city wall over which Paul was lowered in a basket. The large Umayyad Mosque in the centre of Damascus is of interest not only because of its age and beautiful mosaics, but also because it incorporates parts of the Christian Church that preceded it on that site; the mosque has even retained the Christian baptismal font and what early tradition claimed to be the head of John the Baptist. Beside the mosque stands the tomb of Saladin, reviving memories of Crusader times. In the Damascus Museum I studied the archaeological finds from Ras Shamra, where the mother of all Western and Semitic alphabets was created, and marvelled at the richly decorated synagogue of

Dura Europos, which had been transported there from its third-century site near the Euphrates.

Although my air ticket covered the leg from Beirut to Baghdad, I chose to travel overland in order to see the countryside. From Damascus to Baghdad I took the Nairn bus. This bus company had been established after World War I by two New Zealand brothers who had shown great initiative in providing transport straight across the desert that lies between Syria and Iraq. In earlier times, the land route taken by traders and armies had avoided the Syrian Desert by following a dog-leg route that passed much further north through the ancient oasis city of Palmyra.

We left Damascus at about 4 o'clock in the afternoon, and with the same driver behind the wheel arrived in Baghdad twenty-four hours later. On the way I had a long talk with a Kuwaiti schoolteacher returning from a long vacation in Europe. He was so appalled by what he judged to be the moral degeneracy of a decaying Christendom that, on learning I was a theological teacher, seriously put it to me that I should become a Muslim.

It was early the next morning, and still in the midst of a featureless desert, that we reached the border of Iraq; there, to my dismay and discomfort, my visa was judged not to be in order. The bus was held up for a whole hour awaiting the arrival of a senior immigration official, who finally let me proceed with the bus, provided I reported as soon as possible to the police in Baghdad. Right after breakfast the next morning, I duly took a taxi to the police station to have my problem sorted out. A police officer studied my passport, scratched his head, consulted his colleagues, and finally indicated with a beaming smile that I was to follow him. Although he was quite a tall man with an air of self-importance, I observed with some amusement that as we drew near the office of his superior he seemed visibly to shrink, entering the higher presence in an obsequious manner.

There he explained his solution to the impasse and was suitably praised. At least, that is how I interpreted the Arabic dialogue that took place. The difficulty was that I had applied for my visa to the Egyptian Embassy in Sydney, where they had stamped an Egyptian visa in my passport and superscribed it in English: 'Acting on behalf of the Department of Iraqi Affairs'. Unfortunately, no one on duty at the border could read English.

At last I had gained entry into Iraq, only to find that I now had to apply for an exit visa. This process normally took eleven days, but since I planned to stay only four days permission could be granted immediately, provided I went outside and paid a little boy conveniently stationed there with a camera to supply me with new passport photos.

Now I was free to explore Baghdad and its environs. The Ba'ath Party was already in power, and although Saddam Hussein had not yet taken control the atmosphere was quite tense: a dining-room waiter with whom I struck up a conversation suddenly fell silent when I mentioned local politics. And when, along with two Italian archaeological students, I hired a taxi to visit the ruins of ancient Babylon, we found we had to pass through police checkpoints about every 20 miles (32 km).

But it was truly exciting to walk among the broken-down walls of dried brick that are the sole remains of ancient Babylon; these are the walls that once enclosed the fabled Hanging Gardens, one of the Seven Wonders of the Ancient World. The Ishtar Gate at the city's entrance was being restored to something of its former glory, and from the ruins we could see the nearby Euphrates River and a large hill of earth that had been the ziggurat immortalised in the biblical story of the Tower of Babel.

After spending much of my stay at the Baghdad Museum, I boarded an Air Iran flight that conspicuously refused to carry any Iraqi citizens. The highlights of my time in Iran were visits to the Teheran Museum and the heavily guarded vault containing the crown jewels, and a trip south to Shiraz and Isfahan. Shiraz is a centre of traditional Iranian culture; there I marvelled at the monuments erected to celebrate its great poets, as well as visiting its mosques and extensive bazaar. After taking a taxi north to explore the impressive ruins of Persepolis, the ancient royal palace destroyed by Alexander the Great, I decided to stay overnight at a local hotel. Alerted by my guidebook to the nearby tombs of the ancient Persian emperors at Naqshi-i-Rostem, I walked several miles next morning to see the tombs sculptured into the cliff face. There I also had my first glimpse of the remains of one of the small fire-altars associated with the indigenous Zoroastrian faith.

Next I flew to Isfahan, the showplace of Iran. There are sights one can never forget: the Royal Square, opening into the blue-tiled Royal Mosque at one end and the bazaar at the other, surrounded by artists, coppersmiths and artisans of all kinds busily plying their trades. I vowed that on my next visit, should it ever take place, I would stay at the magnificently decorated Shah Abbas Hotel. The end of my Iranian adventure came all too quickly, and with Omar Khayyam's injunction – 'Make haste!' – ringing in my ears, I returned to New Zealand just in time for our daughter Judy's wedding.

That was to be the prelude to the birth of our first grandchild the following year. Before that happy event took place I received a visit from Everald Compton, whom I had known in Queensland. He had taken such an interest in the heresy trial that on his many business trips to New Zealand he had interviewed various leading Presbyterians, including my accusers Blaikie and Wardlaw, and had written a pamphlet, *The Trial of Lloyd Geering*. He was now the Session clerk of St Philip's Presbyterian Church in Aspley, Brisbane, and on behalf of his minister and congregation he invited me to be their guest for a week in May. He was also keen to arrange a variety of speaking engagements which, in his view, would challenge the Queensland churches to face up to the real issues of the day.

When I accepted, he asked me to provide a general statement of the topics I would cover, and this is what I wrote:

> The world today is undergoing change of a more far-reaching character than ever before in human history. All over the world the structures which have held particular societies together are breaking down. We may be heading for a new kind of human society on a global scale or we may be heading for such a catastrophe to human society that it does not bear thinking about.
>
> I believe the Christian faith has a vital role to play in the future of human society, but before it can do so, Christians must wake up to what is happening in the world. For some time many Christians have been trying to hold back change. Change cannot be held back but it can be directed. What can Christians do to ensure that the changed human society of the future will be motivated by the highest moral and spiritual values that we know? We are in a situation where Christians are called to move from the rear-guard to play a leading part in the vanguard of change. The first Christians, we are told, turned the world upside down.

In an attempt to fulfil this mission I set off in May 1970, thinking it would consist mainly of talking to his congregation. I was little prepared for what he had planned. Perhaps I should have realised, when he insisted I fly business class, that he wanted me to be fresh for the interviews he had lined up. On arrival I was whisked into the VIP lounge, where over the next three hours I was interviewed by six press reporters and recorded two television interviews. After a short breather at the hotel, I was rushed to Aspley for a buffet meal with the church office-bearers and then taken to the Queensland General Assembly, which happened to be meeting.

When one of my friends at the Assembly moved that as a former member I should be associated with that body and invited to speak, hard-line conservatives objected, and only after a show of hands was I received and welcomed. Even then, two members recorded their dissent by walking out. (The *Otago Daily Times* reported this incident under the headline 'Geering Survives Snub at Church Assembly'.)

The next day was even busier. After spending the morning answering questions on radio talkback shows, I spoke at a luncheon attended by about sixty clergy of all denominations. In the afternoon I recorded a television programme, and then had all too little time to finish preparing my address to the Laymen's Dinner at Ashley, where people were encouraged to ask questions, having been assured they would receive honest answers.

From Friday onwards the commitments continued. Besides preaching at three Sunday services, I attended a Youth Night and an Adult Study Night for the Aspley parish, and gave a lecture on 'God in the Twentieth Century' to theological students. When I preached that Sunday evening to a packed congregation at St Andrew's, the central city church, I was picketed by some twenty members of the Presbyterian Reformed Church, a newly established group of fundamentalists who had broken away from the Presbyterian Church of Australia as a direct result of the 1967 heresy trial. Its minister later interrupted the service by climbing into the pulpit before I spoke and demanding to be given five minutes to refute what I was about to say. Of course his request was denied.

The same group picketed and interrupted the public meeting of over seven hundred that I addressed at the Aspley Football Club Hall. This time the chairman, Everald Compton, shrewdly put their request to the audience, who voted by about three to one that the Revd Douglas Shelton should be given five minutes to state his case. He then declared that I was one of the false prophets whose rise in the last days was foretold in the Bible. After thanking the audience for their tolerance, he and his followers retired to the rear and caused no further disturbance.

In my address, I expounded the thesis outlined above and stated the reasons why I believed the church had to undergo a reformation in its thinking. Two people who had previously been invited to do so made their response. One turned out to be a rather conservative layman and the other an agnostic who lectured at the university. What I found intriguing was that, although they were at opposite ends of the theological spectrum, they effectively joined forces in vigorously attacking what I had said: the one denied that the Christian message *needed* to be reformed (on the grounds that it was as relevant as ever) and the other that it *could* be reformed (on the grounds that it claimed to be absolute and unchangeable).

But the highlight of my visit to Brisbane proved to be the recorded television interview on the *Meet the Press* programme, aired on Channel 7. With four journalists operating in quick succession, I answered fifty-five questions in the half-hour. Short answers seemed to disarm the questioners, who were apparently used to people who either avoided the question or gave ambiguous replies. I believe that in television discussions all questions should be answered as concisely and honestly as possible; but this practice was to land me in trouble.

For example, when asked, 'Do you believe Mary was a virgin?', I replied, 'No'. But when challenged on whether I believed Jesus to be the Son of God, I said, '"Son of God" is a metaphorical term. I think it's got value in it. But if you take it literally it makes no sense.' Asked for my definition of a Christian, I replied:

One who gratefully accepts all that has stemmed from the historical Jesus and that has helped to make him the person he is, and who in response commits himself to live a life obedient to this heritage, seeking to understand it with his mind, and to perform all that it tells him to do with his will.

I found it a very challenging yet rewarding experience to have to think quickly about each new question and give an honest and concise reply. But under such conditions, one does not produce the sort of carefully worded responses that can be composed for the written media. So it was not surprising that the *Courier-Mail* headlined its report next morning 'Theologian says there is no heaven or hell', and proceeded to list all the other elements of traditional Christian belief that I had denied. Yet its leader was not only fair, but indeed supportive:

> In letting loose these ideas among the general public in Queensland, he has done the Church a service. He is challenging the Church to present its claims in clear terms which not only make sense, but also can appeal to 1970-era people.

I returned home looking forward to some peace and quiet after one of the most hectic yet exciting episodes in my life. I assumed that what had happened in Brisbane was confined to Queensland. How wrong I was! In my naivety, I did not realise the events were also being closely followed in New Zealand. My most aggressive critics had received a full transcript of the television interview and began to circulate a shortened version of it with all the negative responses underlined. They then raised the issue in their respective presbyteries. Several presbyteries immediately dissociated themselves from what I had said in Brisbane, although the Dunedin Presbytery (with some recorded dissent) commended me for 'attempting to proclaim the Christian faith in a contemporary way'.

At their request, I wrote a full-length article for the *Otago Daily Times* (reprinted in the *Outlook*), elaborating on what I had been saying in Brisbane. In it I argued that:

> there is a widening gap between the diminishing churches and the increasingly secular community…this was an attempt to bridge that gap…[The church] has come to live a ghetto existence within her own confined circles, with her own form of Yiddish, a churchy language which is quite meaningful to many of those who have been trained in it but deadly dull and increasingly meaningless to each successive generation of the world outside…In her timid ventures into the television medium she has been more concerned with making an impressive showing than she has been with the truth, and programmes have been dubbed 'religious commercials'…We in the church would do well to heed the dictum of Coleridge, 'He who loves Christianity more than truth, will soon come to love his own denomination more than Christianity and he will end up loving himself most of all'.

I went on to declare that the church had an urgent need both to appreciate all that was good in the secular world and to enter into honest dialogue with it for their mutual good; for only thus could the church play a positive role in preventing the world from blindly going forward to global disaster. Indeed, there is nothing in the article I would wish to change today, for once again I find in this early essay the seeds of many of the things I have elaborated on in my later books.

A little later my colleague Evan Pollard, Professor of New Testament Studies at the Hall, came to my support by preparing for the *Outlook* two excellent articles, the first explaining what we mean when we say Jesus is the 'Son of God', and the second examining what led to the doctrine of the Virgin Birth. Since Pollard's main area of research was in the early centuries of developing Christian doctrine, these expositions were very scholarly. Although I lack his expertise, I have no difficulty in agreeing thoroughly with all that he wrote. But being academic and meticulously annotated, his explanations tended to obscure from the average reader their substantial agreement with my short and no-nonsense replies on the television programme.

One of the chief problems throughout the continuing theological controversy was that people were not able to distinguish between historical or factual statements on the one hand, and theological or metaphorical statements on the other. They were all seen as cut from the same piece of cloth. The result was that lay people of all persuasions kept asking for simple, straightforward statements, and those accustomed to the traditional Christian jargon (and thus inclined to the conservative view) were often offended by what they heard.

Around that time, further confirmation of my position came from an unexpected source. Father J. Vink, a Dutch priest and lecturer in Old Testament Studies at the University of Utrecht, was holidaying in New Zealand, and in response to questions from journalists he said, 'Church doctrines such as the immortality of the soul, the resurrection of Christ, and the virgin birth are mythological and are not meant to be taken literally'. He agreed that his beliefs appeared to clash with the teachings of the Catholic Church, but pointed out that Pope John XXIII had opened the door for experimental and open discussion within the church. As was to be expected, however, Bishop Delargey and other Catholic dignitaries reacted strongly to Vink's statements, calling them 'irresponsible and confusing'. Only a dozen years later, however, the Catholic bishops of New Zealand issued a statement to their people that the story of the ascension of Jesus was now to be understood as belonging to the category of myth.

As critical letters began to multiply once again in the *Outlook*, I realised that although I had been speaking in another country, I had inadvertently started a third wave of theological controversy. Unfortunately, my critics simply ignored the positive things I was saying and continued to fasten on the negative.

Just at this time, by happy chance, Victoria University of Wellington advertised that it was about to establish a Professorial Chair of Religious Studies. After some thought I decided to apply, but because of the publicity surrounding my name this had to be done in such complete secrecy that not even my colleagues knew of it. As I was about to post my application, I felt duty bound to confide in Jack Bates, then Convener of the Theological Education Committee, who tried to persuade me to remain at my present post. Yet while my interest in the Chair at Victoria had initially been aroused by pleasurable memories of teaching Comparative Religion in Queensland, I had also come to feel that the church could not regain its unity as long as I was still teaching at the Theological Hall. However, I had so little expectation of success that I neither halted nor delayed an architect's work on a new house Elaine and I were planning to build on a section we had acquired in Opoho. I still assumed I would continue to teach at Knox until my retirement, and was prepared to deal in the most fruitful way I could with whatever opposition I encountered.

Indeed, when I peruse my notes of addresses given during this period, it appears that I felt quite confident about my future. This is reflected in what I said at the annual graduation and valedictory ceremony at the Theological Hall, at which it was customary for the Principal to address the Exit students. I warned them not to think of theology as a body of knowledge that they had satisfactorily absorbed and were now taking away with them to parcel out in small doses to their congregations. Rather, they should think of theologising as an activity – a lifelong pursuit. Theology was something to be *done* rather than something to be *learned*; and it was everybody's business. All people who began to think about the meaning and purpose of life, and who attempted to get their values into some meaningful order, were taking the first steps in the theological enterprise. They were asking, 'Who for me is God?' Then I warned that no belief or theological doctrine of the past could be considered absolute and final. Personal concern for humanity came before doctrines and creeds; drawing on what Jesus said about the Sabbath, I commented, 'Theology is made for mankind, not mankind for theology'.

At the time I was not aware of the full significance of my words; but looking back after thirty-five years, I detect a hint of how my understanding of God was changing. Not only was I affirming the human origin of all thinking about God, but God was ceasing to be for me a knowable objective entity, and becoming more a symbolic word for the mystery of life and the spiritual values associated with that sense of mystery.

Yet no one, as far as I remember, made any adverse comment about what I said to the students. It was a very different matter when the General Assembly met in Wellington two weeks later. There the aftermath of my visit to Queensland came to a head as my critics persuaded the Assembly to pass a motion dissociating itself from statements I had made in Brisbane. I listened to the lengthy debate, but felt it prudent not to participate unless invited to do so. Over fifty people who supported my views asked that their dissent be recorded. Although a motion requiring that all those holding church appointments conform to official church doctrine was to be sent to presbyteries for discussion, another asking the Theological Education Committee to show cause why my appointment should not be terminated was eventually withdrawn. This, of course, was much more of a snub than anything I had experienced at the hands of the Queensland General Assembly. Although I had many loyal supporters, not least among my own teaching colleagues, I felt that I was becoming an embarrassment to them.

News of the Assembly's repudiation of my views did not stop organisations inviting me to speak; in fact, the invitations tended to increase. Thus early in December I delivered the address at the senior prize-giving ceremony at Waitaki Boys' High School. There, for the first time, I began to spell out the very serious challenges that faced young people entering adult life. I briefly sketched four crises already appearing on the horizon: the threat of nuclear war; the population explosion; the pollution of air and water, and limits to the agricultural capacity of the earth; and a break-down in the transmission of the cultural and spiritual values of the past.

Thus I was carrying on with life as usual, and was already planning to take sabbatical leave in 1971, when out of the blue came the telegram offering me the Chair at Victoria University. When I went home to tell Elaine and Elizabeth (our only child still at home), I found they were even more excited than I was. It suddenly came home to me how deeply the whole controversy had been affecting them. The news of my appointment had come to them like an unexpected release from prison.

As this was the first Chair of Religious Studies to be established in New Zealand, and I had become a public figure, the appointment aroused widespread interest. Journalists sought responses from a variety of people. The authorities at Victoria University said they were delighted. Along with some others, Presbyterian Moderator Ian Fraser gave his full approval to the appointment, but expressed regret that I was leaving Knox College. The Anglican and Catholic archbishops preferred to make no comment. It was clear, however, that my critics within the church rejoiced to see me leaving the Theological Hall – and may even have regarded my impending departure as an answer to their prayers.

The *Otago Daily Times* invited me to write an article explaining my decision. This enabled me to say that, although I still believed theological colleges had an important role to play in training students for the ministry, and that I would have been very happy to continue in that context, I had become deeply interested in the new ways of studying religion that were then opening up. Departments of Religious Studies were to play a differ-ent role, fostering free enquiry into the nature of spirituality in human society and researching the religious beliefs and practices of a rapidly changing world.

Some thirty-five years later, it seems odd that I should have been asked to explain publicly why I had elected to move from one post to another; but no doubt that was the consequence of having been in the public eye for a number of years. Frank Haden, then editor of the *Sunday Times*, flew down to conduct quite a searching interview which he then wrote up very fairly, describing me as 'one of the most misunderstood men in the country'. He ended the article by commenting that he now saw the problem I had had in communicating with the man-in-the-pew, for the taxi driver taking him away from the interview had exclaimed, 'But why does he do it? I mean, Christ rose from the dead and that's an established fact, now isn't it?'

The Theological Education Committee made it possible for me to give up my teaching duties at the end of the first term in 1971; all that remained was for the farewell functions to be held. The chief of these was organised by the students, who seemed genuinely sorry to see me leave. But after teaching Old Testament and Biblical Hebrew for sixteen years, I looked forward with eager excitement to the change. Not only would I be leaving behind an atmosphere of continuous tension, but I would now have the opportunity to explore a much vaster area of humankind's religious heritage – not only a highly complex subject in itself, but one in the process of radical cultural change.

Chapter Fourteen

A NEW KIND OF PROFESSORSHIP

The move to Victoria University in 1971 marked a significant watershed in my life because of the new role I was undertaking. Soon after my appointment was made public, an editorial in the *Auckland Star* drew attention to an important fact:

> Victoria University is not setting up a chair in theology…it is breaking new ground for New Zealand in preparing to teach at professorial level, comparative religion…together with its psychology and philosophy. It will be a long step from the chair of Old Testament Studies at Knox College's Theological Hall for Professor Geering. He has gained the appointment in international competition.

Although Religious Studies was already being taught at Canterbury, Otago and Massey universities, this was the first Chair to be established in this discipline, and it originated with a request from the student body. Yet even after the Professorial Board had agreed to the proposal, no action was taken until George Hughes, Professor of Philosophy, and Peter Munz, Professor of History, revived the idea and finally persuaded the university Council to take the plunge. (Several years later, when I was serving on the Council, the Chancellor confided to me with a grin, 'We thought it was time to let the Presbyterian Church off the hook'.)

So off we went to Wellington, a city to which Elaine and I were hardly strangers, since it was there that we began our life together. On this occasion, however, it was to be the first time in our married life that we were wholly on our own – though, as it turned out, not for long. Naturally we were sorry to leave our family behind in the South Island, but one by one they eventually followed us to the Wellington area, and in later years we had the joy of remaining close to all our grandchildren as they were growing up. In an era when families so easily become scattered around the world, Elaine and I rejoiced that our ever-extending family became more closely knit as the years went by.

The physical shift to Wellington took place in the easiest possible manner. Three months before moving we sold our house in Dunedin to my colleague Evan Pollard, and soon afterwards flew up to Wellington for a long weekend to meet with real estate agents. By Saturday we had chosen a house, had it valued by a friend, negotiated with the owner, and by the time we returned home on the Sunday had signed a purchase agreement. As a result, when we drove off the inter-island ferry two months later, we proceeded straight up to our new home in Wadestown, helped the furniture removers to position our belongings, and were fully settled by nightfall. It could not have gone more smoothly.

Even settling in at Victoria was an easy transition, thanks to the impressive way the university cared for its new appointees. Before an independent Department of Religious Studies could be set up, it was necessary for me to work within an established department. I had chosen Philosophy as the one closest to my interests, and I soon became a close friend of George Hughes. He invited me to participate in the weekly two-hour seminar for postgraduate students, which I did for the next two years. Although I lacked the depth in philosophical studies of most of those present, I learned a great deal and occasionally took an active part in the discussions.

Because I was transferring from a church appointment to one in a secular university, I had to think through the personal implications of my new role. Ever since my original 'call to the ministry', my chief concern had been to serve the church in the best way I could. And I had no intention of cutting myself off from the church now; indeed, I immediately linked up with the Wadestown Presbyterian Church, where Elaine and I had been married, and where I subsequently served for many years as an elder.

But because of my high profile as Principal of the Theological Hall and as the centre of a recent storm of dissension, I deemed it wise to play no further part in the higher courts of the church. Thus, although I remained a Presbyterian minister, and my membership had been transferred to the Wellington Presbytery, I never again attended either Presbytery or Assembly. Since a vociferous minority in the church had made it clear that my presence was an embarrassment, I decided I could best serve the church by absenting myself from its provincial and national decision-making, leaving it free to recover the 'peace' I had been accused of disturbing. This decision was made easier by the fact that, shortly before my new appointment was announced, the Moderator of the Wellington Presbytery had pointedly informed me that he no longer had any confidence in me.

Thus I was, in good conscience, free to give all my time and energy to my new responsibilities. It was not long before I received a visit from the Catholic chaplain at Victoria to tell me that Hans Küng, the well-known radical Catholic scholar, was shortly to come to Wellington. He asked me to chair the public lecture he had invited Küng to deliver within the university at very short notice. Having just read Küng's book on the papacy, entitled *Infallible?*, I happily agreed, and was surprised to find that with only twenty-four hours' notice the largest lecture theatre was full. Such was the public interest in Küng! His visit made a very promising beginning to my work, for it was clear that he and I shared a common concern about the future of Christianity in the modern world. In the years that followed I eagerly read most of his books and met him twice more, once when he gave a lecture in St Paul's Cathedral, London.

Beyond the more mundane activities of learning the ropes in a secular university, ordering books for the library, and starting to write lectures, I had to give considerable thought to how I should develop the embryonic Department of Religious Studies. It was my good fortune to be invited to deliver two public lectures that both prompted and clarified my thinking.

That both lectures were later published suggests that I had made a respectable start. The first, my inaugural lecture, was delivered in September 1972, although by that time I had nearly completed my first year of teaching; the topic was 'Why Study Religion?' The second was delivered at the University of Canterbury in 1973, in connection with the celebration of its centenary; I called it 'The Place of Religious Studies in a Secular University, or, R.S.D. in Search of an Identity'. Here I moved on from the *Why* to the *How* of the study of religion.

It is quite clear why theological students should study Christianity; being already Christian, they need to learn as much as possible about the faith they are called to preach. But why should anyone study other religions – except perhaps out of curiosity? That, of course, depends on how one defines 'religion'. For too long we Westerners have thought of religion exclusively in terms of Christianity, such as its doctrines about God, Jesus Christ, supernatural miracles, and an afterlife in heaven or hell. But neither Buddhism nor Confucianism fits into that framework. In today's religiously pluralistic and increasingly secular world, we must greatly broaden our understanding of religion. Indeed, religion has become notoriously difficult to define. Still, I find the offering of an Italian scholar, Carlo Della Casa, very instructive: religion, he said, 'is a total mode of the interpreting and living of life'.

Some of my colleagues consider this to be altogether too wide, yet I find a broad definition is necessary if we are to do justice to the religious diversity and confusion in today's world. Otherwise we are forced to conclude that people can be divided into the religious and the non-religious, and that the latter are discarding religion because they judge it to be obsolete in this modern secular age. Such a judgement then raises the question of whether the study of religion should have any more place in the university than, say, the study of superstition. As I see it, religion, although it has come to be expressed in many different forms, is a universal dimension of human culture. To be religious is to take life seriously, to formulate a meaningful view of reality, and to aim to get the most out of life, not only for oneself but also for others. Consequently, humanism, atheism and agnosticism are just as much expressions of religion as Buddhism or Islam. Indeed, in 1971 James Thrower, a Religious Studies lecturer at the University of Aberdeen, had just published *A Short History of Western Atheism*.

But as soon as one defines religion in terms of whatever 'concerns one in some ultimate way' (to use the well-known words of Paul Tillich), it means that one is no longer looking at religion from the outside; therefore, one cannot help being personally involved to some degree in the study at hand. And of course this also permits the free exercise of one's critical faculties. Over the following years, in fact, I found that many students chose to enrol in Religious Studies courses simply as a fruitful means of sorting out their own beliefs and religious stance.

By reading *The Meaning and End of Religion*, a seminal book by Wilfred Cantwell Smith, I learned not to treat religion as a 'thing', wholly external to the observer. Such terms as 'Christianity' and 'Buddhism' tend to imply this – as if one could examine religion from a totally objective standpoint, much as a geologist studies rocks. Cantwell Smith revealed the error in this approach by analysing religion into two components: *faith* (the internal attitude of trust with which each person or community responds to the demands of life) and the *cumulative tradition* (the beliefs, rituals, sacred texts and so forth in which the shared faith of a community has come to be expressed). Faith is universal to the human condition; it underpins every human enterprise, including all cultural pursuits, and even science itself. The cumulative tradition consists of the objective data created and handed on by each faith community as it walks its path of faith through time. This tradition is continually changing, with new elements being added and others becoming obsolete or forgotten. It is misleading to regard the cumulative tradition as the whole of religion, and to ignore the inner experience of faith that gave rise to it.

Not only have many 'paths of faith' existed over the centuries, but in today's more secular culture many people are exploring personal paths of faith that are only loosely linked with the cumulative tradition of the culture within which they were born. On this understanding of the spiritual dimension of human existence, every person is potentially religious.

With such thoughts in mind, I concluded that the aim of a Religious Studies Department must be to examine this important dimension of human culture. While this quest needs to be pursued as objectively and critically as possible, it also needs to be carried through empathetically, by which I mean 'attempting to enter subjectively into the experience of the particular path of faith one is studying'. I was once greatly complimented, after delivering a lecture on Buddhism, when a Sri Lankan student came to thank me: he said he had never heard Buddhism presented so convincingly. Any Religious Studies Department should be confessionally neutral, providing a balanced approach to the vast and rich heritage of humankind's religious experience in a way that leaves students free to find and test their own religious answers. Furthermore, it needs to promote research, not only into humankind's religious past but also into why the human religious predicament has today become so confusing.

On the basis of this general approach, I set about planning courses suitable for a BA major in Religious Studies. To ensure that students became fully aware of today's religious pluralism, I decided that none of the undergraduate courses should be devoted exclusively to one tradition. A student who took Religious Studies for only one year should receive an outline of the history of all the great religions, with equal attention to East and West. Further, since most of our students were products of Western culture, they should first study the religious traditions of the East, so that they could then turn to the religions of the West (which they sometimes thought they already knew) and look at them through new eyes. The textbook I chose for the first-year course was *Paths of Faith* by John A. Hutchison. Although it covered much the same historical material as the book I had used in Queensland, *Man's Religions* by John B. Noss, I thought Hutchison's approach (which showed the influence of Cantwell Smith in its very title) was preferable.

The second-year courses (to begin in 1973) built on the general survey presented in the first year. One of them introduced students to sacred texts (drawn from more than one tradition). Another examined common religious phenomena across the traditions, such as the practice of sacrifice or the experience of the sacred. The course that became crucial to my general approach was 'Religion in Change'. The ambiguity in the title was intentional: not only did the course examine how the great traditions were coping with the disruptive cultural changes being encountered in modern times, but it also asked whether the religious expression of human spirituality was itself undergoing a radical change.

This was supplemented by two courses at the third-year level, 'Western Religious Thinkers' and 'Eastern Religious Thinkers'. By the time these were introduced in 1974, a second member of staff, Kapil Tiwari from India, had already joined me, and he became responsible for the latter course. Over the years, the course on Western thinkers enabled me to present an in-depth study of such writers as Martin Buber, Paul Tillich, Teilhard de Chardin, Dietrich Bonhoeffer, Rudolf Bultmann and Don Cupitt, with three chosen for any one year. The one who proved most popular with students was the Jewish philosopher Martin Buber, and under the title *The World of Relation*, I eventually published a little book on his spiritual classic, *I and Thou*.

But even before I began teaching these courses to undergraduates, I found myself already launched, though unintentionally, on a practice that was destined to take the work of the Religious Studies Department out into the community. In 1970, while I was still in Dunedin, the University Extension Department at Victoria (later known as 'Continuing Education') invited me to Wellington to participate in a Saturday seminar on 'Secular Christianity and Bultmann'. It was so successful, drawing an audience of about 120, that more were planned after my arrival. In 1971 I led a seminar entitled 'Secular Christianity and the Education of the Person', followed in 1972 by 'Secular Christianity and Science'.

At first I was only one of a team that lectured at each of these seminars, but before long I found myself becoming the sole presenter. We soon arrived at a format that the participants found effective. The day was divided into four segments: in the first three, my lecture was followed by the answering of questions, while the fourth was devoted wholly to group discussion. Masterton, Nelson and Blenheim soon became part of an annual circuit in the Wellington area. By 1974 the Continuing Education Department at Auckland University had invited me to do the same for them, and this was followed by an invitation from Waikato University to run seminars in Hamilton, Matamata, Tauranga, Whakatane, Taupo and Gisborne. Eventually I was presenting more than a dozen Saturday seminars a year in the North Island: three each year in Wellington and in Auckland, and one a year in many provincial towns.

Late in 1971, and before I had the opportunity to judge how much of my time should be devoted to lecturing both within and outside the university, I was invited by the editor of the *Auckland Star* to write a weekly column for the *Saturday Weekender*. After thinking it over, I agreed to a three-month trial. The result was that I wrote a 600–900 word column, entitled 'Religion Today', every week for the next seventeen years, during the last two or three of which it appeared in the *Sunday Star*.

Thus I produced nearly nine hundred columns, the equivalent of about eight full-length books, and covering a wide variety of topics related to theological, ecclesiastical and current affairs. It was a demanding discipline, and I am now surprised that I managed to keep it up, even during holidays and periods of study leave overseas. To achieve this through extra-busy times, I always kept the editor supplied with a pool of three columns which he could draw upon. For me, it became a valuable exercise in writing – learning how to be concise, lucid, and readily understandable to the general reader. And although short articles cannot penetrate to any great depth, the exercise forced me to delve into many topics I would not otherwise have thought much about.

Only twice did I have articles rejected by the editor, and one of those occasions had an interesting sequel. When I asked the editor why he had not used my article on 'Four Prophets', he said it was too political and not sufficiently about religion. The four prophets I had chosen were Moses, Jesus, Muhammad and Marx. Most likely it was the presence of the last in an otherwise august company that was deemed offensive. On request, I later developed this article into a Saturday seminar, in which I sketched and compared the long-term influence of each of these men. It finally appeared as a longer article in the *Dominion* in 1990, under the title 'Culture Clash in the Middle East'. In it, I proposed that the influence of Moses was reflected in the rise of Israel, that of Jesus in the dominant role played by the 'Christian' nations of the United States and the UK, that of Muhammad in the Muslim nations, and that of Marx in the Ba'ath socialist party then ruling both Iraq and Syria. Given that tensions in that region have increased considerably since 1990, my concept of the clash of four value systems makes the article even more relevant today than it was then.

This brief account of the various activities that resulted from my move to Wellington may give the impression that I was becoming overburdened. In fact I rarely felt under any pressure, and in comparison with my last few years at Knox College, I felt myself living a relaxed life. Certainly, there was little time for general reading, but this was mostly because I had to find time to read about a hundred books a year in relation to my work. The weekends were nearly always free for gardening, odd jobs, and church. I have always enjoyed working with my hands and fancied myself something of a handyman, despite having no specialist skills. Over the years I have painted four houses and three holiday cottages, done a great deal of interior decorating, and established several gardens. During the

week, Elaine and I often went to New Zealand Symphony Orchestra concerts and to Downstage Theatre as well as the cinema. By 1972 Elaine had
returned to full-time work as a speech therapist, and we soon developed
the habit of meeting each Friday evening for a meal at the Royal Oaks
Hotel, transferring after a year or two to the University Club.

Not everything went smoothly, of course. One wintry Sunday morning in 1973 we received a phone call from our daughter Judy, then living
in Invercargill, with the tragic news that her three-month-old son Neil
had suffered a cot-death. Elaine and I immediately flew to Invercargill,
where we had been only two months before to celebrate Neil's baptism.
This was a sudden and cruel blow, and like most cot-deaths impossible to
explain. Such occurrences do much to undermine the belief that we are
being continually watched over by a caring and loving God.

Neither was it always plain sailing with the development of Religious
Studies in the educational world at large. At the time, for example, most
primary schools followed the Nelson system, whereby schools were officially closed for half an hour each week to allow volunteer teachers to
introduce pupils to the Bible and Christianity without violating the Education Act of 1877, which specified that education should be free, compulsory
and secular. The word 'secular' had been included to avoid the sectarian-
ism then rife in New Zealand. That being no longer the case, many people
thought the time was ripe for a change in the way religion was taught in
our schools. The Department of Education therefore organised a conference in Christchurch to which it invited such interested parties as teachers,
parents, and the Council for Christian Education.

For this conference I prepared a broad-ranging paper entitled 'The Religious Content of a Liberal Education in a Secular World'. After defining
religion in much broader terms than any of the traditional forms, including Christianity, I stressed its importance for a well-rounded curriculum
that aimed to prepare young people for life. Then I suggested that there
should be lectureships in Religious Studies at all Teachers' Colleges. This
would enable teachers at the primary level to deal more adequately with
religious questions as they arose naturally in the classroom environment.
Not until secondary level did there need to be a specific place in the curriculum for courses in religion and culture, for which specially prepared
teachers would be required.

Although these suggestions were favourably received by most – since we would be largely following the example of Britain, where religious studies was a compulsory subject – this new venture was finally stymied by two extremist groups: the conservatives, who preferred the status quo whereby only Christianity was taught; and the secularists, who opposed any mention of religion in the official school curriculum. This temporary alliance of two opposing groups echoed the experience I had had in Queensland years earlier, and cost New Zealand a great opportunity to develop a form of education that could have promoted tolerance and understanding in our increasingly pluralist society. It might have lessened the current tensions, bigotry and personal violence which we rightly deplore.

Throughout my lifetime, I have observed that the increase in personal freedom enjoyed by the individual has unfortunately resulted in an increase in crime and personal violence committed by a minority. With this in mind, when I was invited in 1974 by the New Zealand Council for Civil Liberties to deliver the J.C. Beaglehole Memorial Lecture, I chose as my title *The Religion of the Individual in the Modern World*, and was highly gratified to see the address subsequently published.

Here, for the first time in print, I argued the importance of the term 'Axial Period', coined by the philosopher Karl Jaspers to refer to the era 800–300 BC when the world's great religious traditions had their origin. I also drew on the seminal essay 'Religious Evolution' by the sociologist of religion, Robert Bellah, who had discerned five stages in the evolution of religion – primitive, archaic, historic, early modern and modern.

Because this lecture was aimed at promoting the cause of civil liberties, I fastened on Bellah's statement that the historic religions 'discovered the self'. I tried to show that Christianity, Islam and Buddhism, in particular, revealed an increasing rejection of tribalism in favour of an interest in the individual person, culminating in the individualism that had marked the Enlightenment and post-Enlightenment periods of Western culture. As a result, the great value now placed on personal freedom and human rights had led to a succession of movements for the emancipation of the oppressed. Looking back thirty years, I can see this lecture as the précis of the book I was to publish in 1980, *Faith's New Age*.

In 1975 I was granted conference leave to participate in the quinquennial

Conference of the International Association of the History of Religion, to be held at the University of Lancaster, in the UK. It was a great opportunity to meet many scholars I had previously known only by their books, and to hear papers chosen from the rich smorgasbord being offered. A day trip to Hadrian's Wall enabled some of us to view the ruins of the Roman camp and the extensive bathhouse, as well as those of the Mithraic temple where the soldiers worshipped. The latter ruins were a powerful reminder of how widespread Mithraism was at a time when Christianity was still competing with other faiths within the Roman Empire.

Since airfares to the UK were then much cheaper if one remained for a minimum of three weeks, I took the opportunity to stay on for a fortnight and move around Britain. First I visited my friend Harold Turner, who was then teaching Religious Studies at the University of Aberdeen after similar tenures in Sierra Leone, Nigeria and Leicester. He had been one of my mentors in student days, and had succeeded me as the minister of Opoho; our paths crossed many times. From there I travelled on to Inverness, the Isle of Skye and back to Edinburgh, before returning to London to take trips out to Winchester, the cathedrals of Guildford and Salisbury, and Stonehenge.

Little did I know then how soon I would be seeing Harold Turner again. Early in 1976 the University of Otago informed me that it wished to award Honorary Doctor of Divinity degrees to both Harold and me at the May graduation ceremony. While I judged that he deserved this honour more than I – in addition to his later academic career, he had been responsible for establishing two residential colleges for students in Dunedin and was the founder of the Otago University Bookshop – I was nonetheless grateful for this recognition from my alma mater in view of the previous decade of scathing criticism I had received from many quarters, including some in academia. Furthermore, I was invited to deliver the graduation address on that occasion. Since Harold Turner and I were both teaching Religious Studies, I took the opportunity to sketch the importance of such departments in a modern university.

This event took place amid a number of milestones in our family history. In January 1975 our daughter Elizabeth was married. During the year the wife of my brother Fred died. In December my father celebrated his one hundredth birthday, and was delighted with his telegram from the Queen. In January 1976 Elaine's father died unexpectedly in Auckland, taking us away from the holiday we were enjoying with our two daughters and their husbands in Te Anau. And the following month, my father died in Dunedin. Such joyful and solemn occasions in rapid succession were reminders of the swift passing of time and the rapid disappearance of the preceding generation.

In attending these and other funerals during the 1970s, I became increasingly aware of how out of touch the traditional funeral rites were with modern religious thinking. The solemnly repeated words 'In sure and certain hope of the resurrection to eternal life' were beginning to sound rather hollow. But I also observed that a change in funeral procedure was beginning to take place. By the end of the century, the change had become manifest to all: less and less was the ceremony a solemn send-off to the next world; and more and more it became a grateful and almost joyful celebration of a life that had come to an end.

Later in 1976 Elaine and I each had to undergo surgical operations, from which we recovered only just in time to set off to the UK for the study leave already planned. We were fortunate to find a small flat in Marylebone, just 100 metres from Oxford Street. This enabled us to move around London easily, very often on foot, and we got to know the inner city very well. While Elaine took a postgraduate course in speech therapy at Guys Hospital, I made King's College my base, a choice due largely to my friendship with Peter Ackroyd, the Professor of Old Testament. I attended postgraduate seminars at both King's College and the London School of Economics, and made regular use of several libraries. I was then gathering material for my research on religious change, and became particularly interested in what had been happening in the nineteenth century. After discussing my work with Lady Collins, who was then in charge of the religious section of Collins publishing house, I came away quite unexpectedly with a contract to supply her with a trilogy of books. As I shall explain later, that trilogy never got written, although I did complete the first volume by 1980.

We did not stay in London all of the time. Because the owner of our flat wanted to refurbish it, we had agreed to vacate it for three weeks. We used this time to travel around Europe on a rail pass, spending several days in each of Paris, Mainz, Florence, Venice, Valencia and Madrid. It was a time rich in new experiences of scenery, museums, art galleries and historic churches. What struck me most, both in Europe and England, was that the great cathedrals had almost ceased to be places of worship and were increasingly becoming tourist meccas. The small congregations that still gathered in them for services were faced with such immense financial problems that the church at large was fast becoming a 'society for the preservation of historic buildings'.

Since we held round-the-world air tickets, we took a fortnight on the return journey to spend a few days in each of Budapest, Istanbul and Bangkok. The first gave us a little direct experience of life in a communist country – and one of particular interest because of our connection with the Hungarian community during our time in Brisbane (as described in Chapter 8). The visit to Istanbul increased my knowledge of Islamic culture and the way it was responding to secularisation: Turkey had been the most powerful Muslim nation until the secular revolution led by Kemal Ataturk and the 'young Turks'. The visit to Bangkok was my first contact with Buddhist culture on a grand scale – a level of civilisation to which the golden monuments there bear impressive witness.

In Singapore we were the guests of Jim and Jan Veitch. Jim had been a student of mine for seven successive years, and was soon to become a colleague. Not only did he invite me to deliver a lecture at Trinity United Theological College, but one of his Chinese colleagues also took us on a fascinating tour around Singapore to visit examples of new religious organisations of mostly Buddhist and Taoist origin. This made me realise that Singapore had become a microcosm of the world's religious diversity, and stunningly demonstrated the variety of ways in which traditional religions were attempting to cope with change.

After returning home in 1977, I used all my available time to write the book on 'Religion in Change' for which I had a contract with Collins. Since my research to date had led me to conclude that humankind had, in modern times, entered a vastly different cultural world from that which existed when the great religious traditions were founded, the major part of the book set out to trace the radical transition in Western religious thought from the late Middle Ages to the present day.

In the course of my study, and drawing initially upon the work of Jaspers and Bellah (as mentioned above), I constructed a paradigm or historical model of three successive cultural eras through which human-kind has lived. These I subsequently named the Ethnic or Polytheistic; the Transethnic or Theological; and the Global or Humanistic. These eras were divided from one another by two thresholds of radical religious change, the first being Jaspers' Axial Period, centred on 500 BC, and the second signalled by the transition to the modern world during the eighteenth-century Age of Enlightenment. When in 2001 I slightly revised the text for an American edition, I simply called this the Second Axial Period.

This idea is admittedly a subjective formulation which is open to debate. That is why, in my preface to the book, I claimed it to be only one perspective on the history of religion and the nature of religious change. Nevertheless, this simple paradigm revealed itself to me out of the very material I had been studying. In spite of some academic criticism of the concept, I have found it increasingly illuminating in the attempt to understand both the diversity of religious experience in the past and the confusing chaos of the present – so much so that it is referred to or assumed in all my later books.

Such a template also helps us to understand how and why the traditional forms of religion, including even Christianity, are being undermined by the spread of a global, humanistic culture commonly called 'secular'. This term should not be interpreted as 'non-religious' but as 'this-worldly', for religious thought and endeavour must now fasten attention on *this world* (as the only real world) rather than on *other-worldly* goals. In this third religious era, we are becoming aware of what all humans have in common, irrespective of class, race, religion, gender or age; and in our growing concern for human rights, equal justice for all, and international peace, we are continuing to manifest a genuine religious zeal.

The book was finally published in 1980 as *Faith's New Age*. The publishers rejected the title I would have preferred: *God Comes Down to Earth*. I had tried to show in the last three chapters that each of the two axial periods of change had seen a distinct shift towards 'this-worldliness' or secularisation, and that this shift in modern times owed much to the Christian doctrine of the Incarnation. That is why, after referring to Nietzsche as 'the prophet of the new age', the book ends with the words: 'There is a new sense in which it is possible to say – God comes down to earth.'

In both the UK and New Zealand, this book received more serious attention than my previous two. It was widely and for the most part very favourably reviewed, and frequently praised for its lucidity and simplicity. Yet it was not as widely read by the public as I had hoped. This was partly because it lacked the prior publicity of the first two, and partly because it was written at a textbook level. But this latter fact earned me a warm letter from James Thrower, lecturer in Religious Studies in the University of Aberdeen, telling me it was just the book he had been waiting for.

Only a month or so after the book was published, Elaine and I returned to London for a second period of study leave. On this occasion we had been granted the use of one of the William Goodenough flats in Bloomsbury, intended for visiting scholars. But as it would not be available for three weeks, we hired a car and toured around England, Scotland and Wales.

Starting with Cambridge, Ely and Norwich, we travelled north through York and Durham on our way to Edinburgh, passing through Galashiels, the home of my maternal grandparents. Then it was on to Inverness, a tour around Loch Ness, and up the east coast again before crossing over the Highlands (looking very dour indeed) to the quaint fishing village of Ullapool. After spending a night on Skye we drove down to Oban, from where we crossed over the Isle of Mull by bus to spend time on the island of Iona. We were excited to have the chance to visit the monastic buildings then being restored by the Iona Community founded by George McLeod, particularly as he had stayed with us in Opoho on one of his visits to New Zealand.

Time was now getting short, and we had much more to see. We hardly stopped in Glasgow, preferring to see the lovely Lake District before heading south to walk around the walls of Chester. Then we turned westward into Welsh-speaking North Wales, passing through the university cities of Bangor and Aberystwyth before driving down the Wye Valley to Bath and Wells. From there we headed back along the motorway to London, having enjoyed one of the richest experiences of our lives.

Once established in our flat, we settled down to work. Much of my time was spent in the British Museum, which then still housed the British Library. We had not been there long when on the radio we heard of a minor stir being caused by the publication of Don Cupitt's book, *Taking Leave of God*. I already knew of this bright young Cambridge lecturer, having read his *Christ and the Hiddenness of God* in the early 1970s. During our study leave in 1976 we had seen him on television, but were a little disappointed that he seemed more conservative than we had expected. On reading his new book, however, I was quite excited by the way he broke new ground, speaking of God as 'the mythical embodiment of all that one is concerned with in the spiritual life'. On hearing of the wrath of the Anglican hierarchy, then publicly descending upon him, I immediately rang him and was invited out to Cambridge to spend the day with him. He had read my books, and we soon found we were on much the same wavelength, although he had far greater philosophical expertise than I. Despite living at opposite ends of the earth and seeing each other only on rare occasions, we began a friendship that continues to this day.

Once again, Elaine and I planned to use the trip home to see more of the world. First we flew to Athens for four days to explore the Parthenon and some of the Greek islands; we also celebrated Christmas there, along with two former students who had been among the first to major in Religious Studies at Victoria. From there we flew to Egypt, where we found Cairo to be a real culture shock, partly because of the chaotic traffic and partly because of the living conditions. But we had a wonderful tour of the ancient pyramids and tombs, with ten other travellers from at least five countries. It was the last day of 1980, and we celebrated it by sharing a meal at Groppi's, a restaurant that became famous during World War II. We delighted the Egyptians by standing to sing *Auld Lang Syne* at midnight.

From there we flew to Jordan for a fortnight, where we enjoyed the peaceful atmosphere after the chaos of Cairo. A rental car enabled us to explore the wonderful ruins of Jerash, the East Bank of the Jordan Valley, the 'rose-red city' of Petra, the mediaeval fortress city of Kerak, the biblical sites at Madaba and Mt Nebo, and to drive up and down the steep sides of Jordan's 'Grand Canyon'. On paying a visit to the University of Jordan, I was entertained by the staff of its Religious Studies Department, and was interested to learn that all students, whether Muslim or not, were required to take a basic course in Islamic culture.

On our return to Wellington, I settled down to work through my final three years before retirement. But to explain some of the further overseas experiences of those years, I must backtrack to something that occurred before I went on leave. A former student came to tell me that he had joined the Unification Church, and to invite me to a meal with his small Wellington community, then living almost on the university campus. The full name of the church is 'The Holy Spirit Association for the Unification of World Christianity', but its members are popularly known as 'the Moonies' after its founder, the Revd Moon, a former Korean Presbyterian minister who attempted to syncretise Christianity with Korean Buddhism.

As a result of this personal contact, I was invited in 1979 (with all expenses paid) to the annual International Conference for the Unity of the Sciences (ICUS), to be held in Los Angeles in November. These conferences were based on Moon's conviction that if international scholars of all disciplines were brought together in discussion, truth would manifest its power to surface and flourish, thus promoting the unity of humankind. Over five hundred scientists and scholars from seventy countries were brought together for a week each year, the cost of $700,000 being met by the International Cultural Foundation, financed by Moon himself.

On first receiving this invitation, I suspected it was a subtle way of trying to convert academics to the Unification Church; but despite my misgivings I agreed to go, after being encouraged to do so by my friend Fred Sonntag, Professor of the Philosophy of Religion at Claremont University, California. In fact, I found it one of the most interesting conferences I have ever attended. I met up again with Harold Turner and Ninian Smart, and had the opportunity to meet Sir John Eccles (formerly of the Otago Medical School), as well as the philosopher Walter Kaufman, at least four Nobel Prize winners, and the founder of the Club of Rome. Participants enjoyed total freedom of speech, the sessions were arranged to fit their interests, and at no point did the Unification Church attempt to direct proceedings or promote its own specific doctrines.

On my return I wrote a two-page article for the *New Zealand Listener*, describing both the Unification Church and the unusual conferences one would not normally associate with such a sect. In late December 1981 I went to Maui in Hawaii to attend a conference on 'God: the Contemporary Discussion'. Although financed by the Unification Church, the conference was wholly organised by leading scholars from the UK and the United States. It brought together 160 academics from thirty-three nations, representing a wide diversity of beliefs – Catholics, Protestants, Jews, Muslims, Hindus, Buddhists, agnostics and atheists – and included some leading theologians and philosophers.

When invited to the 1982 ICUS conference in Philadelphia, I took the opportunity to stay on for two weeks and pay short visits to Princeton University, the Union Seminary in New York, and the Harvard Divinity School. I made personal contact with scholars in all three places, but was particularly concerned to spend some time with Wilfred Cantwell Smith at Harvard and persuade him to come to New Zealand in 1983. Let me explain the somewhat complicated reason for this.

The year 1983 was to be my last in full employment. Although I still felt very fit and alert, it was then the university practice to retire at the end of the year in which one turned sixty-five. Since it was my good fortune to have been born in February, I could therefore retain my post for most of my sixty-sixth year. Now, it had become the custom of those teaching Religious Studies in the five New Zealand universities to hold a conference each year, and in my honour the 1983 conference was to have a more international character. And it was to this end that I had been commissioned to invite Cantwell Smith, based on his great international reputation in the study of world religions.

Thus, in August 1983, an International Religious Studies Conference on 'Religions and Change' was held at the Central Institute of Technology in Upper Hutt, under the auspices of the Continuing Education Department of Victoria University. Along with our chief guest, Wilfred Cantwell Smith, I was invited to give a keynote address, which I entitled 'Our Global Religious Future: The Process of Conflicting Tendencies towards Unity and Diversity'. I enunciated a simple thesis: 'In the religious experience of humankind two opposing tendencies can be observed – the one towards diversity and the other towards unity. Certain values flow from each, but perhaps the greatest value of all arises from the interplay between the two'.

On this occasion, I let my imagination range more freely than at any other time in my career; so much so that on finding the lecture took one and a quarter hours to deliver, and fearing that I had bored the company with this strange assortment of ideas, I felt so embarrassed that I never looked at the lecture again, until now. Reviewing it a little more than two decades later, I find that to illustrate the thesis I had assembled bits of information I had been mentally collecting over the years from many different sources.

First, I argued that the ecumenical movement was a counter to the natural tendency of every religious tradition to diversify and fragment. Then I suggested that these two opposing movements were simply the manifestation in the area of religion of a phenomenon basic to the universe itself. The universe consists of physical energy which shows two opposing tendencies: an explosive one (since the 'big bang' the universe has been expanding) and a unifying one (gravity pulls objects together). Similarly, biological evolution shows a great capacity to multiply species and yet enables a species to adapt to its environment and thereby increase its chances of survival. Against this cosmic and biological backdrop, I went on to show how languages, cultures and religions exemplified the same two opposing tendencies. Whether any great value is to be gained by such all-embracing generalities I do not know, and I am sure that this view will be scoffed at by many academics; but it does help me to see that we humans do live in a *universe*, where everything is connected and subject to the same basic forces.

Just prior to this conference, I had been invited by the German Ambassador to New Zealand to become one of twenty overseas guests of the Bonn Government to take part in the celebration of the five-hundredth anniversary of the birth of Martin Luther. This small company was drawn from around the world to meet in Nuremberg, where the celebrations began. From there we were taken to places associated with Luther's conflict with the Roman Catholic authorities – Coburg, Augsburg and Worms. The places where he was reared and began his career – Magdeburg, Erfurt and Wittenberg – were in East Germany and hence beyond the authority of the Bonn Government. Nevertheless, we were taken to Berlin for three days, one of which we spent in East Berlin. Although it was an exciting and valuable experience, I was led to wonder, as I observed modern secular Germany and the largely empty Lutheran churches, whether Luther's more lasting legacy was not in his unifying of the German language through his translation of the Bible.

As retirement loomed, Elaine and I began to look for a holiday home. Having sold our property in Cromwell a year after moving to Wellington, we at first looked for something similar in the general vicinity, but gave up the search when we realised that nothing like Central Otago is to be found in the North Island. In the end, we took great delight in buying a section on the Hemi Matenga rise in Waikanae and having a cottage built there. This time Elaine played the major role in choosing the shrubs for the garden, while I was very happy to supply all the labour and to paint our new home inside and out.

This cottage appeared in the television documentary made at the time of my retirement. Entitled 'Labelled a Heretic' and presented by Alison Parr, it sketched my career, focusing on the so-called 'heresy trial' and including interviews with Bob Wardlaw and me. For the very first time in that long saga, Elaine and our family were introduced and given the opportunity to voice their feelings. I was agreeably surprised when Elaine consented to do this, for being a rather private person she had suffered emotionally more than any of us from the public exposure we had experienced during the previous seventeen years. That it had continued to dog us even during the relative quiet we had enjoyed during my time at Victoria University was illustrated by the succession of profile articles now appearing in the press, which, concluding with this documentary, made my retirement a rather public affair.

I was not looking forward to retirement – as so many others seem to do – since I was in something of a quandary as to how I would deal with the sudden dearth of useful activity. My parish ministries and successive teaching posts had engaged me so fully that my work had become my life. I felt greatly privileged to have spent my working life performing functions that had almost totally engaged my body, mind and soul. I had, however, been so absorbed by my pursuits that I had not only been somewhat neglectful of my family on occasions, but now feared that I might feel lost without the sense of fulfilment that comes from productive activity. I was soon to find out.

Chapter Fifteen

RETIREMENT?

The transition from Professor to Emeritus Professor proved to be much less of a change than that from preacher to teacher or from Old Testament to Religious Studies. Approaching my imminent retirement with trepidation, I had gone so far as to attend courses that offered to prepare one for the sudden shift from work to enforced leisure. I needn't have bothered! As it turned out, my life went on in much the same way as before, and was certainly quite as full.

For one thing, until my replacement was appointed I continued teaching two of my courses for a year. In addition, I carried on with my weekly column and the Saturday seminars. Instead of having to plan retirement activities, I soon found myself with enough new assignments and speaking engagements to fill the anticipated void. In fact, my two 'major projects' received little attention. I had planned to play more golf, imagining myself on the links two or three times a week; but in fact I have played less golf during retirement than before. The other plan was to write the second volume of the trilogy commissioned by Collins, it now being some years since the publication of *Faith's New Age*. But although I made several starts on this project, inspiration seemed to evaporate very quickly.

Of the many seminars I gave over more than thirty years, by far the most popular was 'Jung, the Unconscious, and God' – the original presentation of which resulted from a chance event. Because I had made some mention of Jung in *Faith's New Age,* my colleague Kapil Tiwari invited me to introduce to a student gathering the BBC documentaries entitled 'The Story of Carl Gustav Jung', narrated by Laurens van der Post. This event proved to be so popular that a repeat performance was requested for the public in a city venue. This success encouraged me to study Jung in some depth.

Jung's model of the human psyche and his analysis of the unconscious helped me first of all to understand myself. Then I found it threw a great deal of light on religious experience, both past and present. To be sure, Jung's theories of the archetypes and the collective unconscious are open to some question; yet they remain useful models for understanding Paul, Muhammad and other religious visionaries. Once we acknowledge the creative power of the human unconscious, which Jung so brilliantly brought to light, the personal integrity of such people remains intact without our having to attribute their experiences to supernatural sources. The archetype of the *self* (not to be confused with the *ego*) enabled Jung to explain the emergence of the concept of God, the rise of mysticism in most religions, and the process of 'individuation' – a term he coined to refer to the psychic growth by which a human being becomes a whole and mature person. All this seemed to me to illuminate the religious search for meaning and fulfilment.

Accordingly, using the BBC documentaries as visual support, I developed a seminar presentation which was so popular that it was repeated in Auckland for five successive years to capacity lecture theatres holding 180 people, and was also requested in several South Island centres. Finally, in 1988 I published my introduction to Jung's valuable legacy in a book entitled *In the World Today*.

This book also contained some lectures from another project in which I became increasingly involved after retirement, although it really started in 1983. John Murray, the minister of the Presbyterian St Andrew's-on-the-Terrace, invited me to offer three lunch-hour lectures during Holy Week to give the many office workers in the vicinity an opportunity to learn what was going on in Christian thought. So on three successive days, and to a full church, I lectured on 'Jesus Reconsidered' – covering in turn the life, death and resurrection of Jesus. Despite the fact that I had prepared these talks very hurriedly, assembling the notes for them in the hour or two before delivery, they proved so popular that it was decided to publish them, and they went through three printings.

This success encouraged John to found the St Andrew's Trust for the Study of Religion and Society, an independent body which, though associated with the church, was intended to form a bridge between the church and the community. St Andrew's is conveniently situated for such a project, being right in the heart of the central business district and adjacent to Parliament. Trustees appointed by the church were joined by representatives of the community such as Sir Guy Powles, who had recently served as the country's Ombudsman. I became the theologian-in-residence at St Andrew's, and was engaged to deliver three short courses of lectures each year.

In the early years, the Trust sought sponsorship from various business houses in the city to finance each lecture series; but this support dried up completely after the 1987 share-market crash. Some years later I found the preparation of three courses a year, along with my other activities, too burdensome and it was reduced to one, or two at the most. To date, the Trust has printed twenty-one booklets of my lectures as well as seven by visiting speakers. Some of the most popular of the early ones were *Science, Religion and Technology, Encounter with Evil, Creating the New Ethic, Human Destiny* and *On Becoming Human.*

In addition to this new role, I was offered a further writing assignment. After publishing an article on Islam that I submitted to the *New Zealand Listener*, the editor invited me to contribute a monthly column on faith and morals, called 'Horizons'. Occasionally, I contributed further articles. For example, on the twentieth anniversary of the theological controversy that culminated in my heresy trial, the editor asked me to describe what it had felt like to be at the centre of such a storm. Up until then I had avoided even talking about the subject; but after somewhat reluctantly agreeing to write about it, I was surprised to find the article chosen for the *Listener Bedside Book No. 3.* Writing for the readership of the *Listener* called for longer and more in-depth articles; and since I found this very satisfying, I continued with my two regular columns until well into 1988, when changes in editorial policy brought them both to an end.

The editor of the *Tablet*, noting that I not only was a columnist in the *Auckland Star* and the *New Zealand Listener*, but also contributed regularly to Radio New Zealand's *Morning Comment* and *Sunday Supplement* and had edited versions of the St Andrew's lectures broadcast on Radio New Zealand's Concert Programme, later complained in his journal that

I enjoyed greater access to the media than anybody else in New Zealand church circles. That is evidently how it seemed to some of my critics, although until it was pointed out I was not aware of it, for I had never sought such exposure.

So much for my regular commitments. In addition, I was asked to deliver occasional lectures and addresses, the more important of which are worth noting – if only because requests to speak on particular topics force one to expand one's horizon of thought. When Victoria University of Wellington invited me to deliver the 1984 graduation address at a Capping ceremony, I discussed the function of the university in the modern world, drawing attention to the central role played by the Faculty of Arts. Important as all the other faculties might be in preparing students for a professional career, I argued, it was the Arts Faculty that was the *sine qua non* of a university, in that it trained students intellectually and culturally, and thereby enabled its graduates to make creative contributions to society.

In October of the same year, the Wellington Regional Jewish Council invited me to participate in a seminar on 'Prejudice and Pride', to which I contributed a lecture on 'The Christian Origins of anti-Jewish Prejudice'. For some time I had enjoyed a very cordial relationship with the Jewish community in Wellington, and had often taken groups of my students to the Orthodox synagogue. After teaching biblical Hebrew to members of the Liberal Jewish congregation, I had been invited to speak in their Temple Sinai and also in the Auckland synagogue.

Because of my Old Testament work, I had long held our rich cultural legacy from Judaism in high regard, and been deeply concerned about the long history of Christian anti-Semitism that culminated in the Nazi Holocaust. Still, when the Wellington Zionist Society made a presentation to me some time later, I had to say in all honesty that my admiration for the Jewish people as a whole did not prevent me from being highly critical of the cruel and unfair treatment of the Palestinian people through the policies of the Israeli Government. And although a few Jews, including the Israeli Embassy in Wellington, have publicly criticised my support of the Palestinian cause as anti-Semitic, I believe it is important to distinguish clearly between a high regard for the Jewish people as a whole and objections to the political activities of the state of Israel.

I could speak about the Israeli-Palestinian situation with a degree of knowledge and experience; but this was not the case when I was invited to comment on the work of the celebrated New Zealand artist Colin Mc-Cahon. Because I know so little about art, it was with great reluctance that I finally agreed to speak about the religious content of McCahon's paintings at the 'McCahon and Christianity' seminar held at the National Art Gallery in June 1989. To my amazement, the address was subsequently published in the art journal *Antic*, and some time later I was invited to deliver the first 'Colin McCahon Memorial Lecture', in Auckland.

By then, however, I had had time to learn more about the man and his work. I found that we were of a similar age and had attended Otago Boys' High School at the same time, though without knowing each other. We never met, and moved in rather different circles, for at the very time he was abandoning Presbyterianism I was embracing it. Yet there were many parallels in our interests, not the least being Martin Buber's *I and Thou*, and the biblical book of Ecclesiastes – to say nothing of the significance of the great 'I AM' as the name of God. We were both involved in the quest for authentic faith in a secular New Zealand, where the traditional dogmas and symbols were becoming obsolete. When I studied McCahon's specifically religious paintings in chronological order, I found that they depicted not only his personal spiritual pilgrimage but also what was happening in the religious life of New Zealand society during the twentieth century. With this in mind, I titled my lecture 'Colin McCahon and the Twilight of Christendom' and, illustrated with slides of his paintings, it was repeated in several other galleries in New Zealand.

When Marja Bloem, Exhibition Curator of the Stedelijk Museum of Amsterdam, brought her McCahon exhibition, 'A Question of Faith', to New Zealand in 2002, I had the honour of speaking at its opening in both Wellington and Auckland. I likened McCahon to Ecclesiastes, on whose words his last paintings drew so heavily, for the two men lived in rapidly changing worlds whose respective religious traditions seemed to be dissolving into unreality. And like Ecclesiastes, McCahon summoned his viewers to face reality, to accept that nothing lasts forever, and to learn how to make the most of life while it lasts.

Now I must backtrack to 1985, when I was invited by the University of Natal in Pietermaritzburgh, South Africa, to contribute to a conference on 'Salvation and the Secular'. I prepared a lecture on 'The Search for a World Theology in a Radically New Age', for by that time I had been deeply influenced by several books by Wilfred Cantwell Smith. His two basic studies, *Belief and History* and *Faith and Belief*, I regard as essential reading for anyone desiring to understand what is meant by 'faith', how it is related to 'belief', and how the two words have changed in meaning over the years. Only recently, Cantwell Smith had followed up these studies with *Towards a World Theology*.

I began by interpreting 'world theology' as the attempt to express in a rationally intelligible way our search for meaning and purpose within the world as we see it. I then suggested that the Yahwist tradition (the earliest stratum of the biblical Books of Moses) was, in effect, the earliest outline of a world theology, even though it was expressed in a mixture of myth, legend and history. It had remained plausible for nearly three thousand years simply because, in the mythical medium of its day, it so brilliantly described the human condition and the place of humankind in the world. But because we had now moved into a radically new age and expressed ourselves in a non-mythological medium, I contended that it had become necessary to enunciate a completely fresh world theology, this time drawing appreciatively from all religious traditions of the past, yet reviewing them in the light of our new knowledge of the universe.

This was my first opportunity to visit South Africa, in whose affairs New Zealanders had become deeply interested because of our strong moral opposition to its apartheid policy. Indeed, some academics from the UK had refused to accept the invitation to this conference as a form of protest. I judged that response to be a mistake, knowing as I did that those who had invited me (including my friend Martin Prozesky) were also strongly opposed to apartheid. This visit enabled me to see at first hand just how cruel and inhuman this policy was, and also to appreciate how many white people were already trying to have it overturned. As it happened, the first real sign of change occurred while I was there: the Sunday newspaper reported that an Afrikaans theologian had at last openly declared that apartheid could not be reconciled with Christian ethics.

While in South Africa I was contacted by the Marist Father P. J. Gifford (referred to in Chapter 12), who was then teaching New Testament in Zimbabwe. He invited me to spend several days in Harare on my return journey. As well as enjoying a fascinating day flying to Victoria Falls to marvel at the scenery and the wildlife in that region, I lectured to students in the Religious Studies Department of the University of Harare. I had the opportunity to meet the son of former Prime Minister Ian Smith and record an interview with him on behalf of Radio New Zealand. I learned how his religious convictions had made him strongly opposed to his father's policies on race relations.

In those early days after Robert Mugabe's ousting of Smith, even many whites felt quite hopeful about the country's future. Great strides were being made in improving general education, and the university was experiencing rapid expansion. When I saw the changes taking place in the rural areas, I formed such a favourable view of the new Zimbabwe that on my return I wrote to Prime Minister David Lange, urging that Harare be chosen as the location for the New Zealand Embassy then being mooted for an African state in that region. My letter was warmly received. Alas, if I had known then what a tyrant Mugabe was to become, I would not have been so enthusiastic.

During my stay at Pietermaritzburgh, Martin Prozesky proudly showed me how useful he found his access to one of the university computers. In those days the high cost of personal computers put them beyond the means of most people, and few of us had any idea of how quickly they would revolutionise so many of our daily activities. But impressed by what I saw, I began to search for an improvement on the electric typewriter to which I had graduated a few years before. So it was that, on a week's holiday with Elaine in Sydney later that year, I invested in an electronic typewriter. With sufficient memory to hold one of my regular articles and even one of my lunch-hour lectures, it was an exciting step forward.

In the meantime, much of my attention was being taken up with a more personal project. When the desirable section next to our cottage at Waikanae came up for sale, I persuaded Elaine that it would be a good place to retire to, given that we had now developed an attachment to the Kapiti Coast area. But since Elaine was still working, having become the District Therapist at the Thorndon Speech Clinic, we needed to keep a foothold in Wellington. So after purchasing the new section, we bought a small flat in Thorndon, auctioned our Wadestown property, and proceeded to plan our retirement home and have it built. All this took a great deal of my time, but I spent many happy hours attending to the details and planting out the new garden.

This was only just completed when Jim Veitch – my former student, later colleague, and long-time friend – invited me to assist him in taking a group of people on an educational tour to the Middle East to study the origins of the Judeo-Christian tradition. While Jim attended to the travel details, it would be my task to provide mini-lectures along the way. Accordingly, we left New Zealand at the end of 1987 with a group of thirty-seven to fly to Amman via Singapore, and then to travel through Jordan, Syria, Egypt and Israel before spending a few days in Italy visiting Rome and Assisi. For me, two of the highlights of the trip were climbing Mt Sinai in the snow, and a sortie into the Egyptian desert to visit Coptic monks who were still carrying on the tradition of the Desert Fathers initiated by St Anthony in the third century.

We were still in Amman, with the tour barely under way, when the announcement arrived that I had been awarded a CBE in the New Year Honours. While I had been made privy to this a few weeks before, it came as a great surprise to our group, and we found our present surroundings a highly unusual setting for a celebration. My chief regret at the time was that the news broke while I was far away from Elaine and she had been left to field all the publicity on her own.

Therefore, when Jim and I took a second tour the following year, I made sure that Elaine accompanied us. In any case, this time we needed her assistance as a hostess, as there were forty-seven in the party. This proved too large a group, however, for it slowed our progress; on all subsequent tours we limited the number to thirty. On this trip we omitted Egypt and Italy, but included Turkey and more of Syria in order to visit sites associated with the journeys of St Paul.

Unbeknown to me, Jim had for some time been planning something else. He had sought academic contributions from my friends and former colleagues, including six overseas scholars, to a festschrift. Naturally I was honoured and humbled by such attention, especially as the essays included the last one written by John Robinson before his premature death. (We had met on his recent visit to New Zealand, when he greeted me warmly as a 'fellow heretic'.) The book, entitled *Faith in an Age of Turmoil*, was presented to me by the Governor-General, Sir Paul Reeves, at a ceremony at St Andrew's Church in August 1990.

Also speaking on that occasion was John Murray, who on becoming Moderator of the Presbyterian Church invited me to address the General Assembly on 'The Theological Challenge to the Church'. Although unsure of what kind of reception to expect, I happily accepted the invitation, for I had observed that few clergy ever attended the seminars I conducted around the country, even though the topics were mostly theological and even biblical. This disappointed me, for the Continuing Education departments of the universities seemed to be outdoing the national churches in providing refresher courses in their field, and some of their parishioners were becoming more *au fait* with current religious thinking than they were themselves. Actually, this reluctance on the part of clergy to keep up with new developments, as other professionals do, had been apparent as early as the 1960s. Was this because they believed there was nothing more to be learned, or were they afraid of new religious thinking?

Thus, in explaining to the General Assembly the reasons for the rapid decline of the church, I described the radical transition taking place in human consciousness as the dualistic world-view of heaven and earth was being displaced by the view of the universe as one vast, evolving, space-time continuum. As a result, I said, the church found itself lumbered with doctrines and rituals that were oriented to a view of reality that was fast fading away. I warned that, if the church did not come to terms with the new secular understanding of reality, its moral and spiritual message would no longer be heard; it would consign itself to irrelevance, ceasing to be a *church* (which permeates and embraces the whole of society) and becoming a *sect* (which holds itself aloof from society). To my surprise, the address was greeted with a standing ovation; but I fear this was largely out of courtesy, for the words seemed otherwise to fall on deaf ears, it being left to the women's organisation to request the text and publish it in their journal, *Harvest Field*.

Only a few months later, it was I who found myself being pushed somewhat reluctantly into the modern world. For some time I had been resisting my family's urgings to replace my electronic typewriter with a computer. On his way north on holiday, my son-in-law, Grant Hodgson arrived at our Waikanae home and deposited his computer in my study, saying, 'Now while I am away, get going!' I obeyed and, after a fumbling start due to minimal instruction, have never looked back. Soon I had purchased a computer of my own (updated three times since), and it radically changed my work habits. Without it, I doubt whether I would have written any further books.

The book I started on straight away took some years to complete, partly because I was not clear where I was going. In some respects the book slowly wrote itself as I worked my way through a fairly logical succession of ideas, all of which stemmed from the conclusions reached in *Faith's New Age*. Whereas Christian tradition had long taught that God had not only created the world and humankind but had revealed to us his purpose in doing so, it was now becoming clear to me that the new knowledge we have gained in the modern world has reversed that order: we humans live in a cultural world of meaning (of which God is the central symbol) that we as a species have slowly constructed for ourselves.

When I set off to explore just how we have done this, I found that it started with the creation of language. (How ironic that, at this late stage, I should discover the full significance of the Fourth Gospel's assertion that 'In the beginning was the word...and the word *was* God' – and that the Bible itself begins with the statement that everything was created by the *speech* of God!) With the advent of language, our ancient forebears were able to compose stories (we now call them myths) by which they sought to understand and explain the natural phenomena they observed. These stories, in turn, enabled them to make sense of life – that is, to create a meaningful world for themselves.

Drawing upon insights I had gleaned from Jung, I suggested that the evolution of the human psyche over a span of some hundred thousand years was motivated by an inner urge to reconcile and unify the chaotic jumble of experiential data that the brain kept receiving. This same urge can be seen in the scientific community's current search for a 'Theory of Everything'. This is the modern equivalent of the emergence of monotheism, by which the concept of 'God' became the reference point to which everything else was to be related.

I then merged Jung's insights with the model of reality designed by the philosopher Karl Popper – a continuum consisting of three inter-connected worlds. At first, only the objective physical world existed, but eventually the evolution of living creatures on this planet gave rise to the subjective world of consciousness, which has reached its highest development in the human species. This second world then created language, ideas, stories, philosophy and science, which together constitute the world of knowledge. It is this third world that occupies most of our attention, provides us with our values, and gives meaning to life. Yet it is a human creation!

As I worked my way through this book, many things became clear to me that I had realised only partially before. We are born into a humanly created cultural world that enables us to become human. And this world in turn has developed into many sub-cultural worlds. But whereas, in the distant past, these worlds were being constructed unconsciously and being attributed to a supernatural source, we are now becoming aware of their human origin for the very first time. Just as our eyes are being opened to this, however, the many traditional worlds of meaning are being eroded, leaving us with the responsibility of consciously constructing a new world of meaning – one that is global, humanistic and this-worldly. Such a world is not here yet, but is struggling to be born.

Because the pursuit of these ideas was leading me to be more creative than in anything I had written to date, I was glad of the opportunity to test some of them out before the book was completed. This came with an invitation to speak at the 1992 Conference of the Sea of Faith Network in Leicester, in the UK. This organisation had been founded only three or four years earlier in response to a series of BBC television documentaries in which Don Cupitt so clearly portrayed what had been happening to religion with the advent of the modern secular world. I read two chapters from my unfinished book to this intellectually critical audience, expect-ing to be told about any glaring errors I may have made. (For similar reasons, when I wrote *Faith's New Age*, I invited critical comment on various chapters from my university colleagues in other academic dis-ciplines.) My presentation received general approval, and a number of the comments that were made proved beneficial. From there I went to Oxford for the Summer Conference of the Guild of Pastoral Psychology, where drawing upon the material of my unfinished book I delivered a lecture on 'The Spiritual Source of our Symbol Systems', which the Guild subsequently published.

Encouraged by the response so far, I continued working on the book after our return to New Zealand. By now, however, our only home was a high-rise apartment in the heart of Wellington – indeed, the very place in which I am now writing. In 1990 we found ourselves spending much more time in Wellington than we had originally expected, and moved here from our small flat in Thorndon. This was partly due to my interests, but mostly because on her retirement Elaine had decided to return to university for postgraduate study. Since the apartment was so central and comfortable, we saw no further need for our retirement house in Waikanae and had sold it just prior to leaving for the UK.

After finding the Sea of Faith Network in the UK such an inspiring community to be associated with, I spread information about it at various seminars I conducted; such was the response that a New Zealand equivalent quickly emerged and organised its first conference in 1993. It is now a thriving network with some thirty branches throughout the country. By the time its second conference was held in September 1994, my book had been completed and published under the title *Tomorrow's God*, although the sub-title, *How We Create Our Worlds*, is a clearer indication of its theme. This fact is appropriately emphasised by the use on the front cover of one of Colin McCahon's paintings, 'Let us possess one world, each has one and is one'.

The only really negative reviews were written by clergymen who found it impossible to accept that the Christian world of meaning was anything but 'compellingly true', just as it was. One of the most favourable reviews came from a theologically literate layman – and that despite his confession at the start that he understood 'God to be an objective metaphysical reality'. Nonetheless, those who make this their starting point generally fail to see the point of the book.

The reason why so many people in the Western world still claim to believe in this kind of God is that they have been conditioned by their monotheistic culture to do so (whereas most followers of eastern religions have not); and to defend this belief they are forced to assume that the Bible constitutes God's self-revelation, just as Muslims assume the

Qur'an to be the revealed will of Allah. These foundational assumptions immediately become questionable when we begin to examine the origin and evolution of all human cultures. This is why *Tomorrow's God*, while it appeared on the bestseller list for several weeks, failed to be understood within church circles and theological faculties, and was chiefly appreciated by those readers who stand midway between traditional religion and hard-line secularism.

During the early 1990s, people at various seminars I was conducting kept asking about the possibility of further tours to the Middle East; and when I was similarly approached by a travel agent, Elaine and I decided to host a tour on our own, with Elaine responsible for the accommodation and the general welfare of the company while I attended to the travel arrangements and gave mini-lectures along the way. In 1996 we set off on what proved to be the first of four such tours – three to the Holy Land and neighbouring countries, and one to Iran.

To avoid cold winters and hot summers, we planned the tours for the northern spring. Moreover, unlike the earlier tours we had been involved in, we arranged these to include the cost of both dinner and breakfast, for the sharing of meals effectively bonded a group of strangers into a harmonious and mutually supportive fellowship. Further, the tours officially ended in the northern hemisphere, leaving the participants free to choose their own route and time to return home.

The Holy Land Tour for 1997 was planned to begin and end in London. At its conclusion Elaine and I went to Oxford, where for three months we rented a townhouse owned by a fellow New Zealander, Mary Prior, whom I had known since student days. Since Elaine and I both had access to the Bodleian Library, and she wished to go there frequently to pursue her research, she pressed me to start writing a new book. Without her prompting, I would never have written the next one.

At her urging, I began to reflect on the approach of the third millennium, then gaining so much public attention. On the one hand, I recognised that the year 2000 has no special significance, since the Christian dating system is a human convention of dubious authenticity. (To make matters worse, in celebrating this apparent milestone the Christian world was unconsciously and somewhat presumptuously placing its stamp on the whole of humanity.) On the other hand, the year 2000 does approximately mark a dividing line between the end of Christendom and the new global era in which the whole human race is being drawn into world-wide interdependence. Indeed, the year 2000 CE (the Common Era, as scholars term it) could with good reason be renamed the year 1 GE.

As I began to explore the prospects for the new global era, I became increasingly alarmed. Because of our self-destructive proclivities and our inability to share the fruits of the earth equally, we humans are ill-prepared for the challenges now facing us. Not only are we frequently at war with one another, but we are at war with the very earth that sustains all life. I was painfully forced to outline some rather frightening scenarios of what may occur during the twenty-first century.

Before I finished the book, however, some dramatic events took place. The first occurred while we were in London preparing to return home. On reading the *Sunday Times* we were quite bowled over by the news that the previous night Princess Diana had been killed in Paris in a car accident. We joined the stunned crowds as they wandered silently through London and gathered with them outside Buckingham Palace. Over the next two days we found it deeply moving to walk through Kensington Gardens among the silent crowds bringing their flowers. On the journey home, we watched the live broadcast of her funeral service while at Singapore Airport.

The following year, tragedy struck much nearer home. On a Thursday evening in November we received a phone call from Debbie Saundry, daughter of Elaine's younger sister Juliet, informing us that her mother had suffered a sudden cerebral aneurism and was on life-support in Auckland Hospital. Shocked, we flew to Auckland next day, and late in the afternoon took part in a family conference that sadly was forced to agree with the doctors that life-support should be withdrawn.

Ordinarily, of course, Elaine and I would have stayed in Auckland to lend our support to the family, but we had to fly back to Wellington that evening for the wedding next day of our grandson Bruce Davies, at which I was officiating. The wrenching concurrence of these two events caused us acute emotional conflict. Elaine had always been especially fond of her only sibling, and being twelve years her senior had the strong feeling that she and not Juliet should have been the one to die first. This unexpected loss may well have triggered the next event.

Four weeks later, Elaine suffered a seizure in the middle of the night and went into such a deep coma that I thought she had died. I rang 111 expecting the worst, but fortunately she recovered consciousness in the ambulance on the way to the hospital. After a similar occurrence the following night, her condition was diagnosed as epilepsy, and the duly prescribed medication kept her from suffering another seizure for the rest of her life.

But epilepsy did entail some changes in our lives. We were to lead a Holy Land Tour in April 1999, and our daughter Elizabeth now took Elaine's place. Elaine accompanied us to London, and on my return from the Middle East, she and I went back to Oxford for a second three-month stay in Mary Prior's apartment. Once again we delighted in exploring the Cotswolds, and enjoyed visits to Bath and Salisbury.

We returned to New Zealand in September, just in time for the launching of my new book, *The World to Come*. Only on reading the proofs in Oxford (where I had begun work on it two years earlier) did I realise that, following on from *Faith's New Age* and *Tomorrow's God*, it completed a trilogy. To be sure, it was not the trilogy I was planning when I wrote the first volume, but rounding off the work with this title on the eve of the third millennium seemed highly appropriate.

Following the launch, Elaine and I set off for a month in California, where I was to deliver a lecture at the autumn meeting of the Westar Institute's Jesus Seminar at Santa Rosa. The founder of the institute, Bob Funk, had visited New Zealand the year before and we had immediately established a strong bond. Up until then, I had been somewhat dubious about the seminar's work, but for quite opposite reasons to those of most of its critics. Having been influenced by Rudolf Bultmann's conclusion that we could know almost nothing for certain about the historical Jesus, I thought that in attempting to recover reliable knowledge of Jesus' sayings and deeds the Seminar had set itself an impossible task. But when I heard Bob Funk's simple and dispassionate account of their academic findings – what he termed the 'voiceprints' and 'footprints' of Jesus – I felt he brought me closer to that ancient teacher than I had ever been. Not only did Bob generously invite me to become associated with the Westar Institute, but he also showed great interest in the book I was then writing. Indeed, Polebridge Press, the publishing arm of Westar Institute, eventually brought out an American edition of *The World to Come* simultaneously with the New Zealand one; later it published an American edition of *Tomorrow's God*, as well as inviting me to revise *Faith's New Age*, which it republished as *Christianity at the Crossroads*.

So that is how Elaine and I found ourselves comfortably settled in a flat in Santa Rosa for a month. Soon after our arrival, Bob and I flew to Washington for a weekend to conduct a 'Jesus Seminar on the Road' (one method used by the institute to spread information about its work through the community) and to preach in local churches. On our return Bob and I, along with Elaine and Bob's wife Char Matejovsky, travelled in the institute's comfortable van to present further Jesus seminars in California's Central Valley.

The conference to which I had been invited was attended by some five hundred Fellows and Associates of the Westar Institute, and had as its theme 'The Once and Future Jesus'. Having published a two-volume record of its search for extant traces of the historical Jesus, the institute was now setting out to explore the significance of its findings for the future of the Christian faith. The conference heard nine lectures (later published under the same title as the conference) from such people as Marcus Borg, Jack Spong and John Dominic Crossan. My contribution was 'The Legacy of Christianity', in which I tried to show that the modern secular world, with all its faults, is already recognisable as a new but genuine stage in the flow of the Judeo-Christian cultural stream; and that the Jesus relevant to such a world was not the divine figure of Christ elevated to a mythical heaven, but the human Jesus being recovered by the Jesus Seminar.

On returning home in November, Elaine and I were immediately off to the South Island to promote the New Zealand edition of *The World to Come*. Since this tour included Christchurch, Timaru and Dunedin, we decided to drive up through Cromwell and over the Lindis Pass on the way home, as we loved Central Otago and had regretted having to sell our holiday cottage in Cromwell on moving to Wellington. But our return to Cromwell had unexpected results. Motivated largely by Elaine's rekindled enthusiasm for the area, we left the village three days later the proud owners of another holiday cottage. Originally built as a motel unit, it stood in one corner of a well-kept lawn edged with oaks, a large cypress, rowans and two tall beeches, as well as a number of shrubs and an apricot tree laden with ripening fruit.

We went home in a state of happy expectation – brimming over with plans for managing our new 'country estate' and caught up, against our better judgement, in all the hype associated with the arrival of the third millennium. (Of course, that event would not really occur for another year, since the Common Era began with the year 1; but few people, if any, were bothered by such inconvenient facts!) On the eve of the year 2000, then, we joined the large crowd on Wellington's waterfront to see the fireworks display at midnight and experience the relaxed merriment of the occasion. The widespread fear that all computers around the world would malfunction because they were not adequately programmed for the date change proved to be a false alarm. Perhaps the dire scenarios for the twenty-first century that I had outlined in *The World to Come* would meet with the same happy fate.

Chapter Sixteen

'THE WORLD IS MY PARISH'

The third millennium seemed more than a lifetime away when I began my professional career, and I never expected to enter it. Yet now it had arrived and I was still very active, having become a freelance writer and lecturer. Not only was this an occupation in which I could draw upon all that had gone before, but I was now free to expand my horizons of interest. Of course, it might seem a far cry from where I started, as minister of a country parish; yet I nonetheless saw my current activity as the legitimate continuation of the ministry to which I had originally felt called. After all, I was still a Presbyterian minister, now with the exalted status of Minister Emeritus, for despite all that had happened I had never felt the need to resign from the ministry.

Strangely enough, I was now speaking and writing about God and religion more than ever, but nearly always in the public arena and only rarely from church pulpits. This fact reminded me of the words attributed to John Wesley: when he went on his open-air preaching excursions and found himself rebuked by his fellow Anglican clerics for ignoring the traditional parish boundaries, he retorted: 'The world is my parish'.

I had even just published a book on the future of the world! In early 2000, reviews of *The World to Come* were already beginning to appear. Once again, some praised it highly and others dismissed it. That was only to be expected, for any attempt to assess what *is* happening and is *about to* happen on a global scale must be somewhat subjective, and its success is dependent on how well one has absorbed and interpreted a broad range of information. Now, six years later (though I take no pleasure in saying so), the world is already being forced to deal with several of the issues I identified as potential threats – terrorism, pandemics, international conflict, mass starvation, and our interference with the earth's ecology.

The year 2000 proved to be a busier one than usual, although Elaine and I still managed to fit in several trips to Cromwell to oversee additions to our cottage, attend to the interior decoration, and plan the landscaping with roses and shrubs.

In February I was invited to be the keynote speaker at the Strategic Thinkers' Conference in Christchurch, where I gave a lecture on 'Taking our Bearings in 2000 AD'. In November I returned to Christchurch at the request of the Canterbury Branch of the United Nations Association to deliver the Grocott Memorial Peace Lecture. This I entitled 'Obstacles in the Way of World Peace' and, amid some general observations, spoke specifically about the explosive situation in the Middle East and the degree to which both the British and the Americans were partly responsible.

This latter lecture drew on an experience that was the highlight of our year – a trip to Iran, which had been initiated by a chance remark to Elaine about ten days before we left for the Holy Land Tour in 1999. Knowing she had long been fascinated by tales of Persia, I casually said, 'I would have loved to take you to Iran, but I suppose we shall never get the opportunity now'. Unbeknown to me, she had evidently mentioned this to one or two of her friends; when we reached Wellington airport to leave for the Middle East, several people, including the tour operator, approached me to ask if it were true that we were intending to take a tour group to Iran.

Their enquiries prompted me, while in London, to investigate the possibilities. On our return home I received valuable assistance from the Iranian Embassy in Wellington. Among other things, I was told that all women, including Western tourists, must have their hair covered at all times and wear robes down to their ankles. I wondered if the women in our group would be willing to accept such restrictions; yet when the time came they did so without complaint.

Soon after arriving in Teheran, where each of the women was provided with a chador, we flew to Meshed, a city sacred to the Shi'ites because of the elaborate mausoleum of the Eighth Imam at its centre. The economy of the city, which has a population of about three million, is largely dependent on the stream of Muslim pilgrims. Our young guide, Madad, wanted us to see the mausoleum at night, when it was brilliantly lit. When we arrived at the shrine, however, he told us that we should pretend to be Muslims, and if challenged say that we came from Bosnia–Herzegovina (which is largely Muslim). Although somewhat apprehensive, we proceeded to enter the gates (males through one and females through the other), where we were searched for weapons. Fortunately no one challenged us and we mingled with the silent worshippers, caught up in the awe-inspiring atmosphere.

That was only the first of a series of unforgettable sights: the treasures in the museums of Teheran, the ancient city fortress of Bam (since then destroyed by an earthquake), the Zoroastrian fire-temples and burial towers at Yazd, culturally creative Shiraz, the ruins of Persepolis, the magnificent Isfahan, and endless mosques, bazaars and Persian rugs wherever we went. In Isfahan we were all accommodated at the wonderful Abbasi Hotel (formerly called 'Shah Abbas', until the Islamic Revolution).

At the site of the ancient capital of Pasargadae we visited the tomb of the conqueror Cyrus (hailed in the Bible as Messiah to the Jews), but were more impressed by the fact that the Iranians celebrated their poets, scholars and holy men more than their army generals. As well as the mausolea of two Imams at Meshed and Shiraz, we visited the tombs and memorials of Omar Khayyam, Ferdowsi, Sa'adi and Hafez. We ended by going to the mausoleum being built to celebrate Ayatollah Khomeini, the architect of the Islamic Revolution.

The year ended with the news that I was to be made a PCNZM (Principal Companion of the New Zealand Order of Merit) in the New Year Honours. Naturally I felt honoured, but also genuinely puzzled as to the reason for the award, thinking I had done little to deserve it. Indeed, I felt a twinge of sympathy with those who wrote letters to the newspaper deploring the news; I was also slightly embarrassed to be receiving an even higher honour than the much more illustrious Colin Meads, one of our rugby heroes.

The New Year Honours were announced while Elaine and I were at our Cromwell cottage, where we remained for three months, apart from the week I spent in Santa Rosa attending the spring meeting of the Westar Institute. This conference was intended to launch a new phase in the work of the Jesus Seminar: the aim was to explore ways in which the Christian faith could be found relevant to the new global age, in the light of the uncovering of the original Jesus as a Jewish sage. Along with other Fellows of the institute, Karen Armstrong, Don Cupitt, Jack Spong and I delivered lectures that were subsequently published as *The Once and Future Faith*.

In my paper I set out how the Judeo-Christian path of faith had undergone radical changes from time to time, adapting itself to new experiences. For example, to do justice to the ongoing influence of the Jewish sage Jesus, the ancient Christian Fathers had radically changed their understanding of God. Their doctrine of the Holy Trinity obliterated the gulf between God and humankind by 'divinising' the human condition. I went on to discuss how this continuing path of faith could adapt itself to today's understanding of the evolving space-time universe in which we live. Finally, I made the daring (some would say preposterous) suggestion that what transcends us now (that is, what is 'God' for us today) could be called the 'secular trinity' – the self-creating universe, the culture-creating human species, and an emerging global consciousness.

It was during this conference that I found myself being urged to write another book, the origin of which was indeed unusual. At the New Zealand Sea of Faith Conference in 2000, I had given a partly tongue-in-cheek lecture entitled 'Christianity without Theism'. Unbeknown to me, this had been put on the Sea of Faith website; from there, someone in the United States had forwarded it to Bob Funk, who asked if he could publish it in the Westar journal, and later urged me to turn it into a full-length book. Although at first doubtful, I agreed to try.

On returning home, therefore, I set to work on this new project, having no inkling that all too soon I was to encounter a disruption of major proportions. Indeed, life just then was running along very smoothly. In late June, Elaine and I used our air points to fly to Australia for ten days, staying in South Brisbane in an apartment overlooking the river and city. We delighted in walking around all our former haunts, seeing our old house in Indooroopilly, and finding one of the sons of our next-door neighbours still living there.

No sooner had we returned from Queensland than a flurry of activity began, with the quick succession of events now seared into my memory because I have relived them so often. It was family birthday time – first for Elizabeth and Judy (just returned from teaching English in China), and then for Elaine herself, who turned seventy-four on 10 August. Five days later came the investiture at Government House. That night our family gathered for a celebration dinner at Shed 5 restaurant on the Wellington waterfront.

We then set off for the South Island by ferry and car, spending the Friday night with our friends Jim and Ann Thornton at Diamond Harbour. After an evening of lively discussion, Elaine complained of a severe pain in her head as she was going to bed. On waking next morning her first words were, 'I'm glad I've got all my functions'. As she had frequently suffered from migraines, we assumed that the headache would soon disappear as it usually had done before, but it continued throughout the journey south.

On our arrival in Cromwell I was surprised that Elaine did not make an inspection tour of her shrubs. Instead, while I was carrying in the luggage, she quietly slipped fully clothed into bed, where I found her asleep. At 9 p.m. she woke, and I gave her a light meal so that she could take her medication; then she settled down for the night. I woke at 6 a.m. on the Sunday to find there had been a heavy frost, and I asked Elaine how she felt. 'Nothing wonderful', she said, and murmured 'Yes' when I asked if she would have some breakfast. On arriving with the breakfast tray fifteen minutes later I found her in a coma. (It was later decided that she had suffered a cerebral aneurism, much like that of her sister Juliet.) I called 111 on my cell-phone and the ambulance (followed shortly by the doctor) was there in ten minutes. Some thirty minutes later her breathing stopped. She had gone out like a light, much as she would have wished, and at her beloved Cromwell.

Naturally, I was completely shocked; it was as if my world as well had suddenly come to an end. More than once Elaine and I had discussed our inevitable deaths, and we each confessed a disinclination to be the one left behind; but since she was more than nine years my junior, I had long assumed that Elaine would outlive me. Evidently she had not been so sure, for now I recalled odd remarks she had made and saw them in quite a different light. At church one morning, only three months earlier, she had leaned over and pointed to a hymn, saying, 'I want that at my funeral', but I thought nothing much of it at the time. On another occasion she said out of the blue, 'If you are left alone, I hope you will marry again.' Although taken aback at the time, I failed to grasp what this revealed about Elaine's inner thoughts. Apparently she was more aware of the uncertainty of her condition than I had ever been.

Of course I coped, as most people do when faced with sudden and dramatic loss. But it was the support of my family and friends that chiefly carried me through. Because we had been married just three months short of fifty years (indeed, Elaine had already been planning the anniversary celebration), I felt this loss even more keenly than the loss of Nancy. But I had also reached a more mature understanding of death than I had possessed on that earlier occasion.

This I later tried to explain, somewhat blunderingly, on National Radio when Kim Hill, in an interview about my book, suddenly asked me how I felt about the loss of Elaine. I replied that it was just because I had no belief in any afterlife that I felt somewhat comforted, for it meant that I did not feel separated from Elaine. All that remained of her was in the influence she had had on me and others. I still find it hard, of course, to accept the absolute finality of death, yet that finality serves to bring home to us the awesome mystery and finiteness of life itself.

During the next few months, I became grateful for the lecturing engagements to which I was already committed. They so occupied my mind that I was prevented from being overcome by the lonely emptiness that comes with grieving. I had to prepare for seminars, the Sea of Faith Conference in September, and the upcoming lunch-hour lectures at St Andrew's. This new series was to focus on the Israeli-Palestinian conflict; and in the lectures, later published as *Who Owns the Holy Land?*, I attempted to set out, as fairly and objectively as I could, the legitimate claims of both Israelis and Palestinians.

Another activity I found very healing was making a start on writing Elaine's story. Most bereaved people want to think and talk about the person they have lost. First of all, I gathered together in an album all the photographs that best portrayed Elaine's life-story – something I had done when Nancy died, and which proved beneficial for the growing children. It was to be a year before I finished writing the book about Elaine. I found that in recent years she had been keeping a private diary, in which she had written, 'Life is a treasure, a privilege, and a fast-fleeting one. Every moment must be lived'. I therefore titled the volume *Every Moment Must be Lived* and published it privately for family and friends.

During the first few months after the loss of Elaine, my daughter Judy, followed by my granddaughter Jessica, came to live with me. Then just at the point when Jessica was setting off on an overseas trip, a strange and unexpected thing happened. In the course of making travel plans to go to Timaru to speak about *Who Owns the Holy Land?*, I rang Shirley White to invite her to have coffee with me as I passed through Christchurch. Only on rare occasions had I seen Shirley since she hosted Elaine and me long ago during the heresy trial; but as recently as the winter of 2000 she had called in to see us when she was briefly in Wellington.

This turned out to be more than a meeting for coffee. In a way that surprised us both, we very soon found ourselves romantically attracted to each other to a degree that one does not expect at our age. I had long assumed that as people age, they become too set in their ways ever to form the kind of deep relationship that can develop when they are younger. How wrong I was! Shirley and I, with the warm encouragement of our respective families, began to share our lives together in 2002, living partly in Wellington and partly in Christchurch. Eventually, in 2004, we decided to marry.

For all these reasons, the book I had started in early 2001 suffered an interruption. But at last I took it up again, and in late 2002 it was published simultaneously in New Zealand and the United States as *Christianity without God*. I know it seems preposterous to suggest that Christianity can exist without belief in God, but I was particularly concerned in this book to explore the common notion of God as a creating, planning and world-controlling super-personal being. I tried to show that not only have ideas about God undergone many changes throughout the Judeo-Christian era, but even the Bible refers to gods and God in a variety of ways. Indeed, the much-neglected stream of Old Testament thought known as the Wisdom or humanistic books treats the term 'God' as a synonym of Nature, and it is in that stream that Jesus the sage is probably to be placed.

As some of the more critical reviews of the book clearly illustrated, many Christians fail to appreciate the revolutionary character of the central Christian doctrines of the Incarnation and the Trinity, let alone the naturalism present in the biblical Wisdom tradition. It is hardly surprising, then, that traditional Christians find it difficult to accept the idea that in accommodating itself to the modern secular world, Christianity must learn to do without an external, supernatural authority that controls history. In a world come of age, we humans must now learn to accept full responsibility for our destiny. A 'Christianity without God' may have no room for a divine saviour, but it reserves a special place for the man Jesus, the sage whose parables of the Good Samaritan and the Prodigal Son will be remembered long after the creeds have been forgotten.

To assist in promoting *Christianity without God*, I was invited to Santa Rosa to conduct a one-day workshop at the spring meeting of the Westar Institute. During the month that Shirley and I were there, I also participated in 'Jesus Seminars on the Road' in such widely scattered locations as Dunedin (Florida), Portland, Seattle and Edmonton. That was my first opportunity to visit Canada, and it was an extra bonus to get the feel of life in Canada's most northern city.

The following year I was invited to Niagara Falls for the annual confer-ence of the Snowstar Institute of Religion, a Canadian organisation that was founded to counter the spread of fundamentalism in the Canadian churches. My subject, therefore, was 'The Origin and Destructive Poten-tial of Fundamentalism' – a topic of increasing concern to me because of the spread of this reactionary ethos in the New Zealand churches. By fundamentalism I mean the acceptance of Holy Scripture as both literally true and divinely authoritative. This modern form of idolatry has come not only to distort both Christianity and Islam, but to threaten human society by inciting its adherents to hatred and violence. That same year I also devoted the St Andrew's lectures to this topic, and these were pub-lished as *Fundamentalism: The Challenge to the Secular World*.

In March 2004 Shirley and I were off to New York, where the Westar Institute was staging its spring conference at the Marriott Hotel in Times Square. Once again I found myself lecturing in the company of Don Cupitt, Karen Armstrong, Jack Spong and other Fellows of the institute. In my lecture, 'A Path of Faith to the Global Future', I pointed out that the values most highly prized in the secular world, when examined carefully, reveal themselves to be the continuation and extension of values that characterise the Judeo-Christian tradition. Such values as love, compassion, justice and freedom exert their authority by virtue of their own inherent worth, and do not need the support of an external divine authority. I further developed these thoughts on my return home, devoting the next St Andrew's lecture series to the theme 'Where is Christianity Going?'

Before returning to New Zealand, however, we flew to Arizona, where I had been invited to speak in Phoenix under the auspices of a society established for the promotion of radical theology. We had accepted the invitation not only as a chance to thaw out after the cold of New York, but also because of the opportunity to view the Grand Canyon. While in Phoenix I took part in the preparation of a set of documentary videos, *Living the Questions*, designed to be a liberal counter to the very conservative Alpha Courses being widely used in churches.

Later in the same year, I was invited by the Wellington Branch of the Royal Society of New Zealand to deliver the 2004 Hudson Lecture. I interpreted this as an interesting honour, for in the popular mind science and religion are antagonistic to each other. So under the title 'How is Science Related to the Judeo-Christian Tradition?', I explored what lay behind the words of the German physicist, Friedrich von Weizsäcker, when he said, 'modern science would not perhaps have been possible without Christianity'. I tried to show that there were many more positive links between the two enterprises than were usually realised.

The validity of such a view was corroborated when, shortly afterwards, I was asked to address some 200 alumni of Auckland University, many of them medical graduates, on the topic 'Playing God'. I was beginning to master PowerPoint, and I devised a presentation showing how we humans had reached the point in our cultural and religious evolution where we were required to make decisions that previously we assumed to be within the exclusive province of a supernatural God. Not only were we prolonging life through medical science, but we were gaining increasing control over issues of life and death by means of contraception, in-vitro fertilisation, euthanasia and genetic modification. It was not God but Nature that now set the limits.

Shortly after this, I was invited by the newly established Centre for Progressive Religious Thought in Australia to spend some ten days lecturing, conducting seminars and preaching in Sydney, Canberra and Adelaide. Shirley and I also took the opportunity to fly to Alice Springs for a three-day tour of the interior. Of special interest to me were the church and small hospital in Alice that now commemorate 'Flynn of the Inland', who had so stirred my imagination as a young minister in Opoho.

One of my tasks while in Sydney was to contribute to a series of public lectures under the title 'God and Me'. And only six months later, as chance would have it, I was invited to deliver the Hocken Lecture in Dunedin for 2005. Since this annual lecture is expected to be of historical interest, and my own life had spanned most of the twentieth century, I presented a personal perspective on the change that has taken place in religion in the course of the past hundred years. It was published as *God in Twentieth Century New Zealand*. Preparation for these two lectures encouraged me to proceed further in this direction by using these as useful abstracts for this present book. But I was already focusing more of my attention on ecological issues. This first began to show in *Tomorrow's God* and I developed it further in *The World to Come*; so finally, I devoted the 2005 St Andrew's lectures to *The Greening of Christianity*.

In some respects, I have found retirement to be the most creative period in my life. It is true that meeting deadlines can sharpen the mind, as I found when I had to write two sermons a week, course lectures, or a regular column. But the freedom one experiences when not under pressure (when lying awake at night, for example, or even when in the shower) allows surprising new thoughts to bubble up from the creative power of the psyche. In short, retirement from formal duties has proved to be a highly rewarding and satisfying chapter in my life.

Chapter Seventeen

HERE I AM!

That completes the story of my life to 2006 – as clearly as I remember it, and as honestly as I have been able to tell it. Of course it has been selective (as all historical writing is), because there is much that I have now forgotten, and many incidents and details seemed too trivial to record. But believing I have nothing to hide, I have recorded my activities and my thinking as openly and frankly as I could, and have not deliberately suppressed anything. Everything I have narrated, along with whatever has been left untold, has shaped what I am as I now write this. I *am* my life-story, for I carry this past with me in the 'I' who now continues to respond to the duties and opportunities that come with each new day.

In this exercise of recalling the past, I have been struck by the frequency with which I was led to significant turning points or major achievements by chance events. Chance plays a dominant role in the life of every person, just as it has in the evolution of life on this planet – on a far grander scale! That is why we so often speak of 'fortune' and 'misfortune', 'good luck' and 'bad luck'. As I observed at the beginning of this book, one's genes and one's mother culture are the two 'givens' out of which personal identity begins to evolve. We are largely the product of these, together with our successive responses to the many chance and intentional events we encounter from birth onwards. Why, I might never have become a writer had it not been for my critics!

But all in all, fortune has been very kind to me – if I may so personify the element of chance. In view of the countless happenings that constitute a lifetime, it is no wonder that we often feel we are being watched over by divine providence – or, alternatively, being plagued by the devil. For the many different ways in which I have been fortunate, I am genuinely grateful. Of course, I have had my sorrows, disappointments and frustrations; but compared with the lives of most people on this planet, mine has run very smoothly. I have had wonderful support from family, friends and colleagues; and apart from a few fairly brief spells I have enjoyed good health – something with such a high priority in life that we enquire about one another's health every time we meet.

In spite of the predominance of chance in every life-story, the evolving 'I' that makes innumerable decisions, great and small, throughout a person's life forms the continuing thread that gives unity to their story. That fact often prompts us to see more signs of purpose in the succession of chance events than actually exist. (That is why we sometimes exclaim, 'This was meant to be!') But as Nietzsche came to recognise, it is we humans who imagine or create a sense of purpose, for there is no preordained purpose in anyone's life. Even the universe itself is devoid of any purpose, just as nature itself is neither good nor bad, but amoral.

When I was nearing the end of my high school years, I was often asked what I planned to be; but I had no plan. In those days of the Great Depression, some of my schoolmates simply 'became' what the first job opportunity led them to – another instance of chance! Having no clear convictions about a future career, I felt more comfortable just continuing what I was already doing; I therefore drifted into university with no clear purpose, but largely because my genes had endowed me with slightly more than average intellectual ability and thereby enabled me to win a scholarship.

As the reader now knows, it was a succession of chance events in my first two years at university that set me on a path with some direction. Clearly, it was chance rather than destiny that first pointed me towards becoming the 'I' that I now am. At the time, I interpreted those circumstances as the call of God to train for the ministry. Many years later, I found myself identifying with the words of Dag Hammarskjöld, one-time Secretary General to the United Nations, that are found in his posthumous little book, *Markings*:

> I don't know Who – or what – put the question, I don't know when it was put…But at some moment I did answer *Yes* to Someone – or Something

– and from that hour I was certain that existence is meaningful and that, therefore, my life, in self-surrender, had a goal.

That is how it was for me. The 'Someone or Something' was a voice I heard within; it certainly did not come from any external source. Soon after that, I found such experiences described again and again in the extensive Judeo-Christian canon. Indeed, that venerable tradition is said to have begun when Abraham heard a voice calling him to leave behind the familiar surroundings of his birthplace and travel to a destiny he knew nothing about. Moses also heard a voice after first being attracted by the sight of a bush burning in the desert. And as a young boy, the prophet Samuel heard a voice in the night calling him by name. Legendary in character though these stories may be, they vividly express what has been a common human experience. In both of the latter two stories, the response was, 'Here I am!' (I rather like the fact that in Hebrew this response consists of a single word, '*Hinneni*'.)

That word succinctly expresses the response I made in 1937 to the 'Someone or Something' behind the voice I heard within, the Presence that has shaped my life from that point onwards; somewhat uncertainly, even reluctantly at first, I responded, 'Here I am!' And thus I was led to the path that the very first Christians simply called 'The Way', a path I have tried to follow ever since, even though it has led to unexpected territory and unsought aggravations.

In the eyes of some of my fellow Presbyterians, to say nothing of Christians from other denominations, I have appeared to wander far astray from the true Christian path of faith. As they see it, I am at best a maverick and at worst an apostate. Of course I have made mistakes and errors of judgement from time to time; but had I not persevered in following the path before me, I would indeed have forsaken my commitment to that original call.

What is this voice I have been hearing and wrestling with all my life? Like the Jacob of old, engaged in his mythic struggle with an unknown assailant, I do not exactly know; but like him, I have sought to find out. I am still content to call that unknown voice 'God'; but I acknowledge that, as Buber observed, this has become 'the most burdened of all human words' because it 'has been misused so much'. If I use the word 'God' at all, I do so in the way Tillich did when he spoke of 'The God beyond God', or as Mahatma Gandhi did when he said, 'God is truth!'

As the path I have been following has led me through a new and ever-changing world, I have discovered that what I keep learning from the Christian heritage unexpectedly lights up with new meaning – notably in my efforts to identify the unknown voice. For example, when Moses asked the voice apparently coming from the burning bush to supply him with a name, the only reply he received was, 'I am who I am'.

Behind this legend about Moses lies an interesting illustration of ancient reasoning. The Israelite scholars of old assumed that the word Yahweh, the distinctive name they used for God, was somehow related to the similar-sounding Hebrew word meaning 'to be'. They concluded that when they used the name 'Yahweh' they were saying 'He is'. From this they inferred that if God were ever to refer to himself, he would naturally say, 'I am'. What is more, because Hebrew tenses do not indicate time, as ours do, but rather whether an action is complete or incomplete, then 'I am' is more correctly interpreted as 'I am in the process of becoming', since the word implies life, movement and change, not something static and unchanging. In fact, it is the same word that is translated by that well-known biblical phrase, 'And it came to pass' (which should be, 'And it was coming to pass'). Moreover, the Hebrew for 'I am' is one simple word, 'Ehye'.

What the ancient Israelite scholars seem almost to have stumbled upon, in attempting to identify God with Yahweh, later proved quite inspirational to people who were walking The Way. Their formulation was taken up by the Fourth Evangelist and put into the mouth of Jesus as a succession of great 'I AM's: 'I am the true vine', 'I am the bread of life', 'I am the way, the truth, and the life'.

In the twentieth century, the dynamic and changing nature of 'God' was emphasised by Teilhard de Chardin, who practically equated God with cosmic evolution itself; and this was reaffirmed by John Cobb and other 'process theologians'. Martin Buber, having earlier rejected the idea of God as an objective being, rediscovered the divine 'I AM' in the deep, personal, living relationship he called 'I and Thou'. Colin McCahon, fascinated by both Buber's spiritual classic and the biblical name for God, painted them both.

251

Rudolf Bultmann and Carl Jung, among others, have drawn attention to the close correlation between one's God and one's self. Each of us establishes a personal identity by finding meaning in human existence and a goal to live for – in other words, by finding and serving our God. We can observe how strong and solid are the letters in which McCahon painted 'I AM'. Done at a time when the artist suffered widespread opposition from within the artistic world, this canvas was insightfully interpreted by one art critic as follows: 'This painting is at once God's assertion of his being, Jesus' assertion of his being, and (inescapably) McCahon's assertion of his own being'.

On my study wall, in front of me as I now write, are prints of two works by McCahon – 'I and THOU' and 'I AM'. Underneath them is a small Greek icon of Christ (as a teacher, not as the Saviour on the cross) and a silver engraving of the Last Supper. Not far away are images of the Buddha and a seven-branched candlestick. These represent some of the chief spiritual influences in my life.

If asked whether I am a Christian, I still answer in the affirmative, for it is from the Judeo-Christian tradition that I have received most of my inspiration and values. But in this post-Christian, globalising world, I think religious labels have for the most part lost any usefulness they may once have had. I am still a Presbyterian minister, for I have no regrets about having said, 'Here I am!' when I did, nor any wish to deny the validity of that original experience. And I still go to church – partly because I value some form of spiritual exercise, partly out of gratitude for all that I have received through the church in the past, and partly for the fellowship of other people who are also seeking to walk The Way.

Throughout my professional life I have sought to be scholarly, yet I have never claimed to speak or write with the authority of a scholar. From my very first book, I made it clear that I was writing not for scholars but for ordinary people like myself, people who were seeking to make some sense of this awe-inspiring yet bewildering universe, and to find some purpose in their lives.

Of course, I am not infallible; and just as they have done in the past, some people will find much to criticise in this story (assuming, of course, that they take the trouble to read it). But, by way of acknowledging the warm support I have received from people who have generously told

me that my sermons, lectures or books have been of some help to them,
I offer this story as a theological tale in the hope that it may encourage
them on their own paths of faith.

Faith should never be confused with any particular set of beliefs. Beliefs come and go; they depend upon where people find themselves, both
in the cultural history of humankind and in their own spiritual journeys.
I conclude, therefore, with Cantwell Smith's description of faith:

> Faith is one's existential engagement
> with what one knows to be true or good.
> It is the committing of oneself
> to act in terms of
> what one recognises as cosmically valid.

Appendix One

WHAT DOES THE RESURRECTION MEAN?[1]

At the Easter season, Christians celebrate two basic events which are inseparable – the death of Jesus on the cross and the resurrection of Jesus. The historical fact of his crucifixion few would seriously try to deny, but of course it is not simply *that* which concerns us, but rather the meaning or significance that the Christian has come to see in his death, in contrast with that of any other martyr.

It is because of the special significance that the Christian sees in the death of Jesus that he or she takes the cross as the symbol of the Christian faith. Christians may vary quite considerably in the way they try to describe that special significance, but they all agree that Jesus died, as all people must die, and that this death has an eternal significance possessed by no other human death.

Now the resurrection is not exactly an event parallel to the death. It can have meaning only in conjunction with the death. Death is *not* necessarily followed by resurrection, but resurrection has *necessarily* been preceded by death. No attempt to understand the resurrection of Jesus is adequate which does not do justice to the historical fact that he died.

The story in St John's Gospel concerning the resurrection of Lazarus can be quite misleading, for this is no real parallel to the resurrection of Jesus at all; and if it is taken as a historical account, then it should properly be called a resuscitation. It cannot be called a resurrection, for resurrection must take death seriously, and in this case Lazarus evidently still had to die the human death that was final.

---

1 This article was published in the *Outlook*, 2 April 1966. Minor editorial changes have been made, including the use of gender-inclusive language.

Of course the simplest explanation of Lazarus is that this is not a historical story at all, but an attempt by the Evangelist to teach the resurrection truth within the setting of the ministry of Jesus. And such an attempt was likely to end in contradictions.

Because resurrection is bound to take death seriously, we must guard against speaking of the resurrection of Jesus as a historical event. History deals with what happens in the lives of human beings. The resurrection did not happen in the life of Jesus, but after the life of Jesus had ended in death. The resurrection of Jesus is *not* a historical event in the ordinary sense of the word historical; what is historical is the impact that the resurrection made upon the apostles.

What was it, then, that gave rise to this impact upon the apostles? It is not as easy to answer this as is sometimes imagined. In fact we must say that we do not know. There is no way of getting behind the New Testament records and standing behind the apostles to witness for ourselves whatever it was. The past is past and no one can re-enter it. The only evidence we have is in the New Testament records where the first Christians unanimously testify to their conviction that God had raised Jesus from the dead.

Because the resurrection does not properly fall within the category of historical event, it is rather fruitless to debate whether Jesus rose from the dead on the same basis on which we usually discuss the historicity of an event. It is more important to ask what significance it has for us that the apostles believed Jesus to be risen from the dead.

Those who read the little book entitled *Secular Christianity* by R. Gregor Smith, Professor of Theology in Glasgow, will probably be surprised to read in his discussion on the resurrection, 'we may freely say that the bones of Jesus lie somewhere in Palestine'.

It is easy to jump to the conclusion that Professor Smith is here quite openly denying the resurrection of Jesus and hence surrendering his allegiance to the Christian faith. Yet he immediately goes on to write, 'Christian faith is not destroyed by this admission. On the contrary, only now, when this has been said, are we in a position to ask about the meaning of the resurrection as an integral part of the message concerning Jesus'.

How can one believe that the mortal remains of Jesus lie somewhere in

Palestine and at the same time affirm the resurrection doctrine by which, according to St Paul, the Christian faith stands or falls?

First let us look at the alternatives. If the mortal remains of Jesus did not return to dust in Palestine, where are they? In view of the story of the ascension, some may be led to reply that they are in heaven. But this leads to the nonsensical position that the material of which this earth is made finds some permanent place in heaven. (It is important to point out, however, that such an answer did not appear nonsensical in the first century.)

The other alternative is to say that in some way unknown to us, either at the time of the resurrection or at some other unknown point later, the material body of Jesus was dissolved into nothing. For this there is neither a shred of evidence, nor any sound reason for supposing it.

It has been traditional to regard the Gospel stories of the empty tomb as a magnificent testimony to the truth of the resurrection. But if they are treated as records of historical events, they are soon seen to be an embarrassment to the more discerning believer, for they describe the resurrection in terms which are at once superficially dramatic but at the same time imperil the real truth of the resurrection.

The story of the empty tomb, like the story of Lazarus, turns the resurrection into a resuscitation story, in which we are left with the unanswered question of what happened to the material remains of the historical Jesus in the end. Further, this story is really at variance with other resurrection stories, such as the sudden appearance of the risen Lord to the disciples gathered behind closed doors.

It is not accidental that Paul never refers to the empty tomb. In I Corinthians 15, he gives an impressive list of the resurrection experiences undergone by the apostles, concluding with that of his own. But nowhere does he mention the empty tomb. Moreover, in the very same chapter he makes a clear distinction between what he calls the 'physical body' and the 'spiritual body'. The physical body is of the dust of the earth. It remains of the earth and returns to the earth. If we believe the incarnation to be real (and are not led astray by a heretical docetism), then the body of Jesus of Nazareth was of the same dust, and when he died, that body too returned somewhere to dust.

The story of the empty tomb, from which presumably that mortal life had come to life again and departed elsewhere, can be only legend – a very beautiful and attractive legend, and one that will continue to speak quite powerfully to us even when we have come to acknowledge it as legend. How early the legend was we cannot tell, but if we make a careful comparison of the empty tomb story in the Synoptic Gospels, in the later Gospel of St John, and in the second century Gospel of Peter, we receive quite a clear impression of the way the legend was gradually expanding in detail and miraculous element.

The Christian affirmation of the risen Lord does not then depend upon establishing *what happened to the body of Jesus* following the crucifixion. It depends upon what the New Testament tells us of *what happened to the apostles*. Here we should note that Paul, the 'thirteenth apostle', is the only one of whom we can say without question that we have his testimony first-hand of how he came to believe in the risen Lord.

In I Corinthians 15, he writes that the Lord *appeared* to him, but in the three accounts in the Book of Acts that describe his experience on the road to Damascus, there is no mention of an appearance of Jesus. What brought about his conversion was the voice of Jesus that he heard.

It has long been recognised that the various ways in which the apostles have described their experiences do not really tally. Some have tried to fit them together like pieces of a jig-saw puzzle to make one complete and utterly convincing picture. But such attempts always fail because they are not one picture but several – pictures which are individual expressions of personal experiences, which in turn have been retold from mouth to mouth before being recorded.

The more enlightening metaphor to use, perhaps, is this: the various testimonies are like a collection of works of art which differ from one another in size, shape, and colour; but by the discerning eye of the art critic it can be recognised that they have all been created by one master artist, who may himself not actually be known to the critic.

So the various testimonies, different though they may be from one another and some even legendary in form, all point back to a common source – namely, the influence of the risen Lord himself. Not even the New Testament suggests that the risen Lord could be conjured up at will. There was no place to which the genuine enquirer could go in order to see the risen Lord for himself. Even in the Apostolic period the apostles rested upon the confirmation achieved by the witness of one another.

And this is the only way in which we can speak of the resurrection of Jesus being a historical event – it was that the apostles themselves quite unexpectedly became transformed men. The change that they experienced was so consonant with what they had known of Jesus in the flesh that they were forced to attribute it to him. And seeing Jesus had been crucified, then the explanation that came most naturally to them was that Jesus had been raised from the dead.

It is important to remember that 'resurrection' talk did not suddenly spring up out of the blue just after the death of Jesus. The ideas of limited and general resurrection had been growing more prevalent among the Jews for at least two hundred years and perhaps much longer. The Book of Daniel speaks of it.

At the time of Jesus it had become a lively issue of discussion between the conservative Sadducees who scoffed at the idea, and the more liberal Pharisees who had embraced the hope of resurrection. Paul himself must have been well versed in this kind of thinking, and his experience on the road to Damascus turned him quite naturally in this direction for an explanation.

So with all the apostles. Indeed, the Gospels tell us that Jesus himself had told them to expect it. Since the influence of Jesus after his death was so strong as to transform them at that point in a way that had not even happened during his Galilean ministry, it is no surprise that they should have described what had happened to them in terms of resurrection. For them the Lord *was* 'risen'. And what is more, when they excitedly shared their experiences with one another and then boldly declared them to all who would listen, they found that others too became changed as if under the influence of the same Jesus. So the church spread, on fire with the spirit or power of the risen Christ. This is the historical fact to which the New Testament testifies.

The chief event that had happened between the Galilean ministry and the resurrection experiences of the apostles was the death of Jesus. Here we must return to acknowledge the special significance that Christians see in the death of Jesus, and to remember that the death and resurrection can be understood only in conjunction. The death of Jesus was a shattering blow to the disciples.

The meaning of the resurrection may be expressed in some such way as this: following hard upon that apparent disaster (and the rather symbolic term 'third day' probably means here as elsewhere in the Bible 'almost without delay') the disciples recognised that the power and goodness of Jesus were more alive in themselves and one another than ever before. This is well expressed by St John the Evangelist in the words he puts into the mouth of Jesus: 'It is to your advantage that I go away, for if I do not go away, the Counsellor will not come to you'.

In this attempt to discuss the meaning of the resurrection, some readers will no doubt be surprised, because they have always been used to thinking of the resurrection within the framework of the pre-scientific three-decker universe of heaven, earth, and hell – where, to put it quite simply, the resurrection of Jesus was regarded as a historical event by which the dead body of Jesus was brought back to life and, after a few appearances on earth, was raised to the heavenly sphere, where the risen Lord now sits and reigns at the right hand of God.

This discussion is not meant in any way to disturb the faith of those who feel quite happy and satisfied with this interpretation. If any such readers have ventured as far as this, perhaps they would be well advised to forget what they have read.

This discussion is primarily for those who know that the mythical three-decker universe is not the real tangible world in which we live, and because of that are genuinely puzzled to know what modern people are to make of such an important Christian affirmation as the resurrection of Jesus. The expression of the Christian faith in meaningful terms for the world in which we live may not be easy, but the genuine enquirer need not turn from the Christian faith as something that is bound to pass away with the gradual recession of the pre-scientific world.

The New Testament witness to the risen Lord turns our attention to human experiences that are historical and as real today as they were for the apostles. Jesus died – he *really* died, for it was a mortal life he shared with us. Yet the same Jesus has been the power of transformation and renewal in the lives of countless men and women almost from the day of his death down to the present day. This is the unanimous testimony of the whole community of Christian believers.

Jesus lived a human life among humans, teaching and ministering. Jesus was crucified by humans and for humans. From shortly after his death, men and women found themselves strangely moved and renewed by the power of the spirit of the same Jesus, and when the Gospel of Jesus Christ is proclaimed, it is still found to speak with power – his power. The Lord is risen indeed!

Appendix Two

THE ETERNITY IN MAN'S MIND[1]

Casual readers of the Bible are in for a shock when they first stumble upon the Book of Ecclesiastes. It does not conform to the usual run of religious books at all. Here, there seems to speak to us not the man of faith – but the sceptical pessimist who finds it hard to see in life anything at all that is meaningful or of permanent value. The presence of this book in Holy Scripture is no new problem. It almost was excluded from the Bible. The Jewish scholars debated it before the Christians inherited this part of the Bible from them. Christians have always been uneasy about it and most have preferred to ignore it. Yet here it is, in the Bible of the Christian Church to this day; and what is even more curious is the fact that it is the only book that has a churchy or ecclesiastical title, for Ecclesiastes means 'the Preacher'.

Modern biblical scholarship has been able to throw some light on the origins of this book. It is most probable that it was written in the third century BC by a Jew in the Egyptian city of Alexandria. Once we know that, we can immediately begin to see some of the factors that led this otherwise unknown Jew to think and write as he did.

In the century that succeeded the lightning conquest of the East by Alexander the Great, there was a rapid spread of Greek culture, which had so recently reached its magnificent flowering. Nowhere, perhaps, could that be seen more clearly than in the growing city in Egypt founded by

1 An address given at the Inaugural Service of the Victoria University of Wellington at Wesley Church on 12 March 1967. As for Appendix One, minor editorial changes have been made, including the use of gender-inclusive language.

Alexander himself. Alexandria became the chief centre of learning. Literature, philosophy and science all flourished there. The city boasted a library of 700,000 volumes.

Now let us look at the Jewish community that rapidly gathered there. In the previous four centuries, the Jewish people had been subjected in turn to the domination of three great empires whose cultures were quite diverse. There was Babylon, with its mythology and astrology; there was the religion of Persia, marked by its dualism of good and evil and its promise of a heavenly Paradise; and now there was the philosophy and nascent sciences of Greece. What was the Jew to make of these?

There were some Jews of course – the die-hards – who shut their eyes to the change and ferment around them. There were others who surrendered their ancestral traditions and became lost to Judaism in the cultural maelstrom.

But in the author of Ecclesiastes we have a man who was frank and honest enough to declare that he did not know where he was. Nothing seemed to add up any more. He was looking for meaning in life. Caught in this maelstrom, he was looking for a firm rock on which he could stand to take stock of himself. But he found everything going around in circles. To him, there was nothing permanent – all was 'vanity', a vapour that disappears before the eyes.

Now the remarkable thing is that no book of the Bible seems to crystallise the problems of our age as clearly and succinctly as this one. One of the chief reasons is that there are certain similarities between his time and ours. We, too, live in a world of change and ferment. The rapidly developing sciences and other disciplines of study have overturned many of the traditional views both of the world and of the human condition itself.

We can, of course, trace the roots of this ferment back to the Renaissance, followed by the Protestant Reformation; but only in our century is the full impact of this mighty movement making itself felt.

At the same time as humankind is being forced to question the traditional answers we have given to life, this revolution in culture is spreading over the whole world, so that the Indian Hindu, the Arab Muslim, the Chinese Buddhist, as well as Christians of all traditions, are being caught up in this cultural maelstrom in which the old familiar landmarks are being swept away.

Instead of the traditional Christian, Muslim, Buddhist and so forth, living in geographical apartness, there is emerging everywhere a new type of human, one quite new in human history. Let us call this creature the secular human.

Secular humans are the product of this cultural revolution into which we are moving, and this secular human is already in all of us to a greater or lesser degree. Today's farmer, however devout a Christian he may be, does not attempt to improve his crops by prayer, but by fertilisers, as recommended by empirical science. Most people, however religious, prefer to entrust themselves to the medical scientist rather than to the faith-healer.

In our world, as in ancient Alexandria, there are those who insist on shutting their eyes to these changes and clinging resolutely to their traditions, if only in part. There are also those who, in face of the bewildering changes, have completely abandoned the older traditions. But while the emerging secular culture has, like an acid, dissolved away so many traditions, and while it has provided in their place a tremendous body of knowledge and new insights into the nature of humankind, it has shed little light on the basic questions of human existence.

That is why the person who is looking for direction, yet finding none, is likely to be amazed to hear so many of his or her innermost thoughts being openly expressed by this ancient Jewish thinker. Let us look at one or two of them.

He tells us how he looked to the seat of justice. Would that not make it clear that life has a moral meaning in that the just prosper and the wicked suffer their due deserts? But he finds it is not always so, for there are just people who suffer more than they deserve and there are wicked people whose deeds never catch up with them.

He then asks if this is so because God is testing humans to see if they are anything more than animals. But he finds it hard to see that humans do have any permanent advantage over the animals, since both humans and beasts are mortal and the bodies of both turn to dust.

He hints that he has heard that the spirit of humans goes upward when they die, and the spirit of beasts goes downward. Is that the difference? But who is to know? The only thing he can do is try to make the best of things while he lives, for that is all he can know about.

Here the words of the Preacher strike close to the bone. The orthodox Christian tradition that the meaning of life is to be seen in the fate of a person's immortal soul does not hold the conviction for us today that it had for our Christian forebears. Indeed, the very sciences dealing with the human condition – anatomy, physiology, neurology and psychology – have led us back to a view of the human condition almost identical to that held by that ancient Jew. A human being is a psychosomatic creature whose psyche cannot live independently from his or her body. The human being has no immortal soul. Because the body is fleshly and temporal, humankind therefore is mortal.

Incidentally, biblical scholars have shown in the past few decades that this was also substantially the view of the early Christians and was why their hope for an eternal destiny took the form of a belief in a future resurrection of the whole person.

But sceptical and pessimistic as Ecclesiastes is, he occasionally sounds a striking and more positive note – 'God has made everything beautiful in its time'. Here he puts his finger on one of the characteristics of human experience that helps us to realise what mysterious creatures we are. We can readily imagine a highly rational mortal creature who has absolutely no aesthetic appreciation at all. But humans reveal a little of their unique nature in their sensitivity to the beautiful. Humans have themselves created beauty in language, in colour and form, in literature, in music, and in personal relationships.

Ecclesiastes goes on from this to say: 'God has put eternity into man's mind, yet so that he cannot find out what God has done from the beginning to the end'.

Does not this strike a relevant note for us in our contemporary predicament? We humans are mortal creatures, tied to a fleshly body, limited to a little bit of this vast universe and experiencing it only for a moment or two of cosmic time – yet we find that God has put eternity into our minds.

Unlike the beasts, we experience self-awareness and we have some understanding in our minds of the situation confronting us. We are tragically aware of our mortality – we know we must die. Yet we have glimpses of the whole human situation, of the vast universe, of time – and even beyond that of the mystery of God. This is our predicament – a puzzling predicament – for as Ecclesiastes says, although God has put eternity into our minds, we cannot find out what he has done from the beginning to the end. We can analyse complex organic substances, and we can split the atom, but the basic mysteries of God lie yet unfathomed.

What then do we do? Ecclesiastes concludes that the best thing to be done is to make the best of life – to eat, drink and enjoy one's life and one's work while it lasts.

But we can say more than that! However relevantly Ecclesiastes speaks to our predicament, he does not have the last word. For this we must turn briefly to the New Testament. But first let us be reminded of the source of this cultural and intellectual maelstrom which has caught us up. The great cultural revolution now encircling the earth arose in Europe. Just as an individual reflects both parentage and environment, and cannot be properly understood apart from them, so no new human culture is born out of the blue. It, too, is a child of cultural parents. The new secular culture now emerging came out of Christian Europe, and in particular it came out of the universities of Christian Europe.

Those universities were founded by the Christian Church for the pursuit of truth and sound learning, in the conviction that these could lead only to the glory of God. The universities centred their activities upon the study of theology – the queen of the sciences – and theology is still the academic discipline devoted to the basic questions of human existence.

Now because this is the root of the new global culture, Christians must be very wary of concluding too quickly that Mother Church has quite unintentionally produced a hideous monster in this secular child which must be quickly overpowered and destroyed. There are sound theological and historical reasons why the secular age has emerged out of the Judeo-Christian heritage. The Christian can welcome the birth of secular culture!

Non-Christians, however, must be wary of concluding that the new secular culture is, like Melchizedek, without father or mother: a kind of parentless Topsy who could grow to maturity only after shaking off the chains of an oppressing, obscurantist church.

The new secular culture could be the undoing of humankind if its origins are not fully appreciated. This is no idle observation, for today it is widely recognised that the human race now has within its grasp the power to annihilate itself; and it is by no means certain that it has the spiritual maturity to prevent such a catastrophe.

Ecclesiastes makes little reference to the traditional Jewish beliefs, and yet at many points he betrays his heritage. It is because he has not wholly abandoned that heritage that he stumbles upon such remarkable insights into the human condition.

Before it is too late to retrieve humankind from possibly absolute ruin, let us look again at the Christian heritage. There is a little story in St John's Gospel which, in its present form, is more of a parable than a historical incident. It is a parable that speaks quite vividly to our situation.

We are told that many of the disciples of Jesus were beginning to have difficulty accepting the truth of what he was saying. Indeed, the New English Bible translates their words as 'This is more than we can stomach!' Thereupon they defected and followed him no more. But the twelve remained loyal, and when Jesus asked whether they intended to desert him too, Simon Peter declared, 'Lord, to whom shall we go? You have the words of eternal life'.

It is possible in our cultural situation today to make the same affirmation as Peter, and at the same time to confess quite openly that many of the formal expressions of Christian orthodoxy of former centuries are no longer relevant to our time. Indeed, Christian theology today is in a more fluid state than it has been at any time since the period of Christian origins.

But this is not all loss. In fact it can be a distinct gain. We are being forced to learn again that Christianity should never be identified with ecclesiastical systems or with a body of knowledge that claims to be divinely revealed.

We humans are always trying to find security in systems and doctrines so that we may be shielded from facing up to our true human predicament – which is that we do not know for certain who we are and where we are going. There is no infallible body of knowledge that gives us all the answers. God remains forever hidden from sight, and we cannot find out what he has done from beginning to end. We are forced again to make the venture of faith. We do not know for certain where it will lead us.

We are led to this point because of the Word that comes to us out of the Christian heritage itself. If there had been no Christian faith, there would have been no European Christendom. If there had been no Christian West, there would have been no emerging secular culture, and we would not be the people we are, asking the questions we do!

Much of the historical manifestation of Christianity is ephemeral and destined to pass away. That is why we must be prepared to see ecclesiastical systems and theological dogmas rise and fall. But at the heart of the Christian heritage there is a Word that speaks to us still; a Word that calls us to make the same venture of faith in our predicament as our Christian forebears did in theirs; a Word that has the power to turn human pessimism into hope and to draw out of the human heart wonder, love and praise.

For such reasons, we neglect the Christian heritage at our peril. For to this heritage we owe the Word that challenges us to commit ourselves to truth and personal integrity, and self-sacrifice for love of God and our fellow humans.

From the Judeo-Christian heritage that found its focal point in Jesus Christ, there still comes to us a relevant and life-giving Word. It is a Word that should disturb people of all traditions and also people who have none. It speaks both to the Christian and to the agnostic. That Word speaks to the eternity in our mind and calls us to venture forth in faith, that by the grace of God each of us may be led to full, mature personhood – and that is a quality of life that might be rightly called the life eternal.

INDEX